To Jess

Love Mum ... ure!

on th... India

xx

No One Cries for the Dead

The publisher gratefully acknowledges the generous contribution to this book provided by the General Endowment Fund of the University of California Press Associates.

No One Cries for the Dead

Tamil Dirges, Rowdy Songs, and Graveyard Petitions

Isabelle Clark-Decès

UNIVERSITY OF CALIFORNIA PRESS

Berkeley   Los Angeles   London

University of California Press
Berkeley and Los Angeles, California

University of California Press, Ltd.
London, England

Library of Congress Cataloging-in-Publication Data

Clark-Decès, Isabelle, 1956–
No one cries for the dead: Tamil dirges, rowdy songs, and graveyard petitions / Isabelle Clark-Decès.
p. cm.
Includes bibliographical references and index.
ISBN 978-0-520-24314-9 (pbk.: alk. paper)
1. Funeral rites and ceremonies—India—South Arcot. 2. Tamil (Indic people)—Funeral customs and rites. 3. Dirges—India—South Arcot—History and criticism. 4. Folk songs, Tamil—India—South Arcot—History and criticism. 5. Tamil (Indic people)—Social life and customs. I. Title.
GT3276.A3S683 2004
393'.9—dc22
2004046047

13 12 11
10 9 8 7 6 5 4 3

The paper used in this publication meets the minimum requirements of ANSI/NISO Z39.48-1992 (R 1997) *(Permanence of Paper).*

The paper used in this publication is both acid-free and totally chlorine-free (TCF). It meets the minimum requirements of ANSI/NISO Z39.48-1992 (R 1997) *(Permanence of Paper).*

Printed on Ecobook 50 containing a minimum 50% post-consumer waste, processed chlorine free. The balance contains virgin pulp, including 25% Forest Stewardship Council Certified for no old growth tree cutting, processed either TCF or ECF. The sheet is acid-free and meets the minimum requirements of ANSI/NISO Z39.48-1992 (R 1997) *(Permanence of Paper).*⊗

For my mother, and for Jim

CONTENTS

ACKNOWLEDGMENTS

I first thank the funding agencies of this project. The American Institute of Indian Studies sponsored fieldwork in Tamilnadu in 1989–1990, and the American Council of Learned Societies did so in 2000. I also acknowledge and thank Princeton University for granting me a Bicentennial Fellowship in 2001. This fellowship gave me the space and freedom to write the first draft of this book. I also acknowledge the people who kindly recommended me to these generous institutions: Gerald Berreman, David Knipe, David Shulman, Lawrence Rosen, and Jim Boon.

I thank all the Tamil women and men who collaborated with me on this project. I was fortunate to meet them, and I hope that this book will show them how much I respect them. Also, I was lucky that M. Thavamani of Gingee was free to do fieldwork with me again. As happened during our past ethnographic research, Mani brought exceptional dedication, flair, and, sensitivity to what was all along *our* study. He also oversaw the painstaking details of transcribing many of the songs and narratives presented in this book. Thank you, Mani, for your patience, generosity, and friendship. My thanks also to P. Srida from Alampoondi for helping me translate some of the most difficult Tamil dirges.

I am deeply grateful to Paul Albert for bringing his formidable knowledge of the Tamil language to all versions of the petition and of death songs I recorded. A visiting scholar at L'École Française d'Extrême Orient in Pondicherry while I was in the field, Monsieur Albert helped me translate these texts on the weekends. We spent more than sixty hours at it.

I have presented various sections of this book at the 1992 Annual Conference on South Asia in Madison; the University of Wisconsin in Madison; the University of Chicago; UC, Davis; and UC, Berkeley (on the occasion of Gerald Berreman's retirement conference). I thank the participants for their questions and feedback.

My colleagues Jim Boon and Abdellah Hammoudi offered helpful comments on an earlier draft. I especially thank Hilly Geertz for suggesting that I rewrite it backward—a suggestion that added one year to the writing process. Marnie Rosenberg and Matt Fox both edited the manuscript at various stages, offering many insights and strengthening my prose. Working with them was both eye-opening and fun, and I thank them both.

I am so grateful to Naomi Schneider at the University of California Press for her enthusiastic support. My sincere appreciation to Bonita Hurd, Cindy Fulton, and Nola Burger for taking good care of this book. Tara Hariharan made it possible for the text of appendix B to be included. Kirin Narayan's and Stuart Blackburn's reviews of the manuscript for the press gave me much to think about. I tried to implement as many of their suggestions as seemed relevant to my focus. I hope they will see their imprint on my revisions. I owe the publication of this book to David Shulman, who sent a miraculous endorsement with characteristic grace and lightness.

When I was just beginning this project I lost my mother and met my husband. Maman, je ne pourrais jamais assez te remercier; nor could I ever thank you enough, Jimmy, for the gift of your love.

Introduction

I first attended a Tamil funeral in December 1990. Although it was more than a decade ago, I have vivid memories of that day. I had been in a village in the South Arcot district of Southeastern India, for a little over three months when the headman of the nearby untouchable compound walked up and down the main street making the following announcement. "Today, Monday the seventh of the month of Mārkaḻi," he proclaimed to the beat of his drum, "Perumal's mother is dead. The burial will take place at four o'clock this afternoon on the village cremation ground." Only after hearing this did I understand that the piercing wails just now beginning to rise from the neighborhood were sounds of mourning. Restless and curious, I followed the clamor to its source and saw the women of Perumal's household, arms linked, huddled in clusters on the ground beside the dead woman lying on a cot just outside the door. Swaying and moaning, they wept, beating their breasts as they cried out in mournful songs. The mood of bottomless sorrow expressed in their "crying songs" was irresistible, and I was soon moved to tears.

The sudden arrival of the *paṟaimēḷam*, an all-male troupe of untouchable drummers, drew me out of my initial empathetic reaction. Drunk and apparently oblivious to the commotion the death was causing, these men positioned themselves directly across the street, ready to drum. The steady rolls of their metallic drum-strokes were so loud and incessant that they instantly drowned out the women's wails. The troupe then began to sing. But their delivery was fun and entertaining, not melancholic and mournful like that of the women. In the characteristic style of Tamil oral performance, the lead singer even engaged in humorous dialogue with the drummers, and the dance steps that accompanied his lyrics were loaded with obvious sexual imagery and innuendo. It was impossible not to laugh at his playful skits, teasing smiles, and occasional hip wiggles. Soon a large crowd of villagers gathered around the courtyard of the mourning household. Incoming women went immediately to join the crying clusters, while children stood on the side of the road giggling at the drummers' show. The men, on the other hand, gathered around the singers and compulsively paid them to chant their favorite "death songs," leaving the scene only to drink arrack—a locally produced alcohol—with Perumal and his brothers.[1]

The women cried and the untouchables drummed and sang almost continuously until the formal arrival of all relatives of the deceased a few hours later. This signaled the commencement of the last rites, and the village barber stepped forward to officiate over the "mouth rice" *(vāykkarici)*, or ceremonial feeding of the corpse by the relatives. Then, as the body of Perumal's mother was lifted onto a bier to be carried to the funeral ground, the drumming and the crying resumed with renewed intensity. At this point the mourning women rose to prevent the men from taking the bier away. But they were firmly pushed back to the house, where they remained, since Tamil women are barred from following the funeral procession to the cremation ground.

Leading the all-male procession, the untouchables danced and sang along the village's main street to the accompaniment of their instruments. The street resounded with the reverberating beat of drumheads, the jingling of bells, and the high-pitched lyrics and drunken exclamations, all of which offered witnesses the opportunity to appreciate the power of sound, as all eyes focused not on the motionless corpse or the taciturn mourners but on those making the noise. When the procession reached the outskirts of the village, the untouchables stopped drumming. The few men accompanying the deceased woman to the grave, overcome with exhaustion, fell silent. Then, at the entrance to the funeral ground, one of the untouchables delivered a long and solemn "petition" to the guardian of the graveyard, imploring him to open the gates of the afterlife for the deceased. Finally, the men buried the dead woman.[2]

Returning home that day, I kept thinking about the various mourning behaviors I had witnessed. While, for women, death had been an occasion to express deep regret, for the untouchable singers it had been an opportunity to act as a comic foil. More evidence was hardly needed to reveal these starkly opposed stances toward death. The women's desperate sobs, stricken faces, and complete absorption in singing were proof enough that they did not take death lightly. Meanwhile the defiant, exultant singing of the untouchables suggested clownish men who refused to feel anything but pleasure in the face of death.[3] The scene brought many questions to mind. Why do Tamil women cry on such occasions, while men drink and commission untouchables to sing? What exactly are the men buying? And why do they laugh during a funeral rite? I also wondered why the untouchables, usually despised by the villagers, are praised and even rewarded with hefty tips for their "jolly" presentation. What attraction do these men exert on their audiences? Finally, why are the mood and style of their death songs so intensely incongruous with the lengthy petition that the same men later make at the entrance to the funeral ground? For there the untouchables, who just before were brimming with comedic confidence, become stiff and insecure.

Since funerals were not then part of my ethnographic interest, these questions faded from my mind. At that time I was studying the patterning and meaning of exorcist, initiatory, and sacrificial ceremonies (Nabokov 2000). But because many of these latter rituals incorporated mortuary symbols and practices into their procedures, I was often led to revisit the Tamil funeral. Each time I did so, I wondered what the mourning behaviors just described meant and how they might relate to the ways women and men actually experience loss. I thus began paying closer attention to them in an attempt to answer some of the questions they raised.

As a result I started recording crying songs, death songs, and petitions. But it was not until I returned to the South Arcot district of Tamilnadu in 1999 that I was able to devote myself to documenting these three genres of funerary performance. Instead of settling in the village where I had previously resided, I rented a small apartment in nearby Gingee, a bustling market town of more than fifty thousand people located 180 kilometers Southwest of Madras. I did so partly out of convenience, partly out of necessity.

In 1991 I had invited (Paṟaiyars) (as local untouchables were then called) to our rented village house, but neighbors scolded me for bringing these "dirty people" into the vicinity. Visiting Paṟaiyars, or Dalits (as they nowadays prefer to call themselves), in their own separate compound *(cēri)* proved no easier.[4] People from the village *(ūr)* do not generally go into the cēri, and my doing so angered them (it was impossible to keep my whereabouts secret). The elderly would complain, as one did when he said, "You are breaking our rules of conduct." To avoid further aggravation—and probably ostracism—I resorted to working with untouchables from a cross-section of villages scattered within a radius of twenty kilometers of Gingee. This way I could interact with them without my immediate neighbors knowing about it. So when I came back in 1999, I opted to live in Gingee because of its convenient location at the hub of my consultants' residences. There I could also socialize with funeral drummers and singers in relative privacy, as untouchables are less visible in townships than in small villages.

GENRES OF CLASSIFICATION

Not all Tamil women engage in the kind of lamenting behavior—or "institutionalized weeping," to borrow a term from the linguist K. M. Tiwary (1978: 25)—described in this book. At family funerals, women from the higher castes (Brahmin, Ācāri, Chettiar, Singh) may, out of sympathy, join a crying cluster initiated by a female neighbor or acquaintance, but if they do so they simply weep. Women from middle, lower, or untouchable castes, on the other hand, do not simply shed tears, but cry out well-made statements that possess a generic structure, and their weeping is tuneful. The tone and delivery style, including the beating of the breast, pulling of hair, and fainting, are so marked that, if a Tamil man uses them, he is immediately described as effeminate and mocked.

The Tamils call this genre of expression *aḻuvuhira pāṭṭu*, or crying songs, a fitting appellation because the women cry out lyrics that amount to what we would call a dirge.[5] Although the women I worked with could not articulate the stylistic organization of crying songs, all agreed that "to get meaning we need two pairs of lines." Like the anthropologist Margaret Egnor, I too found out that "the first pair of lines . . . describes an image, usually positive, and the second pair of lines describes a contrast or outcome, usually negative" (1986: 300). Also like Egnor, I noticed that two more pairs of lines of the same length and of the same pattern often follow, forming what she calls a "stanza." I put this word in quotation marks because the notion of "stanza," a written convention, is completely foreign to my consultants. But Egnor is indeed correct when she notes that "the two halves of a stanza usually duplicate each other, except for certain words," and that the words which differ "almost always belong to the same semantic and grammatical class; often they are synonyms or antonyms" (299–300). This pattern of describing an image and its contrast, then repeating that same image and contrast with variations, gives internal consistency, almost monotony, to Tamil lament.

In my efforts to understand the meanings invested in crying songs, I worked mainly with four women. Two belonged to the Kavuṇṭar caste, an agriculturist caste making up 35 to 40 percent of the population, the largest caste in South Arcot. The other two women were Paṟaiyar, the predominant untouchable caste, comprising 20 percent of South Arcot's population. Three worked as day laborers in farming fields, and the fourth was a landlady. All four women were illiterate and had learned crying songs "two lines at a time" while hearing more experienced women cry in the clusters that form at funerals.

As for untouchable men, not all of them sing at funerals either. In South Arcot only members of the lowest divisions *(Veṭṭiyars)* perform the services: that constitute the Paṟaiyar funeral caste work drumming, singing, erecting the arbor of palms leaves in front of the deceased's house, building the bier, petitioning, and grave digging or pyre building (also see Moffatt 1979: 120). In some colonies, as untouchable settlements are sometimes called, the work is the exclusive right of a particular lineage. But in others the work is taken on by the Veṭṭiyars on a rotation basis for the duration of a year (Racine 1996: 205). Two of the four men with whom I worked were not Veṭṭiyar, however, but were Paṟaiyars who had joined the local paṟaimēḷam out of personal inclination (also see Moffatt 1979: 197). All four men had painstakingly learned the genre of songs called *cāvu pāṭṭu,* or death songs I say "painstakingly" because death songs are not, like crying songs, organized around two pairs of lines, but are composed of hundreds of verses. Dalit men, who for the most part cannot read or write, spend days memorizing each song in its entirety.

The juxtaposition of crying songs, which focus women on painful emotions, and death songs, which call men to celebrate (on the surface at least) death, makes the Tamil funeral a site of polarization par excellence, a place that thrives on contrary, even antagonistic, behaviors and attitudes. Everything—especially what women, men, and untouchables say, how they speak and to whom—seems to suggest that at the funeral people talk at cross-purposes, with the sole common purpose of distinguishing themselves from one another.

Other anthropologists have noted that South Indian funerals express social distinctions. Bruce Tapper, for example, characterizes rites of passage in the nearby state of Andhra Pradesh in this way: "Of all the various lifecycle rituals, funerals are the most revealing of the definition and differentiation of social statuses." Tapper himself does not attempt to explain why "funerary customs mark the major differences in status which are considered socially significant" (1987: 145), but it seems appropriate that any interpretation should begin with South Indian meanings of death.

"Death," one Tamil farmer told me, "causes the soul to leave the body." "Death," he added, "is also the sad occasion to part with someone forever." This separation is represented on the funeral day itself by ritual activities that mostly consist in removing the dead person from the society of the living, a process that culminates with the burial or cremation of his or her corpse.[6] Since death provokes departures, and endings to relationships, it is no wonder that meanings of distinction and differentiation surface in the social organization of the ritual processes that effect this parting. Kinsfolk and not in-laws, for instance, adopt the special conduct that reduces the pollution of death (for example, dietary taboos, shaving of hair and moustache, etc.). In-laws and not neighbors feed and offer ceremonial cloth to the mourning family. The village washerman and not the basket weaver crushes a winnowing fan at the end of the village procession, an act signifying, I was told, that "the living want nothing more to do with the deceased." The village barber and not the potter punches a small hole in the clay pot of water carried by the chief mourner around the grave in order "to symbolize the draining of life." Untouchables and no others build the bier and bury or cremate the corpse. Men and not women accompany the deceased to the funeral ground, and so on.[7] Symptomatic of such meanings are mourning behaviors suggestive of dissociation from ordinary states of consciousness. Men yield to the intoxicating effects of alcohol, and women work themselves into intense emotional states. In this way both men and women are cut off from their normal states of being.[8]

The crying songs, death songs, and petitions that form the discursive background of the Tamil funeral process likewise evoke a reality in which division is the normal order of things. Crying songs and death songs may differ in form and style, but they all speak of individuals cut off from every single person they love. Meanings of separation also resurface in petitions, the third genre of funeral discourse examined in this book. The petition to King Ariccantiraṉ to open the gates of the afterlife for the deceased is no quick formula. This petition *(viṇṇappam)* unfolds in the form of a fifteen-minute-long oral narrative recounting how the first man ended up all alone, segregated from society.

This Tamil representation of death as the model of, and for, existential and social divisions confirms Maurice Bloch and Jonathan Parry's argument that funerals do not reaffirm society's victory over death, as was contended in classic anthropological theories, so much as generate society itself (1982; also see Randeria 1999). But I emphasize that Tamil funeral discourses do not recreate the "bonds" of Tamil society. Nor do they reproduce the meanings of love and fusion recorded by some of the best ethnographers of Tamil society (Trawick 1990; Daniel 1984). Rather, they articulate an ensemble of splits and cleavages within which notions of alienation, difference, and otherness are essential and full of significance. It is as if the ritual practices and genres of verbal expression that center on and surround the corpse were saying that to be social is to be alone and lonely.

GENRES OF NATURE

The data of this ethnography derive almost entirely from conversations with the four women and four men who sang or recited dirges, death songs, and petitions to my tape recorder, and from my transcriptions of these events. Neither in 1990 nor 1999 did I attempt to record funeral songs and narratives in situ. In fact, in 1999 I did not even try to watch a single funeral, so the contextual descriptions I offer are entirely reconstructed from memory and field notes from my previous research visit.

Of course, I am not proposing that anthropologists study cultural productions out of context. I concur with Bronislaw Malinowski's old injunction to pay special attention to the "live context" in which myths, for example, are recounted: the time and place of the narration, the voice and response of the audience, the mood and emotions, and so on. Nor do I question Malinowski's assertion that "in this live context there is as much to be learned about the myth as in the narrative itself" (1984: 198). Moreover, I admire the work of folklorists, like Richard Bauman (1986), who have turned "the performance event" into a fundamental unit of description and analysis. I fully agree that how such events are organized—for example, the distribution of roles among participants, the uses of time and space, and the uses of music and dance—are central to any understanding of "verbal lore." This is because performances never simply express or enact a preexisting text. Performance *is* the text in the time, place, and manner of its actualization. As the folklorist Dan Ben-Amos puts it, "The telling is the tale" (1982: 10).[9]

For two main reasons, I choose not to focus on recording Tamil funeral songs and petitions within their performance context. The first reason is simple. I could not bring myself to observe people in mourning for the sole purpose of fleshing out any relationship of text and context. I was well aware that the performance event—in the case of my research, the funeral and its ritual process—shaped the poetics, delivery style, and multiple meanings of funeral songs for the singers and their audience. I had already seen, for example, how the coming of women into the crying clusters, and their departures, transformed individual expressions of grief into a fluid, unbounded, and de-centered collage of voices. But I was not willing to detail this process, for it would have required me to stand beside a mourning family, staring detachedly at crying women and jotting down all their movements. I also knew that to learn about the dynamics of performance did not necessarily require me to record information like a physicist or laboratory technician. It was just as effective to speak with the singers and petitioners who could identify better than I the several elements of the ritual process that shape their performances.

My second reason for disregarding in this case the context-sensitive recording techniques of performative theorists is that the usual notion of performance does not well describe the Tamil perspective on what is sung or recited at the funeral. The genres of lamenting, singing, drumming, and petitioning described in this book are defined as part of the ritual tasks of caste and gender. Performance in this context is a duty *(kaṭamai)*. Exploration of the cultural logic that organizes the allocation of these tasks reveals that the sorts of "competence"—an idea central to most anthropological definitions of performance[10]—on display in the rituals are culturally specific. To be sure, while an outside observer might describe the different genres of funeral song as involving talent, acquired skill, and artistry, this point of view is elided to various degrees by Tamil mourners and singers. For them, the performance of funeral song genres is embedded in a conceptual framework of caste duties, and these in turn are couched in native social theories that regard such duties as natural. Thus at funerals, women, men, and Dalits perform the "natural" attributes that in the day-to-day life of the Tamils serve to differentiate them from one another and hierarchize them.

When I asked why women lament and men do not, I was reminded that, in day-to-day life as well, Tamil women and men each have their separate tasks. Likewise, at ceremonies the two sexes have their own distinct responsibilities. At funerals, as one man elaborated, "Men's job is to concentrate on the ritual, especially on taking away the body. Women's work is to cry." I also learned that this gender-based division of mortuary roles springs from basic notions of intrinsic difference between the sexes. The difference that most affects men's and women's respective mourning behaviors, I was told, is that men can control their emotions, and women cannot. As many of my consultants said, "Men feel grief but don't openly show it." Or as one man explained, "At the death of his father, a man may begin to shout 'Appā!' [Father!], but he will stop. His sister cannot; she'll keep on crying." These comments corroborate Tapper's observation regarding a Telugu village: "In complete contrast to the women who gather in circles to wail and cry, . . . men are expected to be stoic, brave, matter-of-fact, and in control as they conduct the rituals. They are pressured not to show emotion. If they break down crying they visibly attempt to hold back their tears" (1987: 146).

My male consultants gave consistent, almost generic responses to the question of why men repress their grief. Invariably, they invoked spiritual, biological, and psychological reasons. One schoolteacher told me, "The gods have decided that men don't cry." An untouchable man concurred: "God created us like that, that's all." One man said that men were able to master their emotions because of their "genes and chromosomes." Another man offered a physiological reason. "You see this protuberance," he asked, pointing to what we call the Adam's apple. "This is what stops our tears." Men also argued that "they were too shy to cry," which was why, "when they did cry, they covered their mouths with handkerchiefs." Men also pointed out to me that they were "braver" then women. But when elaborating on this point, they did not separate the effects of biology from the effects of culture. As one man said, "Men work outside the home: that requires courage and composure. Women stay at home; they are the first affected by good and bad events. This is why they are more emotional." Finally, men also explained that their own duties at funerals prevented them from expressing emotions of grief. As a village man told me, "Men are the leaders of the funeral. They cannot afford to break down. They have to be strong. This is especially true of the chief mourner. He has to be brave *(tairiyam).*" Another man agreed: "If we were to cry with women, their tender hearts would simply burst out and melt. It would be pure chaos. We would all be helpless. That is why we control ourselves. We shed tears, or sit in one place immobilized by sorrow; but we do not join the women, because we have to look after everything."

For the most part, women agreed with these explanations. But in private some of my best friends ridiculed them. "Men don't express grief, because they don't feel it," they would say. As one woman put it, "Men have stone hearts. They think, 'Ah, I am also going to die; why should I cry for the dead?'" A Dalit woman agreed, saying, "Men have a hard heart." To my female consultants the best indication that men lack the capacity to feel anything is that at funerals they "drink, sit around, and laugh." As one high-caste woman from Gingee told me, "Men are happy to drink. And don't let them tell you that they drink to forget the grief, for that's not true. They drink at every ceremonial function: funeral, marriage, ear-piercing ceremony. They don't care about the function. For them, death is like a party. They drink and fight." To her, such behavior disproved the theory that women are weak and men courageous. "Why do men drink if they are so strong?" she asked rhetorically.

When asked why it is the untouchables who beat drums and sing at funerals, my consultants followed a similar line of reasoning. They told me that, in the old days, inhabitants of Indian villages and towns were divided into hereditary groups, with each group, or "caste," assigned a profession *(toḻil kula)* and ritual duties from which its members could depart only within limits. Thus members of the washermen caste specialized in washing clothes and performing certain ceremonial tasks at rites of passage and festivals. Men of the barber caste shaved beards and cut hair and fulfilled their own ritual functions. Carpenters made wood furniture and tools. Men of the Brahmin caste served as temple or family priests. Potters supplied earthen pots for day-to-day and ceremonial usage. The untouchables performed their own tasks, too, the most symbolic of which was to drum at caste-Hindu funerals.[11]

In this way everyone performed practical or ritual duties, or both, for local landowning castes. Payments were regulated according to local usage, but they usually entailed a little food each day, a fixed quantity of grain at harvest *(mērai)*, and obligatory presents (often of money and cloth) on the occasion of the main local festivals and major family ceremonies.[12] The point of such explanations was to highlight the central fact that "drumming was the untouchables' work" *(toḻil)*, "their way of making a living." Here I underscore the point that caste Hindus were not the only ones to express this point of view. The untouchables I talked to also told me that drumming was their "business," "their source of income."

None of my caste-Hindu consultants offered explanations of how this division of labor came about. "It is the law *(muṟai)*"; "it has been like this from the beginning of times," they would say. Nonetheless, their commentaries did not lack a social theory, for they evoked notions of fundamental inequality between castes. This was clearly expressed by one Tamil farmer who broke down the eighteen castes of his village into three hierarchical levels: "The untouchables [Paṟaiyars] are in an inferior position *[kaṭai nilai]*. The farmers, clerks, and teachers are in the middle *[iṭai nilai]*; and the priests and artisans are in the superior [literally 'first'] level *[mutal nilai]*." The rationale given for this ranking system, which characterizes the social structure of most if not all Tamil villages, confirms Louis Dumont's claim that it is not possible to understand caste hierarchy without considering the more general question of purity and impurity (1980). The Paṟaiyars rank low, in fact the lowest, I was told, because they are impure, and the artisans high because, along with the Brahmins, they are the purest of all castes.[13] The same caste-Hindu consultants often added that it was because the Paṟaiyars were impure that they came to specialize in unclean *(tīṇṭṭakāta)* tasks, such as skinning and removing animal carcasses, tanning leather and making shoes, sweeping, drumming, grave digging, and cremating the dead.[14]

Apparently, in the Tamil funeral tradition, competence is defined as a function of natural dispositions. Women cry because they are emotional, and untouchables drum and sing because they are impure. This is not to say, of course, that the genres of crying and singing described in this book are seen as being devoid of "communicative skill" or expertise (Bauman 1986: 3). "Who is going to like a woman who brays like a donkey?" a woman once sarcastically asked when I pressed her to expand on the qualifications most necessary in crying songs. Another told me that she might make fun of a woman's dirge that "has no head, no tail," or in other words, no logic. But both women were quick to clarify that a good voice and a well-phrased dirge only make one a singer not a lamenting woman. What is needed first and foremost for crying out at funerals is genuine emotion.

GENRES OF CULTURE

One of my chief goals in this ethnography is to show that such emotion is not straightforwardly "natural," as statements from my consultants often suggest. As an anthropologist, I consider what gender and caste are, what men and women are, what kinds of feelings they experience or express, and what sorts of duties they take on or not; and none of these notions simply reflect or elaborate upon "nature." On the contrary, they are predominantly social constructions. Yet on this issue of culture versus nature, there need be no sharp epistemotogical break between the

Tamils and anthropologists. For all the naturalistic biases in their explanations of gender (and caste) funeral roles, some of my consultants nonetheless seem to intuit cultural bases for differences between women and men. At the very least, Tamil women say that what makes them more "emotional" at funerals than men is not an inborn disposition but such social arrangements as marriage and widowhood.[15]

This will not come as a surprise to ethnographers of Indian society who have long pointed out that the spheres of kinship, marriage organization, and residential rules clearly help constitute men's and women's varying subjectivities. Ethnographers have shown, for instance, that a man is normally expected to remain in his natal house for his entire life. When he marries, he stays with his parents, brothers, and unmarried sisters in what scholars of Indian society call "the joint family." Although the courtyard is eventually subdivided into separate hearths to accommodate inevitable splits between brothers, a man remains "at home" forever. Should he live elsewhere, his ancestral house is still his both legally (as inheritance) and emotionally. A man's life, in other words, is one of stability and rootedness in his birthplace.

By contrast a woman's life is normally one of movement and departure. Upon marriage she must leave her natal home forever, returning only as a guest. Although, at first she visits her family often, over time she returns infrequently—once a year, sometimes less often. If she is widowed, she remains with her in-laws. The grief that such marital residential rules causes women and their kin, anthropologists have noted, is further compounded in North India, where women are married to strangers. Tamil women, who abide by different preferential marriage rules—often wedding not interlopers but cross cousins and sometimes even maternal uncles—do not merely feel grief. They feel *kuṟai*, an emotion that includes a range of feelings corresponding to "deprivation" and "depletion" that is absolutely essential to the proper expression of crying songs.[16]

Untouchability is no less socially constructed than women's emotions. Nor can this category be understood without taking into consideration experiences of deprivation. The four Dalit men who assisted my research on death songs and petitions had lived, and more often than not still lived, in conditions of abject poverty. "We were poor," one man told me. "My mother and my father used to sell firewood, but they had to walk up to 25 kilometers a day to gather the sticks and kindling that got us our daily ration of millet." His wife recalled, "We were so poor that at times we ate only once in three days. Sometimes we had to make do with grass." Another man told me, "My parents worked very hard, but they were not paid enough to feed us. Sometimes they had to steal paddy [husked rice] so that we could eat." One of my consultants recounted that neither his siblings nor he went to school, because "we had no money to buy books. We were constantly in debt." Another man reported that his father had once owned a little piece of land, but it was so arid that the family could not make a living from it. He ended up selling it "for almost nothing."

These testimonies make it clear that in the past very little money circulated among untouchables. Their livelihood depended on the castes that exploited their labor. As the French anthropologist Robert Deliège writes about the Paṟaiyars in the Chettinad region of Tamilnadu, "We know that the untouchables were in a state of 'semi-slavery.' They did not have the right to leave the village to which they were attached and for which they had to carry out a whole series of tasks, both economic and ritual, which were linked to waste, excrement and evil spirits. The relationship was, above all, one of dependence" (1997: 146). Indeed, many of my consultants told me that whatever cash they had mainly derived from the funeral duties they performed for the other castes. Nowadays, of course, rural Dalits have new sources of monetary income—they often work as salaried workers in the fields—but as Deliège states, "The Paraiyars' economy is basically one of subsistence, from hand to mouth as the saying goes" (64). This was certainly the case for the Dalit men with whom I worked. Landless and illiterate, they could never make ends meet. These men thus continued to perform the one sort of work that provided them with a little extra: at funerals they drummed, sang, carried the bier, petitioned, and dug the graves or cremated the corpses.

GENRES OF EXPERIENCE

Tamil funeral performances are genres framed within definite conceptions about proper roles and identities based on gender and caste. But their expression depends on experiences that, although related to their ceremonial context, nonetheless transcend it. Since the dramas that spill over into these genres are existential, so rooted in scenarios of life and death, a method that focuses on a description of performances is liable to miss the subjective dimensions of what funeral participants experience. For although some aspect of a singer's life experience most certainly will emerge during performance, we cannot know with certainty what that experience is like, no matter how carefully we watch the performance (also see Kapferer 1986). To gain access to this experience, we must attend closely to what singers express in words, images, and commentary about their productions. As Clifford Geertz argues, "It is with expressions—representations, objectifications, discourses, whatever—that we [anthropologists] traffic" (1986: 373). Whatever sense we have of how performances build, of how they draw performers and spectators (or intentionally shut them out), we gain it through such expressions, and not by relentlessly gazing at behavior. And we gain it by talking to people.[17]

This does not mean, of course, that people are always (or ever) willing to reveal to the anthropologist everything about themselves. I found that the four Dalit men who assisted me in my research on death songs and petitions were reserved when it came to discussing the pervasive dynamics of exclusion and discrimination they once had faced and, more often than not, still faced. Seldom did they mention that in the past, unless they were working, they were not allowed to walk along high-caste streets. They were denied access to village temples, schools, wells, and tea shops. They were restricted in the clothes they could wear, the paths they could walk on, the people with whom they could eat, and the behaviors they could adopt in the presence of the high castes. As Deliège describes these behaviors, "untouchables had to speak to a superior with eyes lowered and holding their hand to the mouth. They had to cross their arms over their chest - also a sign of humility - and could not raise their voice" (1997: 148).

I also had to come to terms with the fact that my consultants sometimes contradicted themselves. For example, on the one hand, the four men I worked with insisted that performing death songs and petitions required certain skills. An ideal funeral singer should be funny; he should also have a good voice, a sociable personality, and an aptitude for the task. Among other things, an ideal petitioner should never tell a lie. But on the other hand, their comments also revealed that the indisputable qualification for singing death songs hinged on more than charisma or endowment: the Dalit singer cannot perform unless he drinks. As one Dalit man commented, "Without drinking, we wouldn't be able to stand in the sun for hours." Nor would they be able to sing well, no matter how talented. The alcohol makes them feel "less shy," "less dull," and "uninhibited." The best indication that Dalit men need some kind of "help" in executing their mortuary duties, however, comes later in the ritual. When they reach the entrance to the funeral ground, the untouchables are unable on their own to petition on behalf of the dead. No matter how many times they have already recited the story of the origin of death, they told me, they cannot do it without the assistance of a *tuṇai,* a word that glosses as "helper" or "escort."

Such testimonies (and their attendant silences and contradictions) lead me to suggest that performance at Tamil funerals always springs from something more than mere "fitness." It requires and arises from various experiences—of depletion, deprivation, discrimination, alteration, and obstruction—which provide the living context in which women and men create the meanings of their duties at the Tamil funeral.

GENRES OF LIMITATION

This book, then, is the product of the many conversations I had with funeral criers, singers, and petitioners living near the South Arcot town of Gingee. What I learned in the course of our encounters is that, during mortuary rites, women and men are not telling (by lamenting, singing, petitioning, etc.) what is going on: that a death has just taken place. They are telling about themselves. At Tamil funerals, the question "What constitutes a death?" quickly unfolds into the question "What constitutes a life?" or better still, "What constitutes *my* life?" For these Tamil funeral discourses can be self-referential, even autobiographical. In fact, crying songs, death songs, and petitions are personal histories.

One of the answers to the question "what constitutes my life?" as disclosed by these genres is profoundly disturbing. Women and men can grasp their existence only through sad narratives. A life, my life especially, is a story of losses and endings, forced separations, longings and regrets, say these narratives. Life is good only when it is conjugated in the past tense, in a time that is mythic, private, and irretrievable. Then I was connected; now I am alone. Then I was idle; now I have to work hard to make a living. Not that this gloomy answer goes uncontested, for a contrary and more upbeat take on life is voiced too. But the notion that life is a continual waning of relationships and loss of possessions is the first and last word of the Tamil funeral.

Given the circumstances—a death has just occurred—this answer seems reasonable, almost natural. After all, context does matter, and here context is replete with stark facts. But there is a flip side to such pervasive discourses of demise. They limit what the participants say to or about themselves, thereby restricting the expression of their subjectivity and preventing them, for example, from articulating alternative and more upbeat narratives about themselves. This is significant, for the Tamil funeral is one of few places in which women and Dalit men talk about themselves. Whatever they say there has the potential to both organize and downgrade participants' self-understanding. This suggestion is so contrary to current scholarship related to gender and untouchability in Indian society that I must expand on it here.

Much recent literature objects to any notion that women and untouchables subscribe in some way to the ideology that oppresses them. Writing against representations of passivity or submission, feminist scholars, for example, argue that Indian women question and challenge patriarchal evaluations of themselves in various registers, such as trance, stories, personal narratives, everyday talk, and songs, including the genre of dirges.[18] This new emphasis on multivocality and resistance recently has led scholars of caste society to reject the claim made by Louis Dumont (1980) and Michael Moffatt (1979) that untouchables share a deep "cultural consensus" with the higher castes concerning the basic values and assumptions of the caste system.[19] To the contrary, these scholars contend, untouchables do not now—nor did they in the past—endorse the ideals and institutions of the higher Hindu castes, even if they reproduce the same system in their own favor with respect to other members of "polluted" castes.[20] As Oliver Mendelsohn and Marika Vicziany write, untouchables have never simply accepted their untouchability "without reflection or protest" (1998: 21). Throughout history they have actively resisted it with their own weapons, the "weapons of the weak" (19).[21]

This is also what Sathianathan Clarke, a priest of the Church of South India and a lecturer in theology and ethics at the United Theological College of Bangalore, contends. Based on his personal experience as parish priest and social activist in the Chengelput district of Tamilnadu (1998), Clarke explores the Paṟaiyars' communal identity through the dominant symbol of their economic and cultural degradation: the drum. Constructing this instrument as a text of "resistance" and "emancipatory theology," Clarke encodes it with three meanings. To him the drum suggests the unutterable, incommunicable experience of divine power; it is a symbol of community solidarity; and its sound is an articulation of Paṟaiyar pain. The drum therefore works to resist the coopting forces of dominant caste Hinduism and to empower the Paṟaiyar community.

This book takes issue with Clarke's analysis of the role of drumming in Paṟaiyar society. The book also stands at variance with what we could call a feminist reading of Indian women's songs. Not that I maintain that women and untouchables do not protest their lots in life. Nor do I ignore the subversive potential of their forms of expression, which do indeed expose some determining conditions of female and untouchable existences.

But my ethnography follows Paul Willis's study of English working-class culture in showing that subordinate "forms of penetration" are seldom total (1977). Like the rebellion of poor and working-class kids against school authority in England, the discourses of self-understanding presented in my book are partial and limited. At the very least they are turned back on themselves, often unintentionally, by complex processes ranging from women's and men's production of classifications, to conceptions of their funeral duties, and to narratives of decline and demise. The primary aim of this book is to cast some light on this surprising process.

CHAPTER ONE

A Different Grief

No village sound is more disturbing than the shrill cries announcing a death. Even in cases when death has been anticipated, the wails of close female relatives hovering over the dead person, occasionally throwing themselves across his or her body, still come as a shock. Their words "Oh my mother!" "My father!" "My brother!" or "My husband!" uttered with deep rhythmic elongations in a pealing moan punctuated with tears and outbursts of distress, spread rapidly through the neighborhood, and female friends and neighbors quickly gather to "share the grief" *(paṅkiṭa tukkatai)*. The principal female mourner, or the woman with the "right" *(urimai)* to the deceased (the widow, for instance, in the case of a married man), greets the gatherers by beating her breast and exclaming, for example, "Ayyō, he left me and went away!" The arriving women respond with hugs, saying, "Akkā!" (Elder Sister!) or "Ammā!" (Mother!). They may also respond in commiseration, "What a shame! You lost your husband."

The women then drop to the ground and squat together in a formation known as *punai kaṭṭu*. In agricultural jargon this usually refers to the rounds made by bullocks when they are tied together to thresh wheat. In the funeral context, the word describes the tight circle women form around the principal mourner by interlocking their arms in a collective embrace, each woman simultaneously hugging her companions to the left and right. Although the mourner steps out to greet arriving female relatives, the encircling women remain bound to each other, weeping, wailing, and drawling out crying songs. The women break formation only to make space for the newcomers, who rush into the crying cluster as soon as they too "share grief." When the group exceeds ten women, a second cluster forms. As the crowd continues to swell, the number of clusters increases to twenty or more, made up of women swaying, moaning, and crying out dirges beside the dead person.[1]

In fieldwork, as in daily life, we often encounter radical difference, and we come up against things we cannot immediately identify or understand because nothing in our previous experience has prepared us for them. This happened to me while working in Tamilnadu. When I first saw crying clusters, I simply assumed that women were grieving the loss of a relative or a friend, much as we cry at the funerals of loved ones. Later, however, I discovered that the meanings of women's heartbreaking sobs and crying songs went beyond what was immediately imaginable to me.

The Tamil women I talked with revealed unexpectedly that at funerals they do not cry for the dead. They told me, "We may shout to the deceased 'You left me,' 'You left your wife,' and the like, but [we shout] only a few words. For the most part we do not cry for the dead." These women further surprised me when they disclosed that they do not cry for the mourners either. "We share grief out of sympathy or respect for the widow and the daughter," one said, "but we do not cry for them." All agreed instead that they go to funerals to "cry for their own losses." To underscore this point, in these statements these women are not suggesting that they mourn the loss of *their own* long-gone loved ones. "No one cries for the dead," women told me over and over again. "We all cry for ourselves." In this and the following chapter, I focus on the meaning of this puzzling statement.[2]

THE SOURCE OF TAMIL LAMENTS

In his 1915 analysis of Australian aboriginal funerals, the French sociologist Émile Durkheim argued, "Mourning is not a natural movement of private feelings wounded by a cruel loss; it is a duty imposed by the group. One weeps, not simply because he is sad, but because he is forced to weep. It is a ritual attitude which he is forced to adopt out of respect for custom, but which is, in a large measure independent of his affective state" (1965: 443). In some measure the Tamil women I met endorsed this viewpoint. At the death of a close relative, they told me, they have an obligation to wail. One woman said, "If we don't cry, people will speak badly of us. They'll say, 'Look at her, her father-in-law just died and she stands as stiff as a tree!'" Another woman told me, "It is the law *[muṟai]*. We must cry or people will scold us."

Tamil women are also required to cry at the funerals of friends, neighbors, and acquaintances. As one woman explained, "We can skip a marriage, but we cannot skip a funeral. We must share the grief." Actually, this sharing follows the logic of a business transaction: "I cry in your house so that you will cry in mine." One woman clearly expressed this mourning economy when she said, "Crying in a cluster *[kaṭṭi aḻutal]* is a loan *[kaṭaṉ]*, not a gift *[iṉam]*." "If I cry at other women's funerals," she explained, "they'll come to ours. If I don't [cry], no one will come." Another friend reiterated: "Crying is a loan. If I hug and cry [with] a woman in mourning, she'll hug me when I am in mourning." In practice this means that women friends, neighbors, and acquaintances embrace the principal female mourner not only out of empathy but also to mark their presence at the event. One woman told me, "I hug the woman to show her that I have come to her funeral." Another woman said, "We must hug the widow, for this is how she keeps attendance." Apparently, when the funeral is over, the principal mourner makes a mental list of the women who came to "share grief." Of a woman who was absent she might say, "Who does she think she is? What an arrogant bitch!" The woman who told me this added, "The widow will resent the fact that such and such a woman did not show up. She'll ask herself, 'I come to her funerals, [so] why doesn't she come to mine?'"

Although the Tamil women I engaged to discuss crying songs agreed that mourning is a duty, their views radically departed from Durkheimian sociology on the point of the relationship between felt and expressed emotion. These women conceded that a woman's subjective feelings could not always be deduced from her behavior. After all, a woman might go through the motions of crying, beating her breast, pulling her hair, and singing a melodious crying song "for appearance" *(oppuku)*, only as they put it, meaning without any emotional participation. But for the most part, these women insisted, one need not speak of masks and postures to describe the performance of crying songs. Usually women do not merely pose with tear-streaked faces, strike their breasts, and pull their hair to show proper deference. Nor do they fabricate or affect their emotions. They sob desperately and appear completely absorbed in pain because they do in fact feel grief. In short, in the dirges performed by Tamil women, expression of emotion corresponds to what is felt.

Emotions, as many anthropologists have reminded us, do not precede or stand outside of culture. Despite their deep intimacy and physical immediacy, emotions too are part of the many ways in which men and women in a given society shape and are shaped by their world (Abu-Lughod 1986; Lutz 1988; Trawick 1990; Lutz and Abu-Lughod 1990). Nancy Scheper-Hughes succinctly summarizes the most radical assumption of this relativistic position: "Without our cultures, we *simply would not know how to feel*" (1992: 431, her emphasis). Emotions, therefore, cannot be understood outside of the particular social contexts that produce them. Nor can their concepts be viewed as simply "labels for internal states whose nature or essence is presumed to be universal" (Lutz 1988: 5). Though no doubt responsive to physiological reactions and "feelings," emotions are deeply configured within a culture's wider web of meanings and significations, values, and ideals, and thus can in no way be categorized simply as natural. As Margaret Trawick discovered, what her Tamil consultants meant by *anpu* (love) sometimes ran head-on into her own culturally developed feelings about what love is or should be (1990: 92).

Likewise my own research taught me that my consultants' definition of grief did not quite match the one I brought with me to the field. To the Tamil women I talked to, grief was inextricably mixed with the experience of kuṟai, meaning "little," "want," or "deficiency." My female consultants also underscored that the emotion kuṟai is actually the very source and inspiration of their funeral dirges. "Without kuṟai," they would tell me, "we could not cry out our songs." They even defined the aesthetics of their dirges with reference to the depth of a woman's kuṟai:[3] "The more kuṟai a woman feels, the better her dirge."

What kinds of experience does the Tamil term *kuṟai* encompass? Let me preface the answer to this question by pointing out that kuṟai is not unique to women crying at funerals. In Tamilnadu, kuṟai is the catalyst for a wide range of life experiences. "Everybody has kuṟai of some sort or another," a woman once told me. When I asked my consultants to define this word, they used it in the context of their own lives, illustrating it with personal examples of disappointment, deficiency, and regret. A fifty-year-old Chettiar woman from Gingee told me, "I wanted to become a doctor, but instead I got married. This is kuṟai. I wanted one of my five children to go to medical school, but none did. This is kuṟai. I wanted my younger son to study but he did not. This is kuṟai." A woman whose son owned a jewelry store in Gingee explained kuṟai like this: "Sometimes my son has to borrow money to buy inventory. If business is bad, he feels kuṟai when he pays the interests on his loan." Tamil people are also compelled to feel kuṟai when their siblings do not buy them gifts or when their relatives fail to invite them to a marriage. When a Tamil woman finds out that her husband has a lover, she may yell out to him, "What kuṟai do you have with me?" In other words, "What is wrong with me? What is it that I don't have that this other woman has?" Apparently, Tamil people also feel kuṟai when they cannot fulfill the needs of friends and loved ones. One young high-caste woman told me, "At his daughter's engagement, a father promises to give ten sovereigns of gold to his in-laws. Later he can afford to give only five. He feels kuṟai because he is short."[4] The feeling of kuṟai is so broad and pervasive that my village friends took it for granted that I had experienced it too. At the end of my last fieldwork trip, one of my neighbors, a young man, wanted to buy my radio. I gave him a good price—so good that he asked me if I harbored kuṟai over our transaction. I reassured him that I felt none.

To summarize, the paramount experience of kuṟai is that of feeling unfulfilled, slighted, shortchanged, inadequate, or disappointed. This experience often commingles with the feeling known in Tamil as *aṅkalāyppu.* Implicit in the experience of aṅkalāyppu is an act of comparison, in which others appear to be better off than you. As one woman explained, "See! This boy is studying, but my son is not. This is aṅkalāyppu. See! These women got a good deal on a sari, but I did not. This is aṅkalāyppu. See! These people are doing well, but we are not. This is aṅkalāyppu." She made a point of stipulating that, unlike envy or jealousy, aṅkalāyppu is not malicious. She said, "It's not that you don't want others to do well, but that you despair over your own inability to succeed." "This sense of inadequacy," she added, "only fuels your kuṟai." Thus this critical self-appraisal underlying the sorrow of aṅkalāyppu adds to the negative tally of disappointment that constitutes kuṟai.

In the context of death the experience of kuṟai corresponds to feeling acutely deprived of the love and gifts of food, clothing, money, and so on once provided by the deceased. This came to light when a young high-caste woman who had recently lost her father told me, "I feel kuṟai because my father raised me and married me well." An untouchable widow confided, "I feel kuṟai when I think of the past, of my husband, of the things he did for me." Such definitions flowed easily from Tamil women, suggesting that grief, for them, is inextricably linked with the feeling that they have been cheated out of a relationship that once grounded and completed them. The same feeling organizes the poetics of their crying songs.

Tamil dirges use the vocative case, often addressing the deceased from the perspective of his or her particular kinship relationship to the singer. At the funeral of her mother, for example, a woman is likely to intersperse among her lyrics the words "Oh my dear mother!" She is also likely to eulogize. Her dirge, however, does not praise what her culture defines as "a good person." That her deceased mother was an honored and respected member of an occupational or social group is of little value to the crying woman. Tamil dirges constitute a self-centered language: they always identify the dead in terms of who they were and what they meant "to me."[5] The mourning daughter might therefore continue her song by praising her mother for what she did for her daughter. As a woman told me, "We do not cry to the dead 'You were great,' 'You did so many good things,' and the like. Instead we cry words like 'You took good care of me.'"

In her dirge a mourning daughter does not merely describe how her mother used to love or spoil her. She makes emotional comparisons *(oppāri)*—the common Tamil term for the crying-song genre—and juxtaposes this golden past with the desolate present in which she finds herself, now without a mother's emotional involvement in her life. The woman quoted above best captured the nature of these comparisons when she told me, "What we most say to the dead is this: 'You took good care of me, but now you are gone. I am completely alone. Who is going to watch out for me.'"[6]

Not all Tamil dirges praise the dead. Some songs accuse them of not caring about the singer. In these cases, women may address their complaints with questions like "Why aren't you protecting me?" and "Why am I suffering?" The complaints may also be directed to the gods, particularly to Yamā, the god of death: "What did I do to you?" "Why aren't you sparing me from grief?" "Are you a god?"[7] Whether they praise, accuse, or question, Tamil dirges nearly always focus on painful feelings of loss over a kin relationship that was (and could otherwise still be) fulfilling and centering.

What about my warning that it is impossibile to understand emotions outside the particular social context that produces them? Do some of us relate, perhaps even instinctively identify with, the inner state defined by my Tamil consultants as kuṟai? I, for one, have come close to feeling it since my mother passed away three years ago. Like the prototypical orphaned daughter of Tamil dirges, I grieve for what I have lost: a luminous and generous being, a wise and sympathetic confidant, an unconditional source of support, a spirited grandmother to my daughter, and so much more. When I long for my mother's phone calls, visits, gifts, and invitations to shop, travel, and lunch together in fancy restaurants, I can feel kuṟai suffusing my grief. But like many anthropologists, I remain leery of the proposition that emotions can be felt across cultures (but see Rosaldo 1984). I am not even confident that their full configuration and experiential impact can be translated. At the very least, in order to ascertain, the full meaning of an emotion such as kuṟai, we must do more than elicit practical definitions of its gloss in more or less artificial contexts. We must explore cultural understandings of the situations in which it arises as well as explore the ways of talking about these situations (see Lutz 1988; Abu-Lughod 1986).

The name Yamā in the previous paragraph should serve as a case in point: the Tamil emotion of kuṟai is inextricable from the experience of people whose worldview includes this god of death, a divine power to whom cries, complaints, and prayers may be addressed. The point is that emotions are not feelings pure and simple, but feelings within a culture that casts them in a particular form and imparts to them a quality all their own.

Indeed, when we delve further into the Tamil language of dirges, we realize that crying songs represent kuṟai as resulting less from death and more from the marital practices and relationships that affect Indian women. In fact, according to Tamil dirges this grief is never simply a consequence of death, but almost always ensues from the dislocations in women's lives caused by kinship arrangements and the relatives who enact them. This helps explain why we in the West cannot necessarily feel the kuṟai of lamenting Tamil women. Such grief is associated with life circumstances, forms of social organization, and gender experiences that are foreign to us. Kuṟai is also associated with a particular symptomology, etiology, and "cure" that stresses the necessity to cry out laments and make others suffer for you—in short with a configuration of meanings that are strange to us because they are intended to negotiate and create a social reality that is not ours.

CRYING SONGS

In Tamil folk taxonomy, crying songs are classified according to categories of social relationship. There are songs that lament the loss of a father, mother, and so on. The singers I worked with insisted that they have songs for every category of kin. In reality, though, the roles of "daughter," "sister," and "wife" are most important. Of the 133 dirges that I recorded, 20 are addressed to the father, 25 to the mother, 16 to the elder or younger brother, and 43 to the husband. Although each of the four singers I recorded had lost at least one child, I heard just 9 dirges for children. Not one singer offered a lament for the categories "mother-in-law," "elder sister," or "younger sister." When asked why the losses of parents, brothers, and husbands evoke more comparisons, my consultants unanimously answered, "Because such losses bring us more kuṟai than any other."

Crying Songs for Mothers and Fathers

"Parents are the first gods," these women often told me. "They gave us life and did whatever they could to raise and marry us. Whether good or bad, they were our parents. They took care of us when we were young; they fed us, cleaned us up, clothed us, protected us, and taught us everything we know." Such a conception of parents—so common in India (see Lamb 2000: 46)—results in children feeling bereft by the loss of a mother or father. The magnitude of their loss is movingly conveyed in the following dirge, sung to me by Ellamma, a married Kavuṇṭar woman whom I will discuss in the next chapter:

> There is a road on a hill, my dear mother!
> I—a young woman—walked along the way.

You told me the sky is the witness, my dear mother!
You promised a mango tree.
The sky is not the witness, my dear mother,
And there is no mango tree.

There is a road on a hill, my dear mother!
I—a young woman—walked along the way.
You told me the earth is the witness, my dear mother!
You promised a flower tree.
The earth is not the witness, my dear mother,
And there is no flower tree.

Decoding the poetic metaphors of her stanza, Ellamma explained, "Parents are everything to us. They are the world. They are themselves the sky and the mango tree, the flower tree and the earth. When we walked on the road of life [in other words, when we grew up], the light of the sky guided us, the mango tree and the flower tree provided us with shade, and the earth grounded us. When parents are gone, there is no more world; the sky, the mango tree, the flower tree, and the earth have all disappeared."

Crying women also focus on the nice things their parents would do for them were they still present. Many dirges employ the conditional tense to suggest that if the mother, for instance, were there she would listen to her daughter's problems, spare her of chores, feed her well, and shower her with gifts. I collected six variants of this conjectural voice regarding "what might have been," which always highlight the daughter's feelings of deprivation. For example, Archana, an untouchable widow whom I discuss later, sang:

In the north, there is lightning [bis].
Windows are shaped like plantain flowers.
In the north, shops sell bangles.
Near these shops, I am crying.
If you were here, my dear mother,
You would ask the price of these bangles
And tell me to extend my right arm.

In the south, there is lightning [bis].
Windows are shaped like coconut leaves.
In the south, shops sell honey.
Near these shops, I am crying.
If you were here, my dear mother,
You would buy me honey
And tell me to feast.[8]

This is how Archana explained her dirge to me. The daughter's birthplace is a village where it rains, which one infers from the presence of the lightning. Because rain in Tamilnadu is an indication of prosperity, the daughter comes from a well-to-do household. Ornate windows are further evidence of her privilege. These details suggest that the parents spoiled their daughter, regardless of whether they were actually rich or poor. Since her mother is now no longer there to indulge her with luxuries like bangles and honey, the daughter is compelled to cry.

Neither of the last two dirges specifies why the parent—in this case the mother—is absent. Such lack of specification is characteristic of the genre: Tamil dirges generally give no clue as to why loved ones are missing. Since these crying songs are mostly delivered in the context of funerals, and since they describe scenarios of ending—the crumbling of a cosmology, the cessation of relationships, and so on—the explanation is obvious: death is the culprit. But my sources maintained that dirges addressed to mothers or fathers (and brothers) are often sung long before parents die. In fact, women may begin to cry them out in their early teens, right after they get married, when their parents are still young and healthy (also see Trawick 1990: 165–66; Egnor 1986: 313). This is because at marriage a Tamil woman typically leaves her home and family of origin in order to live with her new husband in his father's home.[9] This departure prompts the daughter to lament that "there is no more world," and that her mother and father "have disappeared."[10]

Margaret Trawick, who has closely studied these Tamil dirges, notes that "'seeking mother' *(ammāvai tēṭi)* then becomes a natural activity, no matter what degree of maturity the [daughter] has supposedly reached, no matter how distant the world where the mother dwells" (1990: 166). Indeed I also discerned that, in Tamil dirges, the daughter is often traveling on the road leading to home. Trawick further observation that, "In laments, the mother is 'hiding' or 'gone to a foreign land' and the daughters are left seeking is also consistent with my research" (166).[11] In the dirges I recorded, the mother, who occupies the place where life itself is situated, is always unattainable. She is gone, missing, absent, dead, or in the past. At times the daughter is so frustrated by her mother's unavailability that her dirge becomes an accusation. "Why did you abandon me, Mother? Why aren't you helping me? I am suffering!" Here again her laments may employ the conditional tense. For example, in the following dirge, again supplied by Archana, had the mother arranged a marriage for her closer to home, the daughter would not be wasting away:

> If you had married me nearby, my dear mother,
> I would have asked you for a loan of lentils.
> I would have come to you.
> Since you married me ten miles away, my dear mother,
> You left me to wither.
>
> If you had married me close to you, my dear mother,
> I would have asked you for a loan of rice.
> I would have come quickly.
> Since you married me five miles away, my dear mother,
> You left me to drift.

The married daughter's lament gains special intensity at the funeral of her parents. Not that her dirges are different from those she might have sung before. Death is still not depicted through explicit reference. "Seeking mother" or "seeking father" remains a constant preoccupation. And there is still imagery, such as receding landscapes, uprooted vegetation, locked doors, and various other obstacles, that clearly represents inaccessibility.[12] Ellamma sang to me,

> I have black millet grains, my dear mother!
> On the edge of the forest, there is a road.

I set out to see you.
The forest did not yield a path.
My yearnings are deep.

I have red millet grains, my dear mother!
On the edge of the jungle, there is a road.
I set out to see you.
The jungle did not yield a path.
My yearnings are deep.

"Before my mother's death," Ellamma said to clarify her dirge, "there was a path that led to her house. Now the path has become a forest and is full of thorns." Elaborating on this image, she added, "When she loses her mother, a daughter is no longer invited to her natal house—that is why there is no path. Without this connection, she is destitute. That's emphasized by the mention of millet—a poor people's food."

Another of Ellamma's songs poignantly conveys why the loss of a father also causes the married daughter to feel kuṟai and to lament:

From Tiṇṭivaṉam [the name of a town], my dear father,
I would get ripe ginger
And news.
Today I no longer get ginger
Or news.

From Tiṇṭivaṉam, my dear father,
I would get cork
And telegrams.
Today I no longer get cork
Or telegrams.

Ellamma gave me the background to these lyrics too. "When he is alive," she said, "the father keeps in touch with his daughter and sends her fancy crops like cork and ginger. When he dies, she no longer receives those gifts or any news from her birthplace in Tiṇṭivaṉam. To her relatives, she no longer exists. They do not even bother to inform her [via telegram] of her father's death."

Crying Songs for Older and Younger Brothers

The last two dirges above express an implicit accusation. Since brothers continue to reside in the ancestral village, often with parents in the ancestral home itself, they ought to inform married sisters of a father's or mother's death. Since they inherit the family property, they should also invite their sisters to return to the ancestral home on special occasions. And they ought to send them gifts, such as saris, money, and crops. The married, and especially the married orphaned, daughter depends upon such invitations and gifts for her sense of connection with her natal family. A brother is her linchpin to her past. Without him she is at pains to establish and maintain a thread of continuity in her life—especially since, ideally, in Tamilnadu brothers and sisters arrange for their children to marry one another. Among some castes a younger brother may even marry his sister's eldest daughter. A woman with many brothers therefore has a good chance to "reenter" her natal house later on. She feels rich and secure. In contrast, Tamil women who lack male siblings feel poor and vulnerable. A brother is so important to a woman's sense of growth and expansion that, in one of her dirges for her mother, Ellamma does not actually grieve the death of a brother—she does not have any—but grieves because she lacks brothers:[13]

> I have a golden ladle and a plate, my dear mother!
> I have a palace without a brother.
> In this palace, my dear mother,
> I cry by myself.
>
> I have gold earrings, my dear mother!
> I am a ripe vine.
> There is no one to take care of me, my dear mother,
> I am wasting with the vine.

Ellamma explained her lament by paraphrasing, "Mother, you have given me good things: gold ladles, plates, and precious earrings. However, you have not given me a brother, so I am poor and alone. I am fertile, but without a brother I cannot marry my children to his, and so I am on my own in this world and perishing."

When they do have male siblings, crying women lament the fact that their brothers do not care for them. In fact, they might even perform the preceding dirge, in which case it would function as an indictment: "I have a brother but he is not taking care of me, so I am withering." Many dirges are actually aimed at living brothers, commonly accusing them of neglect. A frequent complaint is that, since women marry outside the family, brothers act as if sisters were superfluous, dispensable, even unrelated. Archana's stated it this way:

Thinking I was not needed,
My dear brother,
Thinking I came from a different field,
My dear brother,
You cast me away
Like you sow fenugreek and cumin seeds.

Thinking I was angry,
My dear brother,
Thinking I came from another field,
My dear brother,
You treated me
Like you sow mustard and cumin seeds.

"This crying song," Archana told me, "compares the way a brother treats his sister to the way he grows spices. Much as he throws fenugreek, cumin, or mustard seeds into the air, he tosses his sister's heart away. Because he rejects her, she reminds him that they are *cahōtarar* [the state of being brother and sister, or literally, 'same womb']."

Some dirges warn the brother that there are limits to what a sister can endure. Another of Archana's songs stated:

Little brother from Kumpakōṇam [the name of a famous
  temple town],
Little brother who makes a living by building temples,

If a temple falls, it will be repaired.
If your sister's heart is broken, it will never mend.

Little brother from Māyavaram [the name of a town],
Little brother who makes a living by building forts,
If a fort falls, it will be repaired.
If your sister's heart is broken, it will never mend.

Many dirges for brothers revisit the plight of the orphaned daughter, evoking how a woman's connection to her birthplace is irrevocably lost upon the death of her parents. The dirges also suggest that, when her brothers do invite her back home, the sister feels unwelcome, as though she is a stranger in her own house. In the dirge below, her brothers' wives impress upon her that now they own and run the place where she grew up. I collected five variants of this dirge by Archana:

On the top of my elder brother's house,
There is a flag of a swan.
It bears my brother's name.
But his wife says,
"This flag is mine,
It does not bear your brother's name."

In the courtyard of my younger brother's house,
There is a golden flag.
It bears my brother's name.
But his wife says,
"This flag is mine,
It does not bear your brother's name."

Crying Songs for Husbands

Like dirges for parents, crying songs addressed to husbands, Ellamma once commented, focus on remembrance of the past *(kaṭanta kālam)*. As the widow reflects on memories of her former life with her husband, these memories give rise to a lament essential to the reminiscence—the lament that those remembered times are now irretrievable. When her memory stirs intimate details, the widow makes a pronouncement that seems to echo silently in other dirges: she cannot resurrect this past in the present. Ellamma sang,

> Under the *margosa* tree, my dear husband,
> You would read a silver book on the sand bank.
> Today, I cannot hear the sound of this silver book.
> I cannot hear my Bīma's voice.
>
> Under the banyan tree, my dear husband,
> You would recite the alphabet on the sand bank.
> Today, I cannot hear the sound of the alphabet.
> I cannot hear my Arjuna's voice.[14]

One of Archana's dirges makes a similar complaint. In this particular dirge, however, the widow evokes the past by means of a different comparison:

> On the silver mountain,
> My dear husband,
> A silver pigeon is cooing.
> I can hear that pigeon,
> I cannot hear my husband's voice.
>
> On the rocky mountain,
> My dear husband,
> A crow is cawing.
> I can hear that crow,
> I cannot hear my husband's voice.

Like other categories of dirges, a lament for a husband tends to give less expression to a woman's personal grief and more to her dread concerning the social and existential changes she is about to undergo or has already experienced. At the death of her husband, a woman does not merely lose a spouse, she becomes a widow. This transition is one of the most dramatic in Tamil society. It can be understood only against the backdrop of the Hindu ideal: the married woman, or *cumaṅkali*, who produces children, preferably male, grows old with her husband and dies before him. When a husband dies first, however, the widow *(muṇṭai)* undergoes a ceremonial removal of her special marriage insignia known as the *tāli.* This signifies both the death of an "other" and the death of a "self," because the widow-making ceremony constitutes a transitional rite that strips away all of a woman's privileges, which were based upon her active status as a married woman.

After this rite a woman can no longer beautify herself. She cannot adorn her hair with flowers, rub her body with turmeric paste, and dot her forehead with vermilion powder. Nor can she wear bangles, anklets, toe rings, or fancy saris. Finally, she must eat very little so as to reduce her sexual desire and make herself thin and unattractive. The widow must be plain because she is not permitted to remarry or have sexual intercourse with anyone. Since she has lost the auspicious powers of a married woman, she becomes an omen of bad luck and must be avoided. The widow is also condemned to a life of material insecurity: her survival (if her sons cannot yet support her) depends on her in-laws, for whom she continues to live and work—caring for children, performing household chores, working in the fields, and so on. A Tamil village woman conveyed the widow's sad fate when she told me, "Without the parents, at least life can go on. Without the husband it cannot. There can be no pleasure whatsoever."[15]

This social practice makes it unsurprising that, at the funerals of their husbands, women cry for themselves, setting up comparisons between the strongly contrasting experiences of being married and of being widowed. Ellamma explained this in the following dirge:

> My lord, you brought me a five-hundred-coin necklace.
> Today in the troubled courtyard,
> I am withering like a dried-up bud.
>
> Oh king who brought me a three-hundred-coin necklace,
> Today in the crowded courtyard,
> I am wasting like a worn-out rug.

The first two lines praise the wealth and generosity of the husband who bought an expensive (five-hundred- or three-hundred-coin) marriage necklace for his bride. The last two lines describe life after the removal of the necklace, upon the death of the husband: the widow lives in a "troubled," "crowded" house where in-laws give her a hard time. Without affection, good food, and legitimate sexuality, she is forced to wilt ("a dried-up bud") and waste away.

In the following dirge sung also by Ellamma, the widow yearns for the times she went down to the river and smeared her body with turmeric. She laments the fact that, now that her husband passed away, she is forbidden to beautify herself:

If I go to the riverbank with turmeric paste,
My husband,
The brahmins in the water will say,
"She has cut her marriage necklace;
She is a widow."

If I go to the water tank with turmeric root,
My husband,
The brahmins in the water will say,
"She has lost her marriage necklace;
She is a widow."

The final two crying songs that I transcribe here, also sung and explained by Ellamma, go further than mere depiction of the widow's pitiful plight. They question a cultural verdict that pronounces widows sexually unattractive and ritually impotent, and that leaves them economically bereft.[16]

I dug a square well,
My dear husband,
and planted wild chamomile.
That well did not work.
I, the wild chamomile, am wilting.
Why?

I dug a corner well,
My dear husband,
And planted jasmine.

That well did not work either.
I, the jasmine, am wilting.
Why?

You would smooth out a small corner,
My dear husband!
And thresh sacks of priceless rice for me.
Now am I to pick up the leftover grains?
My dear husband!
Is that fair?

You would smooth out a small corner,
My dear husband!
And thresh sacks of expensive cereal for me.
Now am I to pick up the rotten grains?
My dear husband!
Is that right?

At the death of her husband, a woman loses her power to perform auspicious deeds. That is why the well she digs has run dry. The widow cannot even grow flowers (wild chamomile or jasmine). They wither, like her. In the last two stanzas, the widow remembers how her husband used to provide her with the very best kinds of food (expensive rice and cereal). Now she is reduced to scavenging for leftovers or eating spoiled food. Questions such as "Is that fair?" and "Is that right?" convey the widow's sense that her lot is not only painful but unjust as well.

MAKING PEOPLE CRY

Although I have closely adhered to the Tamil way of classifying dirges, my presentation of crying songs is somewhat misleading. While certain themes, motifs, or entire laments are appropriate only for certain kinds of relatives—a lament suitable for a dead son, for instance, would not be suitable for a husband—many are actually interchangeable. By changing kin terms and descriptive phrases to fit the circumstances of the deceased, a dirge for a mother can also be sung to a father or husband. Likewise a song for a brother can be addressed to a father or mother. In other words, there is a formulaic nature to the language of laments that allows for a certain interchangeability that belies somewhat the folk taxonomy of dirges according to kin relation.

My presentation is also insufficient in its suggestion that women's dirges have definite beginnings and endings—an appearance of wholeness—when in reality they do not. Women do not insert headings, pauses, or any other kinds of markers into their songs. They combine dirges as they would string beads on a necklace, singing them in a single breath punctuated only by sobs. As a Tamil music teacher confirmed, "There is no division in oppāri. Women keep on lamenting continuously without taking breaks." This element of continuity is neglected by Margaret Egnor, who seems puzzled by the "problematic" or lack of "semantic relationship between the different stanzas of a given song." She notes that "the images described from stanza to stanza present no temporal sequence of events, nor are they . . . all drawn from the same domain" (1986: 300). Indeed, I emphasize that the women mix and merge not just stanzas but entirely different dirges. What gives coherence to their performances is less "a parallelism of concept" or "some abstract quality," (300) than the experience of kuṟai. Kuṟai is the lived emotional current on which the flowing stream of oppāri pour forth one after another.

This experience is the paramount feeling that one has less than before, that one has been denied or deprived of something vital to one's well-being. We can understand why this feeling is so pervasive in Tamil society and why it resurfaces consistently at funerals. Death is the most extreme of all frustrating and dispossessing experiences. Men and women alike—indeed everyone related to or acquainted with the deceased—feel robbed of their associations.

The dirges we have examined, however, suggest that death is particularly taxing on Tamil women and often cheats them of more than just a loved one. They lose past identities, entitlements, immunities, and even the right to perform simple grooming practices like the application of turmeric to their bodies. Men, on the other hand, are less deprived by the death of close kin. When their parents die, they inherit the ancestral home. When their sisters die, their ritual, social, and economic standings do not change. When their wives die, they can remarry as soon as they want. In startling contrast to women, men seem to actually *gain* from death—property, status, authority, another family, and so on. Ironically, death completes rather than depletes them. This perhaps helps to explain why men do not lament at funerals. They cannot vocalize sentiments of kuṟai, not simply because they are "too shy" or "braver" or "in control of their emotions," as some told me, but because they do not experience the irreparable losses and dislocations suffered by women.

To the extent that they deplore the specific practices that deprive women not only at death but at marriage as well—patrilocal residence, patrilineal rules of inheritance, the ban on widow remarriage, and so on—crying songs seem to support recent arguments that Indian women's songs often contest the patriarchal power structure of Hindu society.[17] Egnor offers a similar view in her interpretation of the crying songs she recorded among Paṟaiyar women of the Chengelput district. She writes, "Crying songs are protest songs in a general sense—they protest not only the personal sufferings of the singer but also the rules of hierarchy themselves (1986: 334).[18] Likewise, Vijaya Ramaswamy concludes her study of Tamil dirges by stating, "'Oppāri' is essentially the product of a patriarchal society in which women lament their personal and material loss" (1994: 33).

Although Tamil dirges do offer a critical commentary on women's lives, what A. K. Ramanujan (1991) called a countersystem, I do not consider them to be political in the sense of a full public protest against female subordination.[19] If dirges are subversive, it is in a subtler register. Lamenting women largely entreat only the dead to listen to their complaints. They even seem reluctant to engage with anyone outside their all-female enclosures. This reluctance is evident in their body language: their tight, arm-linked clusters exclude the exterior world, and their bent backs partition them from the staging of more public funeral activities like the beating of the drums, the building of the bier, the formal arrival of the in-laws, and so on. During interviews, women revealed that they are not merely withdrawn but oblivious to all that is going on around them. If I asked them to recollect particular aspects of the funeral, they would reply impatiently, "When we cry out, we cannot see anything. We close our eyes. We are not looking around. We are not interested in what other people may do." That women are self-absorbed and unaware of their surroundings is also evident in their responses to my question about where they position their crying clusters. "How do we know?" they would reply, sometimes adding, "We cry wherever we happen to be."

Women also seem unwilling to disclose the topic of their comparisons, and they act as if they do not want to be heard by outsiders. Leaning their upper bodies against one another, sometimes resting their heads for comfort on each other's shoulders, they speak in indistinct and muffled voices. Their addresses to the dead, continuously interrupted by unsynchronized weeping, are inaudible. As their wails drown out the lyrics, what emerges is an inarticulate plaint. It is virtually impossible for anyone on the outside to make out the words of their dirges.

Nonetheless, there are certain moments of the funeral process when the main female mourner makes an effort to be heard and understood. During the funeral ritual this occurs immediately after the appearance of a significant kinsman. As soon as her brother arrives, for example, the mourning daughter or widow rises from her cluster to greet him with tears. She walks towards him with exaggerated formality, beating her chest and directing her lament to him. She follows him while he pays respect to the dead, forcing her words upon him and pressuring him to hear her. Inevitably in her solo dirges, she voices the kind of complaints that I included earlier. If she has lost her mother, the woman communicates her anguish over the prospect of losing contact with her natal home. If she has lost her husband, she decries the imminent cutting of her marriage necklace.

At that moment, a woman's intent is to move her audience. As the singers I worked with often told me, "The mourning daughter or widow wants to make people feel sorry *[iraṅku]* for her." That the woman is confident that she will succeed is confirmed by the following lyrics: "If I begin to tell my kuṟai," my widowed friend Archana once recited, "the gods will come down; their tears will flow into the oceans." And one of Ellamma's dirges begins, "If I were to tell my kuṟai, the fruits would fall; the cobra would shed tears."

The whole world, the gods, and the plant and animal kingdoms are devastated to hear a woman lament; it is much the same with her human audience. Although a woman's brother might be able to endure her heart-breaking lament without shedding a tear—his face locked in a rigid, almost stoic, expression—not many mourners can resist the impulse to weep. I observed that at funerals the very onset of a solo dirge forces nearly everyone within earshot to surrender to the mood of hopeless yearning it imparts and to cry.

If a woman does not know how to move listeners to pity, she might be taught to do so on the spot. I recall the lesson my friend Ellamma gave to a young widow at her husband's funeral. Not knowing any dirge, the mourning woman had cried something like, "I brought you so many sweets and fruits from Madras, but you died. Without warning us, you passed away!" Ellamma took it upon herself to admonish the woman: "Why are you worried about what you did for your husband? You should be concerned about what he did for you. And why are you blaming him for his death? It is not his fault if he met an untimely end. No one knows when Yamā [the god of death] will come." Then Ellamma instructed the widow, "If you say that you have lost someone who took good care of you, people will commiserate with you. They'll cry for you. If you don't, they'll criticize you." Some of the women present disapproved of Ellamma's intervention. One neighbor said, "At funerals women should be free to express whatever kuṟai they feel. No one, and especially no woman, should interfere." However, most of my female consultants agreed that Ellamma had appropriately emphasized the expressive mission of crying songs. "If we show that we are bereft, that we have been unjustly abandoned," one woman agreed; "people will be taken over by our grief." She added, "They'll feel sorry for us." When I asked why women wanted to be pitied, she replied, "We derive comfort *(āṟutal)* from people's commiseration. We are touched by the fact that they suffer for us. We appreciate their words of concern and the fact that they tell us, 'Don't cry!'"

I am belaboring this discussion because the notion of "making people cry for you" clarifies the forms of protest involved in Tamil solo dirges. The purpose—and as just illustrated, there is a purpose to these songs—is "to make others feel sorry for me so that I feel better." To the degree that they purport to move others, or at least effect some kind of emotional change in others, for the singer's own comfort, these solo dirges are manipulative. And they can be effective. The next chapter shows how in day-to-day life some Tamil women do soften abusive kin by lamenting to them. But my hunch is that, at the funeral itself, solo dirges are not concerned with reforming or punishing people. Nor are they aimed at transforming "the system," or at modifying the social roles acted outside the temporal boundaries of this ritual. I believe that the function of solo dirges begins and ends with their exegeses. They attempt, just as women say, to induce emotionality, to conjure, in particular, intense feelings of pity and commiseration. It is as if women were saying—and let us not forget the timing and circumstances of their communication—that the best antidote to experiences of separation and divestiture is to entreat all sentient beings, be they gods, animals, or humans, to feel and empathize with one's loss.[20]

MAKING ONE'S SELF CRY

A. K. Ramanujan once noted that in Indian classical literature, "Stories are told performatively—they are not merely utterances, they are part of the action, they change its course, but affect the *addressee*" (1991: 43; his emphasis). Hence this great translator of Indian texts was surprised to find a Tamil tale in which "an old woman tells her stories, her family secrets, only to lighten herself, not to enlighten anyone. Nothing is said about her cruel family being converted, becoming kinder; only she has changed, unburdened of her sorrows." As Ramanujan adds, "In this Tamil folktale, the tale of woe is told to express and affect the speaker's own mood, to change one's own state. It is cathartic for the teller in the tale. Such a notion of catharsis is not part of Indian classical aesthetics" (43).

With this in mind, I suggest that, if we look too closely at solo dirges and their functions, we might miss the larger meanings of Tamil crying songs. As I have already indicated, most women do not cry out to an audience. They lament in clusters with no apparent need of communicating messages to anyone. For all its emphasis on address, vocative words, second-person pronouns, and so on, a Tamil lament is not a dialogue, at least not one with the living. Nor is it simply a monologue with the dead or with the self. Rather it is a kind of therapy. Women cry out songs or else they suffocate, wither, and burn. In order to understand how the meaning of the Tamil lament tradition goes beyond its intended effect on an audience, we must delve still further into the root experience of this practice, into kuṟai itself.

Both lament texts and commentaries suggest that the sense of deprivation that fuels women's dirges induces physical pain, specifically a burning sensation in the stomach called *ericcal.* Understanding this sensation's onset and impact was not easy for me. There comes a point at which cross-cultural research on the somatization of strong emotions is limited by the fact that the anthropologist does not, and in my mind cannot, feel the symptoms reported by her consultants. All she can do is listen to those who, for example, are willing to describe how "their stomach burns when they feel that they have no father or mother to take care of them," or when "their brothers fail to give them saris or money."

My consultants explained that the only way to "cool off" this burning sensation is to "throw out" feelings of kuṟai. As one of them put it, "The burden of our heart has to come out; only then do we get relief." "Conversely," she added, "if we cannot open our mouths, we burst. We bubble up from rage." Another woman agreed: "If women are in a situation that they can neither express nor keep to themselves, they feel boiling hot *[kotippu]*. They feel anger *[āttiram]*." To these women, *talking* about one's kuṟai is not the optimal way of "throwing it out." As one stated, "Talking does help. Instead of letting them confuse us, we must talk about our problems. Like here, for example, like now I speak to you, Isabelle, and I feel better. I do get some support and relief from it." Yet she was quick to add, "When women talk, what's troubling them is not coming out; but when they wail, the real problem comes out." Another woman told me the same thing: "If I talk to you about my problems, you'll comfort me, telling me that things will get better. But if I were to sit and cry out my songs, I'd completely pour my heart out and cool it down." The singer Ellamma was of the same opinion: "If we sit down to cry out, all our kuṟai will completely go."[21]

These comments resonate with Ramanujan's insight that in Indian women's tales "a story is a form of existence, it cannot be neglected, killed, or wished away. It has a life of its own and insists on being told and kept alive" (1991: 45). Likewise a Tamil woman's lament needs to come out or it will burn and consume her. But my consultants' exegeses also suggest that a Tamil dirge has the sort of "magicality" and "instrumentality" that Ramanujan imputes not to Indian women's expressive genres but to classical stories (or texts)—the kind of stories usually told or written by men. Yet like great Indian narratives, Tamil dirges produce results. At the very least, their delivery allows women to "use up" their sorrow. This is especially the case when women cry together, for in the clusters they can cry as long, intensely, and unself-consciously as they need to.

I emphasize, however, that the process of "crying one's heart out" is not any more natural or spontaneous than the attempt to make people cry for oneself. Both behaviors are contrived, because the act of lamenting does not simply let out emotions, it also induces them.

Further conversations with my consultants revealed that gestures associated with the delivery of crying songs incite and magnify the Tamil emotional and bodily manifestations of grief. While not physically painful, beating the breast, beating the mouth, and pulling hair, for example, exacerbate "the burning sensation in the stomach": "they cause women to feel more heat and anger." Likewise the intoning of dirges intensifies feelings of kuṟai. "As soon as we open our mouth to compare," one woman told me, "we feel bereft and we weep." She also added that, "with each line [of our dirges], the sense of loss increases and we cry more."

Such dynamics are consistent with Owen Lynch's description of the old Indian theory of emotion known as *rasa* (1990). "In this theory," Lynch writes, "the major purpose of dance, drama, ritual, and poetry is not mimetic, cathartic or didactic; rather it is catalytic. Aesthetic forms ought to activate an emotion already present in participating members of the audience who must cultivate their own aesthetic sensibility" (17–18). The difference is that, in the Tamil lament tradition, dirges ought to activate the emotion of kuṟai not only in the mourners who may stare at crying women but also in the women themselves. Not that women do not feel this emotion to begin with, for we have seen that without kuṟai they cannot cry out their songs. But women must cultivate or nurture the feeling that they have been rejected, abandoned, excluded, cut off, and so on. Only when their kuṟai grows and takes over their bodies and consciousnesses, "filling them up," can women "throw it out." The Tamil lament tradition rests on the principle that "I have to feel much worse before I can get better."

Working oneself into a state of kuṟai can be soothing and purgative. The Tamil women I worked with clearly contended that the act of crying out their laments reduces, even eliminates, if only temporarily, their symptoms and feelings of deprivation. "The beatings of our breasts," they would say, "both heighten and lessen our anger." "As we cry," they would add, "resentments accumulate and pour out like water flows out of a well." All these women agreed that this peculiar cathartic process is more effective when women cry together. "When a woman wails or beats her breast," I was told, "another one is moved to do the same." Likewise a woman's tears inevitably make her companions weep. In this way, I came to understand, the crying women work themselves up into the extraordinary, heated emotional state that paradoxically "cools off" their kuṟai.

We can appreciate why women are required to join the lamenting clusters initiated by friends, neighbors, and acquaintances. They need one another in order at once to catalyze themselves and purge themselves of their disappointments. However, while a woman's lament serves to intensify and allay the feelings of others who join her wailing, women still do not merge into a kind of *communitas.* They may cry together, but they do not really share grief. This was made clear by a woman who told me, "Women use each other to pour their hearts out, that's all; they are not united." That women do not lament in unison may seem paradoxical. After all, they all mourn the same subjective losses as daughters, sisters, and wives in Tamil society. But women do not incorporate strictly common experiences into their lamenting practices. They also fill up their crying songs with individual feelings and circumstances.

CHAPTER TWO

Songs of Experience

Songs in the Tamil crying-song genre recount much more personal experiences than the survey in chapter 1 might imply. Tamil dirges move beyond a simple demonstration of women's gender roles to describe some of their most intimate situations. They voice not only the common losses women suffer at the deaths of parents, brothers, and husbands but also the particular disappointments they feel in their daily lives and over the course of their lifetimes. Dirges are never actually about common experiences, social trends, or gender dynamics. Instead they almost always describe the personal lives of the women who express them. As the women I worked with told me, "Our dirges have no head or tail [that is, no meaning] without our feelings about our circumstances and closest relationships." This statement would not surprise Margaret Trawick, who has long argued that, in Tamilnadu especially, "an artistic performance is not an object that can be grasped in isolation from the life of the performer. Rather, the artistic act is continuous with the actor's ordinary life; it is a rendition into greater meaning of that life, and is as much dependent on it as a rosebush is dependent on its rose" (1991: 224). Because "what persons are and what they say," to quote Trawick again, "turn out to be hardly separate things" (1988b: 324), and because personal feelings must be considered in order to grasp why dirges are sung and what they mean, this chapter analyzes the genre within the context of women's intimate lives.

Although formulaic and traditional, Tamil laments nonetheless cultivate a meeting of culture and individual sensibility. Individual women are able to assert their unique personalities by selecting out of a wide cultural repertoire those dirges that resonate most profoundly with their own emotional dilemmas. As indicated in chapter 1, they also recompose some songs extemporaneously, drawing on their favorite themes, metaphors, phrases, and structures to fuse their own struggles with the prototypical experiences of the daughter, sister, and wife described in dirges. In this way a woman's lament repertoire becomes a personal statement about who she is and what she yearns for.[1]

Both the form and the purpose of the genre accommodate different personalities and different social or intimate circumstances. In chapter 1, I described how Tamil women might lament at funerals to move others to pity them or to seek relief from the burning sensation that pain and anger cause. These two broad objectives might also provoke women to lament outside the funeral context. And yet, because characters and life situations vary, when women do lament in day-to-day life neither the motivations nor the consequences are ever quite the same as in the context of funerals.

Underneath the distinctive and sometimes contradictory applications of the genre, however, runs a constant theme. When a woman laments, she usually (but not always) takes a journey—a narrative journey—during which she recounts a critical condition in the first person and intermingles her dirge with that particular condition. In this respect her dirge functions almost like a diary. By likening lamenting to keeping a kind of journal, however, I do not mean that a woman's dirge is simply a record of something that has occurred in her life. It is a chronicle, certainly, but also much more.[2]

Many scholars have argued that autobiographical narrative forms—including those that strive to recount events with "facts" rather than poetic images (like Tamil laments)—are not objective records of what happened to people but after-the-fact reconstructions of life experiences (e.g., Bruner 1987: 12).[3] As Jerome Bruner writes, "When somebody tells you his life . . . it is always a cognitive achievement rather than a through-the-clear-crystal recital of something univocally given. In the end, it is a narrative achievement. There is no such thing psychologically as 'life itself.' At the very least, it is a selective achievement of memory recall; beyond that, recounting one's life is an interpretive feat" (13).

Such accomplishments of narrative and interpretation rarely occur in a cultural vacuum. No matter how personal or idiosyncratic—and it always seems to be both—the articulation of one's life story draws on broader narrative models (literary, oral, audio-visual, etc.) for recounting one's life. The implication is that the stories we tell or write are inevitably shaped by our particular culture's autobiographical conventions (as well as by many other literary and mythical conventions people may draw upon). Stories therefore carry certain cultural assumptions about what a person is, for the discourses a culture makes available for describing the course of a life are replete with notions of personal growth and change (Rosaldo 1976; Langness and Frank 1981). For example, contemporary Western autobiographies almost always begin with the category of life called childhood, focusing in particular on relationships with parents and siblings, because our current concept of self and personality development is inextricably linked with early family dynamics. If someone were not to mention these dynamics and their impact on him or her, the account would not fit our expectations of autobiography, since the life experiences described would be devoid of the proper context.

The language of crying songs can be seen as a cultural model for Tamil women to use to talk about themselves and their lives. This model, as noted in chapter 1, is different from models prevalent in contemporary Western cultures for personal development or change. To be sure, childhood also looms large in this model, as lyrics of laments suggest that relationships formed in early years continue to affect a woman's sense of self. But instead of a formative base for future growth, a starting point for what is to come, childhood is depicted as the end of the good life and, therefore, the end of life itself.[4] Whatever happens afterward—and recall that future events are narrated in a spatiotemporal dimension completely disconnected from the past, so women have no continuous identity—is a descent into unfulfillment. In dirges Tamil women tend to grapple with the tension between the "then" of events and the "now" of recollection as a way of drawing out, over time, their sense of depletion. Not every lamenting Tamil woman makes use of such temporal contrasts. Some traffic with other kinds of comparisons. But the result is the same. Instead of progress or simple maturation, what is evoked is dearth, decay, and death.

Understanding what goes into the shaping of autobiographical discourses is critical, because these accounts have the potential to control life experiences. To quote Jerome Bruner again, "The culturally shaped cognitive and linguistic processes that guide the self-telling of life narratives achieve the power to structure perceptual experience, to organize memory, to segment and purpose-build the very 'events' of a life. In the end, we *become* the autobiographical narratives by which we 'tell about' our lives" (1987: 15, his emphasis). I find Bruner's argument convincing. Because people invest their very identities in the life narratives they fashion, those narratives come to act as models not only for conduct but also for the ongoing integration of new life experiences. The language of comparisons, with its emphasis on memorable experiences and devolution, becomes the framework within which Tamil women both view their lives and live them. In the end, then, women become what they cry about. The life stories of the four women I worked with and the narratives of their crying songs illustrate this point.

ELLAMMA

Not every Tamil woman belonging to the middle or low castes—Kavuṇṭar, Paṟaiyar, and so on—that lament at funerals knows a repertoire of dirges. I discovered in the field that the majority do not. A woman confirmed my finding when she said, "Among ten women in a cluster, two may be very good singers, two or three may lament adequately, and the rest don't know the dirges. They may shout 'Appā! [Father!]' or 'Ammā! [Mother!]' or cry continuously without words. Some women don't cry at all." Another woman corroborated these statistics. "On average," she said, "four out of ten women know crying songs. The others shed tears."

A shabbily dressed woman with work-worn hands and gnarled joints, Ellamma was said to be one of the best singers of dirges in the Gingee area. When I met her in 1990 at a village funeral, she had a plain look with irregular features: a large nose, thin lips, missing teeth, and the thinning white hair of an aged woman. Yet there was something striking about her face. Neither age nor fatigue could mask her attentive gaze and a smile full of vitality. When she heard I was interested in women's crying songs, she insisted that I record her on the spot. As I felt uncomfortable thrusting a microphone in front of her at a family wake, we agreed to meet again in the privacy of her home.

I remember vividly the first time I paid her a visit. The road to her village was unevenly surfaced, and the occasional pothole or stone against the metal wheels of my motorcycle would throw me off balance. Although I kept my eyes on the road, I could see from a distance the rocks and boulders piled high around her village. There had been talk that this walled-up world with red soil and few trees could not support its tallied population of one thousand inhabitants. I noticed many abandoned houses, the absence of men, and signs of poverty.

Ellamma was not home at the time, but word of my arrival spread quickly to the peanut fields where she was working. When she joined me on the front porch of her tile-roof house, I realized that this frail woman in her late sixties or early seventies (she did not know her age) defied many Western stereotypes of Indian women, as well as the expected conventions of her own culture.

In her youth she had run away from her husband to live with another man. As if this desertion were not scandalous enough, this other man, who over time begot her children, was not a Kavuṇṭar as she was but hailed from a higher caste. Ellamma violated other taboos of caste society as well. She served as the village midwife, a job usually performed only by women from the low-status barber caste because delivery requires contact with impure substances like blood. "Tending to a birth," Ellamma told me during our first postmortem, "is polluting. But I've never minded this work. After I deliver a child, I go home and take a bath. What is the big deal?" That Ellamma had no fear of biological processes or their negative social connotations was further evident in her willingness to "share the grief." She would often travel alone by bus to nearby villages and towns to lament at the funerals of relatives or acquaintances. "I cry at all funerals," she told me, "except those of the Paṟaiyar [untouchables] people, because I don't know them—they live separately." Yet she denied that she was a professional crier. "How could I get tears for someone I don't know?" she protested with an expression of reproach on her face.

My relationship with Ellamma proved immensely valuable. She knew hundreds of crying songs and was able to do what most Tamil women could not: she could sing dirges to me. The other women who offered to perform crying songs for me quickly discovered that they could not. Because lamenting behavior occurs only in situations like funerals where feelings of kuṟai run high, most of these women found it impossible to burst spontaneously into crying songs outside of the proper emotional context. Feeling "cold," "flat," and intimidated by my presence, as one woman admitted, they could not garner the necessary energy or inspiration to lament. Over time a few of these women did get used to the odd situation that I put them in, but then they faced another problem. They could not perform without exhibiting the behaviors usually associated with lamenting. Inevitably these women would be induced to sob. Embarrassed by their wails and tears, they would usually stop singing after the first few lines. Over time, many devised ways to communicate their lyrics to me, often by reciting them without any melody. However, such arrangements were not necessary with Ellamma, who could sing dirges to my tape recorder without any apparent inhibition. She could perform her dirges without emotionally engaging with them. I realize now that, had I worked *only* with Ellamma, I might have missed the essential detail, as stated before, that crying songs are framed genres with defined emotional and experiential configurations. Ellamma, unlike most women, could step outside the frame that usually binds these songs; in this as in other ways, she herself was outside the norm.

Adding further value to my research, Ellamma was also a brilliant translator. Other women could not—or would not—comment on their lyrics and dismissed my questions with remarks like "Tell American people that it is just a song." Ellamma, however, gave attention to each line, explaining the many metaphors and poetic images encoded in her laments. Then she would annotate these explanations with social commentary so that I might grasp both the textual and the contextual significance of her comparisons. It was as if Ellamma clearly understood the ethnographer's predicament—the distance that I had to traverse in order to get a feel for the unfamiliar experience of crying songs. Working with her in 1990 energized me so much that I devoted a great deal of time to taping and transcribing approximately seventy dirges from her repertoire, despite the fact that women's crying songs were not at that time the focus of my research.

Ellamma was still alive when I returned to Tamilnadu in 1999. My heart jumped when I saw her again and noticed the toll that age had taken on her body. No longer able to stand up straight, she walked facing down with her head and torso twisted to one side. I later found out that the village kids called her "Koṉai" behind her back—a word that means "hunched back." Yet, despite her handicap, Ellamma still worked from 7 A.M. to 2 P.M. as a daily laborer in the agricultural fields, often followed by an afternoon shift at the local mill, where she cleaned husked rice.

She agreed to help me again, only this time she brushed aside my suggestion that I should meet with her in her home and said instead that she would come to mine in Gingee. She occasionally showed up as early as 6 A.M. "so that," she said, "we can begin our work early." When she recited dirges she had sung for me in 1990, I realized that ten additional years of lamenting had rendered her laments a bit more abstract, if not more opaque. Ellamma had also become harder to interview. She eluded many of my questions, often launching into a crying song out of the blue and as if on automatic pilot. She was even more difficult in a group setting. When someone interrupted or contradicted her, she would retaliate with a long-winded story that allowed her to remain the center of attention. It soon became apparent that Ellamma's insistence on meeting in my house came from an essential need to be alone with me. Yet she had outgrown our ethnographic conversations. She was no longer interested in elaborating on texts or cultural contexts—she wanted to speak about her personal life. As I let her take command of those situations, though, I began to understand that Ellamma's autobiography was intimately related to the story line of her laments.

In presenting Ellamma's story in the following pages, I have taken the liberty of "narrativizing" it, to borrow a term from Urvashi Butalia (2000: 11). That is—to paraphrase Butalia's own explanation of this term—I have removed the questions I posed whenever I did not understand Ellamma's account or when I needed more chronological information to follow it, and have let the text run as one continuous narrative. I have also deliberately transformed the transcript of my conversations with Ellamma into a "readable" text. To this end I have deleted repetitions, digressions, hesitations—anything that would have made her story hard to read. In what follows, much more about that story has been lost: the particular inflection and the body language, which sometimes tell a story different from the words. Also missing is what Butalia calls "the conscious 'shaping' of the interview by the interviewer, who is usually in a situation of power vis-à-vis the person being interviewed" (12). Given this, I make no pretense of presenting Ellamma's account in its pure form. And yet I hope that I have preserved its overall tone and narrative form. Here is how her story began.

I was the firstborn. My parents had five children. We lived in Madras but often returned to my mother's village to visit my māmā *[Ellamma's mother's brother], who had married a girl from another village. The girl died soon after giving birth to the only one of her four children who survived infancy. I was twelve when she passed away, and my parents brought me to my māmā's house to look after the baby girl. When I came of age, they wanted to marry me to my māmā. [Although not common, marriage with the maternal uncle is acceptable among certain Tamil castes.] At first he refused, because he thought he was bad luck. But neighbors and relatives convinced him that I was taking good care of his baby, so we got married. He was much older than I was; but I did not mind, because he was wealthy.*

When I turned fourteen, I gave birth to a baby girl. A few months later she got sick, and I took her to a nearby village for treatment. She died there. People wanted me to bury her on the spot, but I took her back home instead. As I walked back to our village, carrying her dead little body in my arms, I cried out my first song. No one had ever taught me how to form a dirge; the words just came to me. I still remember what I sang.

At this point Ellamma stopped her narrative to sing:

I came to sweep the doorway,
My precious child.
I found a diamond.
After my diamond closed its eyes,
My precious child,
I found sorrow.

I came to sweep the garden,
My precious child.
I found a jewel.
After my jewel closed its eyes,
My precious child,
I found grief.

Before resuming her story, Ellamma offered the following commentary:

When I was a young woman, I came to my māmā to do domestic chores, like sweeping the doorway. I worked hard. The reward for my labor was my baby. She was precious, like a diamond, to me. When she died ['closed her eyes'], I was miserable.

When I reached home, the neighbors told me, "Don't cry! It is just a baby," but I could not stop. My husband was away then, and I cried even harder because he was gone and I was alone with my dead baby.

This was only the beginning of my troubles. Around that time, a young man from the Mutaliyār caste started to follow me whenever I went to work in the fields. He pursued me everywhere. I had no reason to report his conduct to my māmā. I was not doing anything wrong. I was not even talking to this man. But people began to gossip. They had the nerve to say that the baby that had just died looked more like this man than my māmā [Ellamma's husband]. Like this, they fabricated [cōṭi] *stories.*

Then my mother came to live with us. I heard my māmā say to her, "Your girl is misbehaving. She has too much sexual energy. Don't feed her too well and she'll stop roaming around." I was nice and plump then, but they began to feed me only a bowl of porridge a day, and I lost weight.[5] *I was sad but I did not cry. I thought, "Let my māmā do whatever he wants. Let me die by his hands!" One day he caught a fish from the lake and my mother cooked it. When she was not looking, I helped myself to some rice and fish curry. She caught me and scolded me severely. I just threw the food on the floor. My māmā yelled at both of us. That was the day I left his house.*

I went to the Mutaliyār man's house. He did not know what to do. The man who had gotten me in all that trouble was now thinking, "If Ellamma moves in, I'll never be able to get married." He just wanted to play ["graze" is the word Ellamma used]; he was not serious about me. His elder brother, though, took me in, and I lived with these people for four months, working every day in their fields. I was not happy there. The Mutaliyār man constantly reminded me that I had ruined his life. Seeing that I was miserable, his elder brother told me that I was free to go. When I left, he gave me four measures of rice so that I could eat.

I wanted to go back to my parents' house in Madras, but the [younger] Mutaliyār man would not let me move out of the village. He wanted to keep me for himself. He found a place for me to live, and I worked hard as a day laborer in the fields of a village landlord. I did not want people to think I was living the life of a prostitute. I cried a lot in those days. I would think of the situation I was in, and tears kept on flowing. A year later the Mutaliyār man built a house on a government plot and we moved in together. Then I bore three children, all of whom died. When I realized that the fourth one—a boy—was going to make it, I thought, "This child is enough for me. I can raise him on my own." So I told the Mutaliyār man to get married.

It took him a while, but he finally found a bride. Right before his marriage, I told him, "Don't come back for at least a year. Don't come back until you have a baby!" Shortly thereafter his wife became pregnant. He shipped her back to her parents [it is customary for a Tamil woman to give birth in her mother's home] and showed up at my door. His wife gave birth to a boy, but he would not go to her. I told him to do so, but he wouldn't listen to me. So a few months later, I went to his wife's village with a basket of gifts. I persuaded her to come back. But she did not like it here, and so she returned to her mother's place. The Mutaliyār man made no attempt to get her back. Two years later he was actually thinking of getting married again [polygamy is illegal but not uncommon in Tamilnadu]. I went back to his wife and said, "Look, I have already wasted my life. Don't waste yours. Go back to him." She came back. But a few months later, her baby boy died and she hanged herself.

By then I was carrying another child of the Mutaliyār man. I agreed to feed him [which also means "to have sex with him"], and he moved back in with me. After the birth of our second boy, who survived, we had a girl. We now had three children together, but the Mutaliyār man did not want to provide for them. He filed a court case, contending that they were not his but my māmā's. He lost the case. My māmā lied, saying that he never tied my marriage necklace, and the village Brahmin priest corroborated his deposition. And so the Mutaliyār man was forced to acknowledge the paternity of my three children. Then his elder brother caused additional problems, claiming that since we were not married our children could not inherit their father's share of the family estate. I went to court to testify that I had no children from my māmā. We won the case, and my children were recognized as legitimate heirs of their father's property.

But the father of my children was making no provision for me. I realized this the day our village president died. While alive, our president had had a long-standing relationship with a Muslim lady to whom he willed nothing. The woman was left alone and completely destitute. On that day I overheard the father of my children say to a friend, "That will also be Ellamma's fate." His words hurt me so much that I immediately closed the door and poured my heart out. Who do you think I cried for? I cried for my māmā—I thought of his wealth, of his property, of the material security I could have had with him. The father of my children kept knocking at the door, but I did not open it. I kept on crying, and neighbors ran to listen to me. This is what I sang:

> *What you said has lighted my entire body afire.*
> *I am burning like a hot pot of oil.*
> *The fire of the hearth at least goes out sometimes.*
> *Because I am bound to you, my fire never goes out.*
> *The blacksmith's forge at least goes out every few days.*
> *It will take an eternity to put out and soothe my woman's heart.*
> *With jewels I was a vine that was full of life.*
> *Now there is no one to take care of me.*
> *I am dying with the vine.*
> *With precious stones I was the plant that was full of life.*
> *Now there is no one to embrace me*
> *I am dying with the plant.*

Ellamma is the woman who, in chapter 1, instructed a young widow on how to elicit pity with lament. Ellamma would undertake this sort of instruction even in the fields, so that her female coworkers might learn to do the same. She was not always pleased with the results. "These women are stupid," she once commented. "They forget what I teach them." Perhaps she was hard on her pupils because she herself was such a diligent student of comparisons, always making a point, for example, of listening to what other women sang at funerals so as to learn more crying songs.

My sense is that she was not stocking up dirges simply because verbal talent and the ability to play with poetic forms are highly valued in Tamil society. Ellamma herself might have had a deep appreciation for original metaphors and new images. But she also intuitively understood what James Fernandez calls the "persuasive power of tropes" (1986). She knew that the richer her comparisons were, the more convinced others would be of the truth of her lament. This was her objective, the reason she applied herself to her craft. Ellamma might have sometimes cried out dirges to assuage her kuṟai, but she lamented principally to move others to cry for her. In doing so she made her dirges an arsenal from which she could fire shots at anyone who tormented her.

Whenever someone close to her mistreated her, she would summon up a dirge on the spot to denounce his or her behavior. In this respect Ellamma was not alone. As the next case studies show, Tamil women from time to time lament in day-to-day life to complain about relatives who abuse them. To be clear, however, such behavior is not considered good form. I was often told that women should not cry out dirges outside the funeral context and especially not within earshot of others. But Ellamma had no such qualms; she even had the nerve to lament on auspicious occasions of the Tamil calendar year. For instance, once during the happy festivities of the Tamil New Year, (Poṅkal), her second son brought her some special delicacies—in this case, apples and oranges—as is customary on that day. But when Ellamma helped herself to an apple, her son scolded her, arguing that the fruits should be saved for his sick wife. Ellamma finished her domestic chores and went to a neighboring hill to collect wild rush. From there, she saw her firstborn son arriving from Madras for the family celebrations. Ellamma rushed down and greeted him with the following lament:

> Instead of the apple that I fancy,
> Son whom I bore!
> Should I, your mother, eat river mud?
> Instead of the food that I love,
> Little king whom I bore!
> Should I, your mother, eat the mud of the pond?
> Because I carried you when you were little,

Today my shoulder slopes,
My hip tilts.
Because of you I lost my strength.
Because of you I endured hardship.
Now, my little man, there is no one to call me "mother."

Ellamma also lamented the day her nephew got married. Apparently the young man had neglected to alert her that his new bride had arrived at the village for the marriage ceremony. This was a critical omission, because the formal arrival of a bride calls for special evening celebrations. Feeling ignored, Ellamma went home and, alone in her house, cried out that her nephew had spurned her because, as she explained, "I do not have fancy clothes, I am not rich enough for him." Here is how she wove this feeling into her dirge:

If I were doing well, young man!
I would go to your wedding
Wearing black, wearing silk.
To your eyes, the black would glitter
Like a brilliant light.

If I were doing well, young man!
I would go to your party
Wearing red, wearing silk.
The red would glitter
Like a brilliant light.

As Ellamma saw it, her weapon of choice worked. After they heard or were told about her songs, the father of her children included her in his will, her firstborn son bought her apples and oranges, and her nephew invited her to the ceremonial dinner. But not everyone in the village was prone to feeling sorry for Ellamma. Her female coworkers complained that "she whines all the time and speaks too much." As one woman put it, "No one can shut Ellamma up. No one can win an argument with her. When she starts a fight on the job, the only thing to do is to walk away and ignore her." Neighbors resented the high interest rates that Ellamma apparently charged on her cash loans and her demands for costly security deposits, often in the form of a brass pot. And Ellamma's occupation as midwife remained a source of malicious gossip: many whispered that she was greedy and had no principles.

Ellamma must have known that rumors of her complex reputation would reach me, for she often defended herself: "I am an old lady. I can't work as fast as my coworkers. They need to help me." She also justified her temper: "I don't wait to tell what is on my mind. I settle accounts on the spot." She never alluded to any money-lending activities, but on one occasion she offered her reason for tending at births: "People say that I deliver babies for the money. Sure, I get ten rupees and a measure of rice for cutting and tying the umbilical cord and cleaning up the place. But I do this work as a kind of charity. There is no barber woman in our village to do home deliveries. Not everyone is rich here; the poor can't afford a hospital birth that costs two to three hundred rupees. Childbirth is dangerous to the mother. Someone must help out. That's why I have been delivering babies around here for the past forty years. People keep calling me because I have lucky hands."

In this way Ellamma let me know in no uncertain terms that she was the victim of malicious gossip. She also hinted that she was needy, not greedy. The word *poverty* figured prominently in all of her self-descriptions. She often told me, "I go to bed hungry. The boss only feeds us *kañci* (rice gruel). It is not enough. I am so poor that I just want to die." That she craved more food of better quality was obvious one morning when I took her out for breakfast in Gingee. This little woman of no more than eighty-five pounds proceeded to gobble down all the vaṭais, tōcais, and pūris she could get her right hand on. She ate so much that she made herself sick. Nor was she above asking me for help. Whenever we parted, she would press her right palm against mine in hopes of finding a bill, for this was our discreet way of transacting money. Sometimes she would point to her torn sari or broken plastic bangles, her eyes imploring me to replace them.

My hunch is that Ellamma was neither worse nor better off than her neighbors. The difference was that she never missed an opportunity to deplore her life circumstances. This is not surprising: the expert at lamenting, the constant crier of dirges, had internalized the emotions of her comparisons. Kuṟai—that feeling of utter depletion—had become her main, and perhaps sole, way of being in the world. It guided not only the way she talked about her life but also the very way she talked to and related to others. Imploring people to feel sorry for her had become her primary mode of social interaction. And in her attempt to convince others of her losses, Ellamma simultaneously persuaded herself of the truth of her lament.

According to her narrative, she began this pattern the day her father's children casually revealed that he had not included her in his will. According to Ellamma, she had cried, "With jewels, I was a vine that was full of life. Now there is no one to take care of me. I am dying with the vine." Ellamma told me that these lines were meant to say: "When I lived with my māmā [her first husband], I was rich and happy; with the Mutaliyār man I am poor and miserable." This comparison, however, contradicted what she had told me about her māmā. In her account this man does not exactly figure as the good provider that Ellamma in her dirge makes him out to be. He was not particularly supportive when she lost her infant baby. He was not even around. He practically starved her when rumor had it that she was fooling around with the Mutaliyār man. And besides, no one had forced Ellamma to leave her māmā; she had run away of her own free will. Granted, her subsequent relationship with the Mutaliyār had deprived her of basic rights and amenities, but her praise of, and yearning for, her māmā seemed somewhat excessive, if not painfully ironic. In the light of later hardships, her memories of her husband were colored by nostalgia. But there was no going back. Once Ellamma articulated this regret, it took on a life of its own. It became the major leitmotif of her dirges. At virtually any funeral, she would expand on it.

Her lament took on a particular intensity the day her māmā died. As soon as she arrived at his funeral, she told me, she removed her marriage necklace and placed it on his bier. This was a strange thing to do because usually a Kavuṇṭar widow removes her *tāli* not on the funeral day but on the sixteenth, or last, day *(karumāti)* of the funeral cycle. Ellamma's gesture was even stranger considering that she was not really her māmā's widow. Although her children's father had never married her, she had lived with the Mutaliyār man for over forty years and essentially was his wife. Ellamma explained her behavior: "Why should I have not removed my tāli? My māmā was the one who tied it, and he had died. I had the right *(urimai)* to be his widow. And why should I have waited to remove it?"

Ellamma took the opportunity of her māmā's funeral to voice publicly what had become the summation of her life. She told me what she cried then:

On the rock I am a bud of jasmime.
I am the bud that does not bear fruit.
If I had borne fruit,
My husband's place would not be able to hold me.

On the fence I am a bud of jasmine.
I am the bud that was not picked.
If I had been picked,
Our house would not be able to hold me.

"The 'rock,'" Ellamma then explained, "stands for my children's father. Because I live with him, I am not expanding, I am alone. If my māmā had not abandoned me on this rock, I would be surrounded by relatives." As she restated, "Had I lived with my māmā, had he picked me, I would be rich in relations. I would not have had to sell sweet potatoes; I would not have had to pound rice and grind flour as I did for the last twenty years. My māmā would have taken care of me." Ellamma added that she sang this particular dirge to her māmā's relatives to make them feel bad for her. She said, "I wanted them to think 'What a shame Ellamma did not get to live with her māmā. If she had, she would be among people of her kind [Kavuṇṭars rather than Mutaliyārs]. She would not feel like an outcaste in her own family. Her children would have a lot of relatives. They would not be strangers to us; they would have married among us. If they had had problems, they could have addressed themselves to us; we would have helped them.'"

But Ellamma's lament did not succeed in eliciting pity or commiseration. In fact, the family ignored her, and no one gave her the respect and consideration due a widow. Her māmā's daughter—the very woman Ellamma had helped bring up—did not even hug her, nor did she present her with the ceremonial sari due a widow. It was a terrible day for Ellamma, who went home feeling completely defeated. There too she got into trouble. Her children were appalled by her self-professed widow status. They scolded her, saying, "Our father is alive, and you go around saying you are a widow! You have disrespected him and us as well!" Many in the village made fun of her: "You cried so well for your māmā. How are you going to cry for the father of your children?"

But Ellamma persisted in behaving like her māmā's widow. Despite general protest, she refused to bear the auspicious insignia of a married woman. Accordingly, she stopped dressing her hair with flowers and daubing her forehead with a small dot of vermilion powder. By that time she seemed to be beyond the point of letting her laments tell her life story. She was living the story line of her comparisons. Once happily married, she had become a poor widow that everyone derided.

And yet I suspect that if her children's father were to die before her, she would assign a different meaning to her comparisons. My hunch is that she would then yearn for her life with the Mutaliyār. This is because, for Ellamma, lament is an opportunist language that exploits the circumstances in which she finds herself in order to make other people cry for her. Her dirges serve her need to be pitied, even if it is to the detriment of past specifics, memories, or former struggles. And so, much as she now praises her māmā, Ellamma might one day very well recollect all the things the Mutaliyār had done for her. In so doing she might even convince herself that this man, too, was good to her.

RENUKA

Tamil women usually begin to join crying clusters after marriage. By the time their parents die, which often happens when the daughters are in their forties, the latter can be fully adept in the genre of crying songs. By then, I was told, women need little effort to reach a state of disappointment, as their hearts are already full of kuṟai. Indeed, by this stage of their lives women have endured many ordeals—separation from natal kin, death of children, disputes with in-laws, and so on—all of which they deplore in their dirges. But as the next case study confirms, what most distresses women, and what they continuously grieve about in their dirges, is troubled marital relationships.

Around sixty years old when I met her, Renuka was of medium height, stocky, and had a broad face, a high square forehead, a strong jaw, and small brown eyes. This Kavuṇṭar woman and her husband, a retired schoolteacher, owned a housing complex on a back street in Gingee, and they sublet the apartment adjacent to theirs to one of my Tamil women friends. I met Renuka when my friend put me up for a week upon my return to the field in 1999. Both my friend and Renuka were unhappily married, so the atmosphere in the stone-wall compound was unbearably tense. There was no escaping the frequent angry outbursts, the loaded silences, and the furtive glances that seemed to ask, "See what my husband is doing to me?" To me the compound felt like a trap, and it most certainly felt worse to the two women who rarely ever left it. Only when their husbands were out did they seem to relax and breathe. They would take those opportunities to get together in the rear courtyard and share their marital misfortunes while washing pots, grinding spices, and cutting vegetables, but always with an ear on the alleyway, quick to detect a husband's footsteps and to change the subject of conversation.

My role in these sessions was limited to listening and commiserating, until I found out that Renuka was a reputed singer of dirges. When I asked her about the truth of this rumor, she let me know in no uncertain terms that she was not about to sing for me. She told me flat out, "I can't lament for you. How can I cry when I am not in a state of *kuṟai*? The words won't come." I tried to tell her that there was no need to cry out a dirge, that I only wanted to know what sort of comparisons Tamil women made at funerals and why, but my response aggravated her further. "How are you going to understand our dirges if you don't hear them?" she replied in a disapproving tone. Then one afternoon she suddenly took it upon herself to sing me a dirge. But as soon as she began, the tears came and she stopped, which, as I have already explained, is the usual pattern of events. Rather than cast a pall on our relationship, though, her aborted lament brought us closer together. Her sobs had brought tears to my eyes and prompted me to reach for her hand—an empathic reaction that I was to learn later is culturally appropriate and even desirable. As I note in chapter 1, when she laments to someone, a woman wants to move her audience. Perhaps gratified by my emotional response, Renuka insisted on sharing her dirges with me from that point on. However, she would only recite them, without any melody or tune, as if she were reading from a book.

Renuka was never able to explain her songs. Unlike Ellamma, she had no feel for the ethnographic endeavor and even less interest in translating cultures—hers or mine. Moreover, this brusque yet big-hearted woman viewed all my questions regarding "social patterns," "gender roles," and similar abstractions as misguided. They could explain nothing important about dirges. When I once made a correlation between her lyrics and what I refer to in chapter 1 as "the orphaned daughter's plight," she asked me squarely, "What does this have to do with my song?" Then she drew me back into her life, demanding my full attention to her conjugal problems. Renuka was the most intense of all my female consultants, and it was impossible to miss the connection between her domestic troubles and the story line of her laments.

Renuka never recounted her life story in the way that Ellamma had. She did not have Ellamma's skills as a storyteller—Ellamma's sense of plot and her flair for climactic denouements. She also followed a different narrative model. Whereas Ellamma strongly emphasized her past as a dramatic counterpoint to her current situation, Renuka was somehow indifferent to the subject of her beginnings. Even the stamp of childhood on her seemed light. What weighed on her, and what was particularly memorable to her, was the tug of the ever present. Over time I did glean a few facts about her life—where and when she was born, how many siblings she had, and so forth—but in her accounts, Renuka always returned to the painful immediacies of her marital relationship. I quote from what she told me at some length:

I was born in the North Arcot district. I had one brother and four sisters. Our mother was like gold. Our father never beat us. In my childhood I did not study. Back then, people did not send girls to school. Even my brother did not get past third grade. Because my parents owned some land, my siblings and I worked in their fields. My job was to tend the cattle, which is why you sometimes can hear my husband yell out, "You're just a stupid cowgirl; don't talk back to me!" Because I was late to come of age, my parents did not arrange my marriage until I was twenty. In the old days [Renuka added for my benefit], we had no say over these arrangements. We had to marry whomever our parents chose. Mine decided on a man who was acquainted with us through common relatives in our village. He was a high school teacher with a good income. My parents thought he would make me happy.

From the very start this man gave me problems. On our wedding day he humiliated me by spurning my parents' gifts. Our first year was miserable. It is not that I was afraid of him [Renuka was referring to his sexual demands], for I was already brave then, but we would clash on every little thing. He is selfish and insensitive, always thinking of himself and never of me. He has never acknowledged that throughout our marriage I did my best to help him out. When we lost our baby girl, I hid my grief so as not to burden him. When we could not support our three children on his salary, I did whatever I could to make ends meet. I bought a cow and twice a day sold its milk to neighbors. At harvest times I went to work in the houses of local landlords. From morning to night I would remove the husk of raw rice or shell peanuts. But my husband never thanked me for taking on these various jobs [Renuka cried]. At times all I wanted to do was run away, but I put up with him and endured his abuse because I did not want to spoil my parents' reputation.

The past ten years have been the worst. My husband is getting old. He knows he is not going to be around forever, and he is taking out on me his fear of dying. Last night he got up at two o'clock to scold me. It is not like it never happened before. In the past he would sometimes hit me or bang me on the wall in the middle of the night because I would not have sex with him. But last night he was positively crazy, yelling out, "When I came home, did you bother asking me whether I ate? You bitch! You're not taking care of me. You see how you are going to cry after I die." I could not sleep afterward. I lay awake the whole night. These kinds of scenes are very hard on me. And they happen more and more. The other day I spilled a tumbler of water near his food. He got mad. I tried to tell him, "It was just an accident," but he replied, "You are just a pig. You'll be slaughtered like a pig after my death." [Renuka cried again.]

He is very needy and always hungry, and I have a hard time meeting his needs. I am getting old too. My neck aches, and I can't wait on him the way I used to. But the main problem is that he is just rude and abusive. For example, last week he asked the son of a neighbor to dig a pit near our septic tank so that he could plant a banana tree. I did not think it was a good location and I told him so. He yelled back angrily, "In which cunt should I plant the tree, then?" Like this, he insulted me in front of the boy. [Renuka cried.] When later that day my son scolded him for that obscene display, my husband said, "I am going out to buy some insecticide for our coconut trees." This was his way of punishing me, his way of saying, "You're so bad that I am going to kill myself."

Who cares whether my husband takes poison or hangs himself? Who cares about him? He fights for any small thing for no reason at all. I have no peace of mind with him. Let him die. This is what I'll sing at his funeral: "What did you keep? What did you keep? Around the house you kept shit." [Renuka laughed, and yet immediately after became serious again.] All four of my sisters have lost their husbands, so I know what it's like to be a widow. I do not want my husband to die. I just wish he wasn't making problems.

Renuka did not recount such episodes with the intention of making me feel sorry for her. She was gratified when I would offer sympathy but was not prone to exploit my reaction. Nor was she inclined, as far as I could tell, to share her unhappy story with people who lived outside her compound—either in speech or lament. Renuka was, in fact, leery of public displays of lament, especially outside the funeral context. "It is not good taste," she once told me, "to cry our lives out before people. I would not do it, no matter what my husband did to me. I don't want people to know that there are problems in our home. If they were to find out, they would speak badly of us. They would soil the good name of our family." Renuka was also fearful of her husband's reaction. "If I were to lament at home in full view of the neighbors," she explained, "my husband would beat me. It would only make things worse."

Whenever she could not endure any more of her husband's abuse, Renuka would cry *alone* at home.[6] As she told me, "When my heart bubbles and destroys me, I simply need to throw everything out." I don't wait for a funeral. I simply wait for my husband to leave. Then I lock myself in the house and cry out quietly." When asked why she locked the door, she replied, "So that no one interrupts me, so that I can cry as much as I want." When I tried to discover what she wailed on such occasions, she said in a firm voice, "I don't know. I never think about what is coming out of my mouth. The words just come out. Everything comes out."

Over time, however, I recorded thirteen of Renuka's dirges, and I was struck by their distinctive and gloomy sense of temporality. Unlike Ellamma, whose dirges at least hinted that if only the past would persist into the present she would be happy, Renuka did not make such conjectures. Nor did she juxtapose events of yesterday and today. Instead Renuka made different kinds of comparisons, ones that evoked the hopelessness, even the inescapable finality, of her current situation. She once contrasted, for example, her feelings of entrapment with the crow's freedom:

When the crow grieves,
It goes far away.
When I grieve,
Where can I go?

When a small bird grieves,
It finds refuge in other nests.
When I grieve,
Where can I find shelter for my heart?

Renuka's lyrics also differed from those of Ellamma on the subject of praise. She seldom complimented the dead—or the living for that matter. In fact, she habitually accused them of neglect and abandonment. As the following dirge suggests, even her mother failed to protect her:

Because I was hot, because I was hot,
I went around the silver mountain,
Where all the hunters aimed their bows.
I became a *vēṅkai* tree, my dear mother,
I became a flower for the hunters.

Because I was thirsty, because I was thirsty,
I went around the golden mountain,
Where all the hunters raised their sticks.
I became a *tavaci* tree, my dear mother,
I became a flower for the hunters.

Since I did not understand this dirge, and since Renuka was usually loath or unable to explain anything to me, I asked my old friend Ellamma to interpret it. Her first reaction was that I had recorded a widow's lament. "The woman in this dirge," she said, "is hot, steaming with kuṟai, like a widow. And like a widow she is also isolated, without protection, which is why she compares herself to a lonely tree and a flower that is vulnerable to sexual predators with 'bows' and 'sticks.'" Later Ellamma offered an entirely different interpretation. "It may be that the woman of this dirge is infertile. Because she cannot conceive, she goes around the mountain to ask the gods for a child. If this is the case, then the hunters stand for the woman's in-laws, who will mistreat her if her prayer fails."

Neither of these explanations resonated with Renuka, who was neither a widow nor barren. "You got it all wrong," she responded to my transmission of Ellamma's comments. "In this dirge I complain to my mother that I am in a state of kuṟai and have no one to turn to. When I despair, when I am 'hot' or 'thirsty,' I don't have relatives to go to. Because I am on my own, all alone, in the wild, 'around the mountain,' I am easy prey for my husband—the hunter, the plucker. The only way I can survive is by hiding my feelings and hardening like a tree."

Throughout most of her married life, Renuka specifically faulted her brother for not protecting her from her husband. At funerals, she often wailed the following dirge, which, although vague in its indictment, incriminated him personally.

Among the dancing deer,
An arrow shot a golden doe.
I was the target of that arrow.
I became the fire of the flame.
There is no water in the river
To put out this fire.

Amid the gathering of deer,
A sword stabbed a golden doe.
I was the victim of that sword.
I became a basket of fire.
There is no water in the pond
To put out this fire.

"I am the deer of this song," Renuka said, "I was playing. But then, when I married my husband, I was shot. I became the target of his abuse [arrow, sword] and anger [fire]. I have no one—not even a brother to protect me from him."

Renuka's dirges are therefore bleaker than those of Ellamma. They express not merely deprivation but a sense of being transgressed and wounded, evidenced by the fact that the majority of her lyrics compare herself with a stabbed deer, for example, or a hunted bird. Such vivid images of injury—physical and violent—are consistent with the way Renuka talked to me about her life. The crucial episodes of her ongoing account, and perhaps its sole raison d'être, address the times her husband abused and brutalized her. Ellamma, on the other hand, never complained that the father of her children beat her up. That Ellamma did not fear this man was evident in the fact that she would complain about the losses he had caused her to whomever was willing to listen.

What Renuka's lament language did share with that of Ellamma, however, is that it had become habitual, so much a part of her self-description that it prevented her from speaking of herself in any other terms. Yet Renuka was more than simply her husband's prey and a casualty of a bad marriage. She was also a relatively well-off landlady, the mother of a boy whom we have seen was quick to defend her, and the grandmother of an adorable toddler who played in her compound all day long. Why did she seldom mention these other facts of her life? Perhaps her omissions were symptomatic of her oppression or depression. But Renuka's lament did not purely express her inner state. It did that too, of course, and I do not mean to minimize her suffering. But a language of lament, as seen in the previous case study, also organizes a woman's subjectivity. At the very least it narrows it, thereby limiting and focusing her experiences. This restricting process may last forever, for once a language of lament is formulated, it persists stubbornly in spite of changed conditions. Ellamma, I previously suggested, would keep on feeling poorer than before, no matter how much cash she might raise, and Renuka would always find herself alone and wounded.

JANAKI

Perhaps as a result of their caste specialization in matters related to death and funerals, Dalit women tend to know more dirges than women of other castes do; they are also considered better singers (Trawick 1988a, 1991; Racine 1995). Renuka told me, "The women from the colony are born with the dirges. They always attract attention at funerals. No one can cry like them. No one has ever cried like them." A Dalit woman was also proud to say, "When we cry, the gods come down to hear us. We have the gift of voice *[kural]*. We know the art of singing. We may not go to school, but at least we have that going for us—we sing well."

Clearly the prerequisites for becoming an accomplished crier of dirges go beyond caste affiliation. Inner disposition and the various emotional characteristics described earlier are also part of the formula. While women from the colony may know many dirges and drawl them well—"with meaning," they would say—they are also subject to the criteria that distinguish much of Tamil lament. Unless they feel kuṟai, they cannot lament. It is not farfetched to speculate that Paṟaiyar women cry well because they suffer more deprivation than women of any other social class. But not every Paṟaiyar woman is willing to bemoan her disappointments. Some may even be reluctant to do so.

In 1990, Janaki, a Paṟaiyar woman from Gingee, gave me the chance to work with a funeral petitioner (see also chapter 4). Married to Janaki's husband's sister, this man must have felt comfortable in her home, for that was usually where I found him. As I got to know Janaki, I discovered that she was not only smart but savvy, especially regarding matters of gender. A large woman with beautiful eyes and a great voice, she missed no opportunity to put men down, and she did it within their earshot. For example, when I asked her brother-in-law why the god Brahmā (who figures in the narration of the petition for the dead) seemed uninformed about the world, Janaki answered in his place, "Gods are like men: they are stupid. This is why they need two wives." On another occasion, she elaborated her views on marriage: "The wife is wiser than the husband. He shouldn't do anything without consulting her, for she knows what's best." It was hard to resist her feminist worldview.

When she understood upon my return to Tamilnadu in 1999 that I was interested in crying songs, Janaki offered to perform for me. She had witnessed my tape-recording of her brother-in-law's petition and was familiar with my mode of working. She was well aware, for instance, that our sessions would produce written transcriptions and extensive discussions. Sadly, however, our collaboration led to the deterioration of our relationship. For one thing, Janaki had difficulty performing dirges before my tape recorder. Like Renuka, as soon as she began her first song she cried and stopped altogether. Unlike Renuka, however, she blamed me for putting her in this odd situation—not in so many words but with reproach nonetheless.

Perhaps because she knew I would pay her and she needed the money, she made a point of learning to perform oppāri without crying. But Janaki would not comment on her dirges—a surprise, considering how smart and verbal she was. "Just publish my dirges as they are," she once told me. "No need for explanations, not even for American people." Renuka too had been reticent to regard laments as if they were pictures of cultural scenes requiring explanatory captions. But at least Renuka gave me a strong clue: by means of her comparisons she transposed her experience in the story of her dirges. What she cryied about was real and personal: it was currently happening to her. Janaki never hinted that her personal life was the subject of her lyrics. Nor did she seem to attribute any significance to them for that matter. "It is just a story," she would reply to my questions about her dirges. "It has no meaning." And indeed her songs recounted epiclike scenarios that seemed more allegorical and symbolic than the realist plots voiced by Ellamma and Renuka. For example, she sang:

Beyond the silver mountains,
Near the place of the prostitutes,
After playing dice for money,
My dear son Ciralan,
You entered the brothel.
Who knows what the prostitute asked?
Who knows what you said?
Just throw two coins to the whore,
That's enough, and come home.

Since Janaki was neither an enthusiastic nor a very good informant, eventually I stopped engaging her on the subject of lament. But since she was intelligent and perceptive in human affairs, I asked her questions about her life, expecting her narrative to tell me something her dirges had not. Initially, this expectation turned out to be a mistake. Her autobiography was no more introspective than her dirges. But telling it eventually led Janaki to explain why she was reluctant to open up.

Janaki did not remember much of her childhood beyond its persistent poverty. She was born in a Paṟaiyar colony a few miles from the temple town of Tiruvaṇṇāmalai. The sixth child in the family, she looked after two younger brothers while her elder siblings and parents toiled in the local fields of caste-Hindu landlords. Although the family owned a parcel of land, it was so small and dry that the one crop of millet it yielded each year was insufficient to supplement their meager wages. "We were very poor," Janaki often told me, "I don't know how we got by." When asked what she remembered most vividly of her early years, she replied without hesitation, "Hunger," and then added: "We did not have enough food. At times we did not even have rice water. Many times I went to sleep without eating."

That Janaki's reminiscences of her relationships with her parents and siblings were infrequent did not surprise me. In general the Tamil women I met had little to say about early family dynamics. Their parents had been wonderful to them, and most of the time there was nothing more to tell. As we have just seen, however, women like Ellamma and Renuka could speak endlessly of their marriages, often beginning their personal narratives with their wedding day, as if nothing had transpired prior to this major life-cycle transition. By contrast Janaki was extremely reserved about her marriage. She was willing to recollect only the relatively frightening yet typical experience that she and many young Tamil brides underwent when their husbands began to make sexual demands on them. She recounted:

At eighteen, I married the son of my father's sister. He was very poor, and I thought that God had fated me to work hard for the rest of my life. At the beginning my husband and I did not speak—we did not say a word to each other for the first three months. I had so much fear. Being married to him was like fighting with Yamā [the god of death]. Do you think he left me alone? Do you think that they bring us [women] only to cook rice? We have to sleep with them [men], make babies, and fulfill their desires. That is why I had fear in my heart. But there was no way to hide. My husband tracked me down everywhere I went. We were living with his eight brothers, their wives, and [their] children, all in one house. To avoid being with him at night, I would go to sleep with my sisters-in-law, but they would arrange for my husband to find me. [Janaki laughed.] Then they would lock the door behind the two of us. I shouted, but no one ever came to rescue me. [She laughed again.] My husband never beat me. He waited for me to come to him. I feared him for three years. Then God made us come together.

The rest of Janaki's account was telescopic. She related how she and her husband eventually moved out of his ancestral home because, as she explained, "there were simply too many of us living under the same roof." The couple moved around a lot, finally settling in a one-room thatched-roof hut near Gingee, where they supported their six children by doing various agricultural jobs. About her marriage of forty-five years, Janaki had almost nothing to say. The little she did report was idyllic: "My husband is a nice man." "He does not drink, does not beat me." "We don't argue." Actually, she portrayed everyone in the same rosy light: "My parents never scolded us." "I never fought with my siblings." "My mother-in-law was good to me." The funeral petitioner I mentioned earlier, to whom she was related by alliance, "didn't lie, always did the right thing." She never spoke of troubled bonds, disappointments, or for that matter, anything that might have explained why and what she lamented at funerals. Even her recollection of her older son's death at age twenty-eight from a convulsive fit while bathing in a pond was relatively flat, as if this terrible tragedy had not happened to her personally.

While in the field, I often wondered whether Janaki was subscribing to a tacit cultural model that defines the Tamil genre of autobiography as an idealized account of one's life and relationships. But I never pondered this possibility too long, for two reasons. First, I do not think that life stories or personal narratives constitute an active genre among rural

Tamil women, not even in informal contexts of intimacy. In villages there is no need to tell one's story: everybody else already knows it. Moreover, for reasons already explained in this chapter, Tamil women are fearful of revealing private personal or family matters to neighbors.[7] Second, I had ample evidence to show that, if a model existed for talking about the past and especially about one's childhood, Tamil women did not employ it to speak about the present. Ellamma and Renuka, at least, were quick to abandon the idiom of praise when describing their current relationships with husbands, brothers, and children. So why did Janaki, a forceful and loquacious woman, not bring up her disappointments? Was she discreet? Resigned? Or was her life truly that good?

I came upon an explanation a few days before I left the field. One sunny morning Janaki showed up rather unexpectedly at my door. This was unusual behavior, because her typically long shifts in the fields did not allow for unscheduled visits. Her arrival was all the more surprising because I had gone to her house the day before to say goodbye. I invited her to have coffee with me on a mat in my rented house, and Janaki told me why she had come. For all the time we had spent together, she said in a regretful tone of voice, we had never really gotten to know each other. I responded that I felt the same way, but that I had sensed all along that *she* was the one who had created the distance between us. She denied that this was the case. Then I reminded her that, rather than sharing her problems with me, as friends do, she had consistently given me a vague and rosy picture of her life. Her reply gave me much to think about. "If I had begun to tell you about my difficulties," she said, "it would all have come out. I would not have been able to stop. I have kuṟai. I have four sons, two of whom I don't talk to because I don't get along with their wives. I struggled so much to raise my children. When my sons ignore me, do you know how much that hurts? I have kuṟai. It is there in my heart, but I don't want to speak about it. What is the use of dwelling on our disappointments? What is the use of getting ourselves all worked up?"

Only then did I understand what Janaki had perhaps tried to tell me all along. The process of rehashing one's sorrow through speech and especially lament was not liberating, cathartic, or even healthful—at least not to her. On the contrary, she implied, it was fruitless or, worse, dangerous and psychologically damaging to brood about problems: it would leave her emotionally unsteady, vulnerable to the sway of sorrow and beyond the point of consolation.

Not that Janaki only cried out dirges of duty or necessity. At times, she lamented for the same reasons as Ellamma. She too had experienced the support and compassion that crying songs could win her. She once told me, "If my son makes me cry, my husband will say to him, 'Why are you making your mother cry?' Then he'll comfort me. 'Why are you concerned about your son? Don't worry—until I die I will protect you.'" Like Ellamma, she knew how to use the genre of lamentation as punishment for critical kin, thereby revealing what her dirges failed to convey at first glance: namely, her desire and predilection for manipulation. "Sometimes," she told me in an uncharacteristic disclosure, "my husband criticizes my cooking. 'There is not enough salt in the curry.' 'The rice is not properly cooked.' We fight, and I lament on the floor of our house. Let him hear my pain and realize the damage he has done, so that he'll think twice before scolding me again."

But first glances are not always misleading. I have returned to Janaki's dirges again and again, and I do not find self-pity or anger in their emotional range. Unlike Ellamma's and Renuka's repertoires, which sound like advertisements for particular nostalgias or grievances, Janaki's dirges, while sad and melancholic, are entirely without sentimentality and wrath. They do not accuse, nor do they conjure a past that is sweeter and more precious because it is gone or never was.

My hunch is that this untouchable woman actually sung not dirges but rather the kind of songs men from her caste have the duty to sing at funerals. That she borrowed or at least drew on these so-called death songs was evident in her lyrics, which recount epiclike scenarios, the very kind of scenarios that, as the next chapter shows, the Dalits usually parody so as to distract mourners from their grief. Death songs also influenced the aesthetics of her laments. The criteria that determine the power or beauty of a man's death song have more to do with talent than inner disposition and emotion. Likewise, Janaki was of the opinion that "what matters about a woman's dirge is not her feelings, but her voice and delivery." This statement, which she often repeated as a way perhaps to preempt my questions about the meanings of her dirges, completely contradicted what my other female consultants had told me. Ellamma, for example, had underscored over and over the point that "the trademark *[urimai]* of a good oppāri singer is her discontentment." And Renuka never failed to remind me that "a woman cannot lament if she doesn't feel kuṟai."

Had I listened more carefully, I might have discerned much sooner that Janaki was not the lamenter that both Ellamma and Renuka were. Unlike these two women who had been fascinated by the language of comparisons from an early age, Janaki revealed a long-standing and deep-seated ambivalence for women's dirges. As a teenager she had made fun of these crying songs, performing them at home with exaggerated emphasis to make her younger siblings laugh. In doing so she imitated Dalit funeral singers, who, as I argue in the next chapter, exploit a similar style of delivery to deride the subjects of loss and attachment. Perhaps Janaki embraced the male genre of funeral singing at such a young age because she already had a sense that it was risky to dwell on disappointments. As she was to discover later on, laments might mollify others, but once out they surge with such force and intensity that she could not stop them. It was safer not to compare. That way, the indictments and the thwarted expectations that dominate comparisons did not define her and her relationships to others. That way she remained in control of herself.

ARCHANA

Unlike Janaki my fourth and final consultant derived comfort from releasing her kuṟai through dirges. This comfort was not born out of the kind of satisfaction that Ellamma felt when she succeeded in making others feel sorry for her. Nor did it result in a desperate outpouring of emotions, as was the case when Renuka lamented alone in her house or in the privacy of crying clusters. It was a quieter and less dramatic kind of consolation that might actually be closer to what most Tamil women feel when they lament.

A Paṟaiyar widow, Archana had high cheekbones, bright eyes, and full lips that made her look younger than the sixty years she claimed. She lived alone in a small thatched hut on the outskirts of a large untouchable colony to the east of Gingee, supplementing the allowance her children provided her by working a few days a week as a laborer in the fields. The work was hard on her back and knees, and she really did not need to earn money, but she wanted extra cash, she said, "so that I can spoil my grandchildren."

What first attracted me to Archana was her generosity and humor. Of course, charismatic and entertaining personalities are a trademark—almost a requirement—of Tamil singers, even when they specialize in dirges. Ellamma, Renuka, and Janaki were, in their own ways, droll and captivating. But Archana was irresistible. She had a natural talent for mimicry, mockery, and especially self-derision, and she rarely missed an opportunity to flaunt her gifts. She performed for me one morning when I was interviewing her neighbor, a funeral singer, on the subject of men's death songs.

Upon my arrival she and her women friends had huddled on the singer's front porch, where they proceeded to giggle and interrupt the interview with their own comments. It was soon impossible to carry on a focused conversation. When I finally surrendered, Archana insisted that she cry for me. Rather than await my reply, this Tamil village widow—and a frequent target of slander—began her typical lament. "I have heard a lot of bad things about me," she sang. "To whom am I going to report them?" Archana must not have felt personally victimized by the malicious gossip, for she produced these lines with such exaggeration that everyone laughed. Someone joked that, because I had brought my tape recorder, "a quality singer was in order." Archana pretended to be offended. Her sense of indignation was so dramatically overstated that her friends and I could not stop laughing.

Archana was not a very good crier of songs. Her voice did not project, and her drawn-out pronunciation of vowels often sounded forced. When catching her breath, she would frequently hiss and cough. Like my other consultants, she was also inhibited by the ethnographic constructs of the gathering. "Here in your home," she would say, "the song is not coming. I am not used to crying in other people's houses, and normally I am scolded for doing so . . . . For the dirge to come," she would add, "I must feel kuṟai." On other occasions, she would tell me that I made her feel self-conscious, a state not conducive to lamenting: "I cannot cry here, because I am afraid of what you'll think of my song."

I tried to tell her that my opinions mattered little, for that was the truth. Although I knew she was conversant in the lament tradition—she knew dozens of dirges and could convey the details of their appeal and meaning—it was the woman rather than the crier of songs that I pursued in Archana. To some extent this was also the case with Renuka, who ultimately was more of a friend than a consultant. But Renuka was intense, and she weighed me down with the sadness of her bad marriage. Archana, on the other hand, was lighthearted, uncomplicated, and without boundaries. I seldom sensed a cultural barrier between us. She seemed to feel the same, for she once declared with her usual exuberance, "Save for our skin colors, you and I are alike, like older and younger sisters." She connected this way with other women as well, for, unlike my other female consultants, Archana had many women friends. Since she seldom was alone, conversations with her usually involved these other Paṟaiyar women, whose perspectives on lament enrich my discussion here.

All these women confirmed what my three earlier consultants had told me in so many ways: they had been happiest during childhood. This claim still strikes me as a good example of the kind of radical differences we encounter in the field. The notion that childhood is the best time in life seems to me to run against most of what Western psychology and its scholarly or popular spokespersons presume about the development of an individual over time. Do we in the West not hold the belief that childhood is when we form oedipal, neurotic, and dysfunctional attachments that plague us for the rest of our lives? The Tamil women I met maintained the reverse proposition: their youth had been blissful, their first relationships (especially with parents) extraordinary.[8]

The traumatic event or the circumstance that had caused them to first experience a state of unfulfillment was their marriage.[9] As one woman put it, "In my mother's place, I didn't know anything about disappointment and sorrow *[cañcalam]*. Only after my marriage did I come to feel the meaning of these words." Even Janaki, who was raised in abject poverty, agreed: "Although my mother was hard up, I was at peace in my natal house—no one to scold me, to tell me what to do. I was happy there."[10] Women who seemed content with their marriages even said, "We may be happy in our husbands' homes, but we were eight times happier in our parents' houses. The love is stronger toward our natal house." Finally, each of the women profiled in this chapter told me that, as marriage marks a sudden end to their state of fulfillment and the introduction of kuṟai into their lives, so it marks the beginning of their laments; "We cry almost all of our dirges after marriage. Before that we had no reason to cry." Indeed the prototypical woman of Tamil dirges laments almost entirely according to this pattern. The woman begins to make comparisons when she marries and moves out of her parents' place. Before that, a woman is not expected to know anything about kuṟai. That is why she has no story to tell, no comparison to draw.

Thus many of the dirges examined in chapter 1 indicate that Tamil lament is born of women's longings to recover their former lives in their natal houses. And yet, as we have just seen, in their actual life stories neither Ellamma, Renuka, nor Janaki made much of the loss of this past. Even Ellamma, who in her dirges often contrasted life with to life without a mother (or father), never hinted that she missed these early days. In contrast, Archana's life story is full of regrets and yearnings for her parents and her long-gone childhood. In fact, her account matches perfectly the prototypical experiences of the orphaned daughter as profiled in Tamil dirges. I have edited the first part of the account that follows into a more readable form. I have paraphrased the second part, which, unlike the first, was recorded over the course of many interviews spanning several weeks.

I was born in the town of Malaiyaṉūr. My father was the headman (talaivar) *of the local Paṟaiyar colony. Besides earning a regular salary, he had land that my three brothers cultivated. We were so well off that we could afford to cook large batches of porridge every day. We never ran out of food, even during the drought. My parents raised me well; they never beat me or sent me to work. I will never forget the days I spent in their house. I think of them more frequently now that my own children are grown up.*

I got married when I was young. I don't know how old I was, but I had not even reached puberty. My husband was the son of my father's sister. I was his second wife. His first wife had left him because she did not like his mother. My husband was much older than I. By the time we got married, his first wife had already given birth to four children with her second husband. That's how old he was. It took me four years to get used to him. At first I ignored him. I did not like him. I did not like being his second wife. I did not like his looks. I was so unhappy that I often ran back to my mother's place. My parents never pressured me to leave. My husband was patient too. He would wait a week or two before coming to pick me up. On the way back home, we would walk so far apart on the path that no one could have guessed we were husband and wife. If someone asked me, "Who is this man?" I would reply, "You tell me!" At this, my husband would laugh; he was a good man. For the first three years of our marriage, I continually ran away. Then one day my elder brother scolded me severely for spoiling our family's good name, and so I stopped. But God only knows why I came back and settled here.

I was fifteen or sixteen when I first got pregnant. First I had two sons, both of whom died in infancy. Then I gave birth to a daughter and then again to three more girls. Finally, I bore my son. My husband and I worked hard to raise our five children. My mother-in-law sent me to work as a laborer in the fields. She was a very cruel person, very mean to my two sisters-in-law and me. She underfed us, giving us a mere bowl of porridge daily. It was never enough after a hard day of work and a long trek back from the fields. I could not say anything to her. My husband never intervened, but my father-in-law would scold his wife. "Give the girls more food," he would say. This man was like gold, but he died very soon after my marriage. My mother-in-law, on the other hand, went on to live ten more years. Ten years of sheer misery! Neighbors would comfort me, assuring me that the old lady was not going to live forever, but this did not stop my tears.

I learned subsequently that, during this time, Archana began to lament at village funerals. "I did not cry for the dead," she told me; "I cried for myself. I was poor and miserable in my mother-in-law's house. Nothing had prepared me for that kind of life. I had had such a happy childhood; my parents and brothers had taken such good care of me. I would remember the past and cry." Not surprisingly, the dirges that most appealed to her, and which she mastered at funerals one at a time by listening to more experienced lamenting women, summoned up the good things done by parents for daughters. She would evoke such things, she once said, "to remember the past." And while working in the fields, she would deride her mother-in-law by singing a different genre, called "songs of mischief" *(kuṟampu pāṭṭu)*. She gave me an example of such songs, giggling so much that I am not sure my tape recorder picked up all its innuendoes:

> Mother-in-law who goes with everyone in the forest!
> Mother-in-law who goes with everyone in the forest!
> Sticking their loins in your pouch,
> Sticking their loins in your pouch.
> Mother-in-law who goes for tribals!
> Will the tribal man sleep with you?
> Will I get to see?
>
> Mother-in-law who goes in the stream!
> Mother-in-law who decorates her vagina!
> The stream is laughing,
> Your ornament is glittering.

Life improved considerably after the death of Archana's mother-in-law. With the help of Archana's father, the couple and their children broke away from the joint family to live on their own. Archana accounted for her father's assistance by saying, "He blamed himself for marrying me to such a poor man. He felt bad for me; he could not stand seeing me work so hard. He bought us a plot of land and built a house for us. He was willing to construct a house made of cement, but my husband would accept only mud walls and a thatched roof. My father continued to provide for us until he died."

His death, which closely followed that of her mother, was a huge loss to Archana, who cried and cried, as she said, "until there were no more tears in my eyes." At his funeral she cried out a dirge different from all others that I recorded. Rather than kuṟai, that complex feeling of loss and want, it expresses something closer to what we might call *grief.* Here, the bereaved daughter rushes home as soon as she is informed of her father's death. The imagery suggests that the path is without obstacles. But when she arrives at her destination, the sight of her deceased father pains her so much that she cannot bring herself to perform simple last rites. Archana recited:

> Today in Benares there was a knife fight.
> They told me the point of the knife stabbed your neck.
> When I set off, my dear father,
> The forest brightened, the black oleanders bloomed.
> I made a beautiful garland of flowers,
> But, my dear father, I could not bear to lay it on your neck.

At her father's funeral Archana also voiced the typical plight of the mourning daughter. How was she going to make it in this world without her parents' kindness and generosity? How was she going to go home, now that they were no longer there to invite her? Whether she addressed such questions to her two brothers I do not know. But after the funeral, they sent her gifts of grain and money regularly, entreating her to visit as often as she wanted. However, Archana no longer liked returning to her natal home in Malaiyaṉūr, because she felt snubbed by her sisters-in-law, particularly by her younger brother's wife. "She is not good to me," Archana complained to me. "When I go there, she is rude; she does not even offer me water." At funerals Archana also lamented that she was made to feel like a thief in her own natal house. As the following song suggests, she was even treated like a thief:

> In the place where I was born,
> There is a golden drumstick tree.
> When I went to pluck it, my dear mother,
> My brother's wife said,
> "The policeman is watching!"
>
> In the place where I was born,
> There is a golden drumstick tree
> When I went to break it, my dear mother,
> My younger brother's wife said,
> "The government official is watching!"

For many years afterward, Archana continued to lament the loss of her beloved parents and her natal home. But then life gave her another reason to cry at funerals: her husband became paralyzed. She described his condition: "He could not stand up, nor walk, nor feel anything. We went to many hospitals to seek treatment, but no doctor could cure him." And so Archana took care of him. She recalled, "Another woman would have left him, but I stayed with him until he died two years later. I fed him, bathed him, cut his hair; I did everything for him."

Throughout this difficult time, Archana often felt the need to lament at home. But no matter how heartbroken, exhausted, or frustrated, she resisted the impulse because "women should not lament at home. . . . It is improper," she told me. Moreover, she did not want her husband to feel bad: "He would have been devastated to hear me cry out." And Archana feared her son's reaction. "If I were to lament at home," she told me, "my daughters would console me, but my son would press his hands on my mouth to shut it. He would scold me." And so Archana saved her laments for funerals, where, amid other grieving women, she could still voice her yearning to be pampered and protected by her parents.

After her husband's death, Archana's life lost its urgency. By her own admission she was doing well for a widow. She had a son, brothers, daughter, and grandchildren who adored her and provided for her. She had many friends who were fond of her sense of humor. Her son was the first Paṟaiyar man from her colony to attend college. After graduation he was to marry his elder sister's younger daughter, so that his education and employment opportunities would benefit Archana's first daughter and granddaughter as well. And since Archana had recently married her two younger daughters to her brothers' sons, who lived in Malaiyaṉūr, she could go back to her natal place in the capacity of mother-in-law.

But Archana missed her husband. "I often think of him and the life we had together," she told me many times. "He was a good man," she said on another occasion. "He never scolded me or checked on me or told me to wear a nicer sari. He would help out with the domestic chores, often bringing firewood from the forest. When I see his photo in our house, I cry. I think of the things he would enjoy and I cry. He would be so proud of his son studying so well. If he were alive, we would go together and visit our son. Now I must go alone, and that makes me sad. I also miss our intimacy."

At funerals Archana compared her life with and without her husband. Doing so relieved her. As she said, "The relief is temporary, for the kuṟai comes back sooner or later, but it helps to cry." Because her kuṟai was (and perhaps has always been) more on the side of yearning and regret than on the side of rage and despondency, her lament was less excessive, less "bubbling hot" than that of an unhappily married woman like Renuka. Moreover, she did not have license to work herself into the state of "heat" characteristic of lamenting women. When she cried too long or too vigorously at a funeral, one of her siblings or children would come to her lament cluster to remind her that she was not alone in the world. Then he or she would take her back home. Finally, Archana did not have it in her to lament in order to cause others to cry. As noted earlier, her general mode of interaction was the opposite of Ellamma's. When she had an audience, she did everything she could to make them laugh.

There was one more sign that Archana's relationship with the lamenting idiom was less dramatic, less intense, and less complicated than that of any other of my female consultants. Although she knew many of the dirges recited by Ellamma and Renuka, she often made comparisons using the language of her own heart, as evidenced by the fact that her dirges did not always rhyme or follow the formulaic dyadic structure of Tamil laments. As this final example suggests, her dirges were more personal than any others I recorded:

> When will I see your golden, beautiful face?
> Without my husband, I have sorrow.
> I want to see, I want to see
> This rich man who came to me.
> I cannot see.
>
> If I look at your picture,
> Will you come and stand by my side?
> If I think of you,
> Will you come and stand before me?

And yet, despite its lighter tone, Archana's lament language is no less constitutive than that of Ellamma or Renuka. If anything, it might have more bearing on her subjectivity; one cannot fail to notice that Archana's life story neatly recapitulates the life experiences typically described in Tamil dirges. Like the prototypical lamenting daughter, Archana has mourned the loss of her parents. Like the prototypical lamenting sister, she has complained about the behavior of her sisters-in-law. Like the prototypical lamenting widow, she now laments the death of her husband. In Archana, the life transitions described in chapter 1, led to a meeting of common emotions with an individual inclination to feel their sadness and, finally, to accept them.

LIVING THROUGH THE FUNERAL

The four women discussed in this chapter used dirges to express different feelings in different ways and with different intentions. Ellamma cried out in public in order to shame those who failed to provide for her. Renuka depended on the genre to find the strength to get on with life. Janaki did not find the process for "cooling off" women's hearts particularly soothing, yet she still employed dirges as a form of retaliation. For Archana, lamenting was neither a way to manipulate nor a means of retribution. She cried dirges to recover the past, to erase the rupture between what once had been and what was.

These distinctive and sometimes contradictory applications of the lament practice are consistent with women's personalities and the particulars of their lives. Crying songs express the inner self and intimate situations. In that sense, despite their formulaic structure, they are personal creations and extensions. They become a woman's unique expression of herself and a way of feeling (or not feeling, as in the case of Janaki) at a visceral level the restrictions or losses of her own life.

Yet, for all its creative potential, the Tamil language of dirges is also restrictive: it limits a woman's articulation of her subjectivity. It does so by imposing a way of speaking about one's life that deprecates who one is and what one has in the present. Margaret Egnor characterizes this way of speaking when she writes of a particular Tamil crying song that it exhibits "the property of waning, of there once having been much and now being very little. The singer laments her loss of wealth, of bodily substance, of time, and of relations" (1986: 318). Much the same is true of the dirges presented in this and the preceding chapter. Either the singer was better off before, or others—the crow, for example—are better off than she is now.

Once a woman inscribes this version of her personal life in this kind of "diary," she adheres to it. As she participates in the funerals of those closest to her, she revises her comparisons by deleting or reinterpreting old contrasts so that memories, even unpleasant memories, are idealized over time. The genre of Tamil lament does not yield steady narratives, but the perspective and tone do remain constant. The singer always claims to have been happier in the past: she would still be content had she not lost her former life.

These comparisons give form to what is perhaps the essential truth of

Tamil lament: the source of a woman's kuṟai is the intensity of her feelings about the possibilities and hopes that have been lost for her. This applies in particular to Ellamma's and Archana's dirges, which are full of regrets about former experiences. But in Renuka's lament biography, she subscribes to a notion that seems intrinsic to the Tamil lament tradition: once a relationship is over for good, it becomes desirable or even vital to one's sense of self. After her brother passed away, her dirges began to praise and express yearning for him. Even Janaki, who would not allow herself to lament, expressed a tendency to long for what was no more. Only when I was about to leave the field did she seem to need my friendship, suggesting that for all her misgivings she too had internalized the language of comparisons.

We have seen how this discourse of yearnings fares outside the funeral context. Although the four women discussed in this chapter did lament in daily life, two of them cautioned that it was not appropriate to do so in public.[11] Some women derive benefits from venting their rage to an audience of neighbors and kin. Ellamma, at least, seemed to be getting what she wanted. Yet most women emphasized the risks associated with lamenting at home within earshot of others. Loved ones might be hurt. Neighbors might gossip. Husbands, brothers, and sons might retaliate.

The men I talked to confirmed these fears, emphasizing how much they did not like their wives, mothers, and sisters to lament outside the funeral context. Men tolerated this behavior in their sisters, sometimes even comforting them with words such as, "I am with you, why are you crying?" or "Don't mind my wife; at least drink some water before you go." Men also allowed their wives to bemoan their sons' or brothers' conduct. But men strongly resented their wives for complaining about *them.* Their immediate reaction, they told me, was to leave immediately, thereby depriving their crying wives of an audience. Some men agreed that, when they returned home, they might amend their ways for a week or two. But most conceded that their wives' laments so enraged them that they became vindictive. One man told me, "Men get angry when their wives cry publicly about marital problems. They think, 'Why is she crying about that?

Whatever wrong I might have done, she should not be bringing it out in the open.'" "Crying out at home," this man concluded, "creates more problems, impelling some husbands to beat their wives even more."

It is no wonder that women agreed that the lament clusters they formed at death rites were the safest place for the cathartic outburst of emotion available to them when in states of kuṟai. In the privacy offered by the tight circles of grieving women, they "can pour out their hearts as long and as loud as they want," as Renuka once said, "without fear." And they could cry about private personal or family matters that could not be shared with anyone or expressed in any other context. Most of the time, men did not hear their complaints, and if they did—for example, at the moment when the chief female mourner greeted them individually—they did not object. In fact, most men did not pay much attention to women's dramatic displays of vulnerability.[12]

The funeral ritual thus remains the main forum in which women undergo their narrative journeys. This is where they tell their stories and weave together their past, present, and future experiences with the connective tissue of their comparisons. This is also where they learn to speak about themselves, as evidenced by the fact that there is an essential, even organic, connection between what a singer laments at funerals and how she talks about her life. In subsequent chapters I show that, in South India, funeral rituals are a major context for the formation of self-narratives. It is as if Tamil culture were saying that one's story—and thus one's ability to know who one is and how to live—can be told only in times of ending. Perhaps because of this particular context, such self-narratives are stories of depletion and personal decline. When death is the cause of the story, the narrative imitates death: life itself imitates death. The continuities between the two genres of personal accounts lead me to suspect that Bruner is correct when he writes, "Just as narrative imitates life, life imitates narratives" (1987: 13).

CHAPTER THREE

Why Should We Cry?

By the time the five or six men who make up the local untouchable band *(paṟaimēḷam)* arrive at the scene of death, the family men are clustered in small groups around the outside of the lamenting circles.[1] Even when they pay their respects to the deceased or build an arbor of palm leaves above the front door to shelter the body from the sun, men express no connection to the female zone of mourning. They enter it only briefly then leave. Whenever they come too close to the women, getting entrapped in their embraces, they remain emotionally distant. Not that the men are silenced by women. While some sink into a drunken stupor, most are possessed of manic energy, furiously pacing the courtyard, ordering youngsters and servants to run for more flowers or palm leaves and so on. Nor are men without their own tasks, for they must organize the funeral ritual. But the men are scattered, disorganized, and without a coherent stance on death. Their most distinctive pose is one of marginality and negative opposition to the women: they stand on the periphery of death and do not cry. With the arrival of the funeral band, this pose crystallizes into a total rejection of grief.

ON AGGREGATION AND FUNERALS

The Dalit men I worked with told me that at death their duties are threefold. Their first responsibility is to inform everyone in the community that a death has occurred. This is their reason for drumming the "death beat" *(cāvu mēḷam)*, which apparently can be heard anywhere within a radius of seven kilometers. The Dalits' second duty is to draw the villagers to the scene of death. This is also accomplished through drumming. As one Paṟaiyar man pointed out, "The drums have the power to gather up people."[2] Finally, the Dalits must entice the assembly to stay throughout the death rite. This is why they sing the genre of songs called death songs. "Unless we sing, people will not stay at the funeral," one man told me. When I asked why, he answered, "Drums do not seduce, but songs do. Songs are like a bridge: they connect people together." Janaki, the Dalit woman described in chapter 2, answered more vividly: "The drums all by themselves would be plain. They would not keep people. The songs are the cosmetics of the mēḷam [here meaning: troupe of musicians], what makes it attractive. They are the point of interest, the centerpiece." Addressing herself to my assistant, she added, "If you and I walk down the street, nobody will pay attention to us; but if she [pointing to me] comes along, everyone will look. Isabelle is to us what the songs are to the drums." Perhaps unsure that I had understood her, she restated, "The singer is the one who makes it all happen. Why? Because he draws people. He gets the attention of whomever passes by, even those who have no business there."

A funeral must be well attended, because a lonely death is a public shame, even a crime. "If people do not have a chance to gather," I was told, "the villagers will say that the funeral is a fraud, that the dead man or woman is stolen." When I asked, "Stolen from whom?" he replied, "From us—the community. We need to see the corpse and say goodbye." I was also told that the absence of a large turnout of mourners would suggest that the deceased was an orphan. A good funeral publicly attests that the deceased was not alone in the world but rich in social relations. Neni Panourgia's observation that, at Greek Orthodox funerals, "the more people that come, the more loved and important the deceased is understood to have been" certainly applies to Tamil death rites as well (1995: 174). This is why it is imperative for the local mēḷam to draw as many mourners as possible. "If the mēḷam doesn't perform," a landowner explained, "people don't come and the funeral is considered to be unfitting or unsatisfactory." "Without the mēḷam," I also heard, "there is simply no funeral."[3]

On the surface such comments corroborate the old anthropological argument that in most, if not all, societies the ultimate objective of funerals is to reassert the forces of social life in the face of death (Hertz 1960; Durkheim 1965). These comments also support the discourse on functionality that states that death strengthens a community's social structure by calling forth feelings of togetherness and solidarity. Indeed, there are many indications that the Tamil funeral ritual does evoke such emotional dynamics. This is most evident at the moment of the formal arrival of the in-laws.

One hour before the funeral procession's departure for the funeral grounds, each group of in-laws (if the deceased is a man, the groups include his wife's kin, his married sisters' kin, etc.) walks in ceremonious succession from the village outskirts to the mourning household. Accompanied by the mēḷam's drums, the in-laws bring *varicai*, which means "order" but also "gift" or "donation." In the context of the funeral, the word must be understood to mean "gift." "Varicai," one man explained, "means *aṉpaḷippu*," which literally translates as "giving out of love." "It is a kind of kindness," he added, "or consolation *[ātāvu]* for the bereaved."

This ritual display of sympathy is expressed mainly in the form of water carried ceremoniously in large brass pots balanced on the head. "The in-laws bring water to wash the body," I was often told. When I pointed out that the family had a well in their courtyard or that water was available nearby, I was inevitably reminded, "The family has no time to draw water, they are in grief." The family is also unable to cook food, because they are in a state of ritual impurity. Thus, the in-laws feed them after the burial or cremation. One man summarized the value of their assistance when he explained, "At death the in-laws do the kind of work that the household's women usually do but cannot do at that moment: bring water, husk rice, cook, and express concern. They do this out of respect *[mariyātai]*." However, the in-laws are not alone in their emotional exhibition of "connection"—another gloss for the Tamil word for "affinity" *(campantam)*—to the mourning family. The village barber and washerman—the so-called children *[kuṭipiḷḷai]* of the village—also help out during funerals, thereby displaying the principles of solidarity and interdependency on which the caste system, like kinship groups, is said to rest (Brubaker 1979).[4]

The argument that funerals uphold social structures, however, has been criticized for its inability to deal with conflict and social change. Clifford Geertz and others have argued that an emphasis on equilibrium and stability fails to explain the dysfunctional aspects of ceremonial behavior and the transformation or even disintegration of ritual systems (Geertz 1973: 142–43; also see Danforth 1982: 27). Such criticism is consonant with my research. My observations suggest that Tamil death rites can be fraught with tension and antagonism. After all, rites gather relatives, and among relatives there are always discord, resentments, and injuries just waiting to surface. I have witnessed brothers, for example, fighting over ritual expenses and inheritance. I have listened to cowives argue endlessly over the right to lead their husband's funeral. Furthermore, there is ample evidence that Tamil death rites are not simply changing, but are becoming sites of contested meanings between castes.

I propose that the main problem with the functional analysis of funerals lies in its assumption that ritual behavior always functions the same way and for the same purpose—essentially to promote social cohesion. My fieldwork on Tamil funerals suggests that a single form of behavior might have more than one meaning. The formal arrival of the in-laws may generate sentiments of solidarity and reciprocity, but the same event also elicits exhibitions of rank and precedence, as evidenced by the fact that varicais proceed according to a strict order, with the mother's brother first in line. Likewise, large gatherings at Tamil funerals may attest to social sentiments, to a desire in particular to reencompass the deceased in a wide circle of social ties. But the same gatherings may also be prompted by contrary, even conflicting, motivations. When they aggregate around the mēḷam, Tamil men challenge the finality of death not by projecting *ideal* images of a cooperative or cohesive society, but by reproducing *real* representations of who they are and how they relate to others.

OFFERING PRAISE

Dressed simply with towels wrapped around their heads and long waist-cloths tucked to fall like short skirts, the funeral drummers position themselves directly across the street from the mourning household. Ignoring the family, they light some dry kindling. Then they hold their drums above the flame to soften the skins. When each barrel-shaped wooden drum *(tōṟikaṭṭai)* has been heated, its player fastens the strap around his neck so that this "big drum" *(periyamēḷam)*, as it is also called, hangs down in front of his waist.[5] The player of the *caṭṭi*, a small but heavy "pot drum," does the same.[6] Because the *palahai* is light, its player simply holds its one-sided round frame vertically in his hands.[7] Once ready, the Dalits beat their drums with sticks that today are often made from bicycle spokes.[8]

It is impossible to ignore, or simply not to hear, the drummers' pounding. The first round of drumbeats is an assault on the auditory sense. The even rolls of metallic strokes are so loud and incessant that, I was once told, "They follow you everywhere." Evidently, people, in turn, follow the beats, for, by the second round of drumming neighbors flock to the house of the mourning family. The women rush to "share the grief," and the men and children gather on the side of the road. Not expecting to be greeted by the family, because, as one man told me, "there is no reason to welcome anyone on a day like this," they stare at the corpse, inquiring about the cause of death and its place and time, and making plans to stay for the funeral.

When the singer *(pāṭuvar)* steps forward, a joyful excitement seizes the assembly of men and youngsters. Bowing, smiling, shuffling his feet to the drumbeats and wiggling his hips, the singer is here to entertain and make everyone laugh. After the third round of drumming, he sings four lines of a high-pitched tune—although to say that he "sings" is not entirely accurate, for there is no obvious melody to the lyrics that he shouts with unpredictable crescendos. As he draws out the last words with exaggerated emphasis, the drums resound like a chorus. He continues to sing "piece by piece" *(tuṇtu tuṇtā)*, four lines at a time, always followed by a round of drums. Here is an excerpt of what he may sing:

At the foothills of the Himalayas, (bis)
Dear wife; your father Iswarar [the god Siva] (bis)
Is doing penance happily!
At the foothills of the mountain, (bis)
Dear wife; your father Karthan [the god Siva] (bis)
Has closed his eyes
And raised his hand [as in a meditative posture].
Dear wife! Your father Gangadharan [the god Siva] (bis)
Is doing penance.
Dear wife, I would like to stop him. (bis)
Please give me permission to stop your father's penance.

Alas! My dear husband! (bis)
Those are not good words. (bis)
They are words of pride.
If you go to the Himalayas [and stop my father's penance],
You will die.

My sweet wife, my father Mayan (the god Viṣṇu)
Will protect me.
My sweet wife!
No danger will come to me.
My sweet wife!
No danger will come to me.

What happened to you? (bis)
Alas, my dear husband, (bis)
What are you saying? (bis)
Have you gone mad?
Your father herded cattle.

Your father took his mother-in-law as his wife.
Your father was born in a shepherd family. (bis)
Your father took a Muslim girl as a concubine. . . .
Your father won't be able to protect you.

Although his lyrics are argumentative and ominous, the singer takes them lightly, mocking them with a racking, inconsolable sob that is unmistakably exaggerated. This prompts the drummers to whistle and laugh. A growing sense of jubilation is reinforced when a couple of bold dancers with bells on their ankles brush against each other in a sexually explicit, even obscene, choreography. Bystanders make no attempt to conceal their amusement. Soon they begin to give the Dalits money to hear specific death songs.

Such donations are well regarded, because death songs are said to praise *(poṟṟu)* the dead. I underscore, however, that the majority of death songs, like the one just excerpted, do not actually eulogize, or for that matter even refer to characteristics of, the deceased. Only when the in-laws bring their donations do the Dalits sing the deceased's "life history" (*varalāṟu* or *carittiram*), commemorating and commending his or her qualities.[9] But the word *commemorate* here also requires some qualification, for what is acknowledged in these biographical songs is not a full personality, or even a character sketch, but an idealizing social identity. The singer essentially gives a synoptic and superlative account of the individual's lifetime public achievements. I offer as an example what was sung in honor of the late Arjuna, a Dalit man I worked with in 1991 (also see Racine 1996: 206–8). One afternoon in spring of 1999, I asked his son—who was also a funeral singer—to expand on those aspects of a person's life that are to be remembered. He responded with an improvised song about his deceased father, as follows:

Mēlpampadi is the best village of the country.
Mēlpampadi is where the singer Arjuna was from.
Renowned and respected, he lived with dignity.
Great and prosperous, he lived like a landlord.

Sunday the 27th of the month of May 1989, he lost his life.
He left the earth and reached heaven.
Renowned and respected, the singer Arjuna lived with dignity.
Great and prosperous, he lived like a landlord.
Whenever he would leave the village wearing his vesti [long white cloth that men tuck around the waist],
He would pass for a Veḷḷālar [a village landlord].
He looked like a devotee of the great god Siva.
He excelled in the art of the theater.
In his profession as drama teacher, he was warmly received.
Everyone in this village, everyone without exception,
And all his students, had affection for him.
I have known him since 1956 [the year the singer was born].
My father shone as a drama teacher.
He kindly transmitted his expertise to me.
My father shone as an acting teacher.
He kindly transmitted his expertise to me.

Whether they specifically celebrate the deceased or not, all death songs are said to commend the dead. As such, they have a kind of absolving value, because praise clears the dead of the sins they committed during their lifetime. One singer explained the workings of such exoneration: "When they are commended, the souls of the dead go to heaven." The commission of death songs by the men attending the funeral is therefore not simply a show of appreciation for the Dalit singer but also an offering, one made out of personal or social esteem for the dead and their living families.

These findings substantiate work by the anthropologist Arjun Appadurai on the linguistic and public expressions of praise (*stōtra* in Sanskrit) in India[10] Noting that "in the Hindu world the paradigmatic or prototypic act of praise is the praise of the divine" (1990: 95), Appadurai lists four aspects of the Hindu construction of praise: "First, it makes praise a ritual offering. Second, it puts praise into a formulaic and an aesthetic framework. Third, its main device is description (often through hyperbole) of the positive qualities of the god or goddess in question.

Fourth, praise . . . is associated with the public expression of the emotional bonds of devotee and deity" (94). As we have just seen, at Tamil funerals praise also functions as a "ritual offering" that employs a "formulaic and aesthetic framework" (in the form of song) expressing "emotional bonds" (sympathy and respect). It makes no difference that the recipient of praise in this context is a dead person rather than a deity, since South Indian Hinduism postulates no absolute distinction between deities and human beings (Blackburn 1988; Fuller 1992: 30; Nabokov 2000). In praise there is a logical conflation of attitudes toward the dead and the gods.

I add one major qualification to Appadurai's formulation. In the context of funerals, the descriptive element of Tamil praise is focused less on its recipients—the dead—than on its dispensers: the men who sponsor the death songs. It is well known to scholars of Tamil culture (including Appadurai himself) that the patrons *(yajamānas)* of ritual and performance (dance, theater, etc.) are lavishly praised for their support.[11] There is evidence that such profuse acknowledgments borrow from the old records of royal acts of generosity (Appadurai 1990: 95; Blackburn 1988: 145–47). In the past, Tamil kings were the model patrons of temple festivals and the arts. Endowment was honored in an extended opening portion of inscriptions, or "praise prefaces," whose central objective was to "identify and glorify" the patrons (Appadurai 1990: 95). The same objective continues to infuse forms of praise associated with contemporary patronage. In his study of a Tamil expressive genre called "bow song" *(vil pāṭṭu)*, for example, Stuart Blackburn notes that, when the singer receives individual gifts of a few rupees during performance, "he interrupts the narrative and announces the donor's name, village and the amount given." (1988: 145–46). The singer's acknowledgment is always flattering, as he multiplies the amount given "by a factor of one thousand" (146).[12]

Much the same happens with death songs. Individuals who commission them are identified and commended. For example, if the donor of a song is a man named Elumalai who is the deceased's uterine nephew, the singer might announce, "Elumalai gave money so that his maternal uncle [māmā] might reach heaven." The same inflationary strategy observed by Blackburn at bow song performances resurfaces in these public acknowledgments. The singer always exaggerates the donor's contribution: if Elumalai paid two rupees for a song, the singer announces that the man gave him four, six, or more.

I have observed that these proclamations increase in number and intensity very quickly. As soon as one man's name and donation are honored, another offers more money for a song. Before long, men are participating in what one singer called a competition. He explained why men rush to outbid each other: "Men can't stand that I compliment someone else. That immediately makes them think, 'Hey, I am not lower than him. I am just as good. In fact, I am better.' Then they give me more money so that I praise them more." Another singer offered a similar assessment: "Men resent the fact that others get honored before them. They compete because they are proud and jealous of each other." This man believes that drinking only intensifies these dynamics. In his words, "As soon as they drink, men fiercely request songs without taking into consideration kinship or social relations. They just want to outdo each other; they just want to be better than everyone else."

As these remarks suggest, the men alone are responsible for these aggressive behaviors. Women do not engage in them—in fact, they do not even pay attention to the mēḷam. Women may subsidize death songs, but for different reasons than men.[13] As one singer told me, "Women do not ask for their names to be praised. They pay for songs as a way to tip us or express gratitude for our services." The same is true for the men of the bereaved family: they seldom commission songs, and when they do so, it is out of generosity or appreciation for the drummers. The men who actively vie for acknowledgment at Tamil funerals include neighbors, distant acquaintances, and particularly in-laws, the very men, in other words, who have come with "donations" intended to help the mourners.

It is not completely accurate to say, however, that the deceased's family is not looking for praise. They may not solicit the Dalits' compliments, but they nonetheless strive for approval. They specifically want people to say that the funeral of their father or mother was a "success," "a good show," that it nicely paid him or her back. This yearning must be understood in light of the widespread Indian belief that providing parents with proper last rites is the most fundamental way to "thank them for bearing us, bringing us into this world, and leaving us some property" (also see Lamb 2000: 46–50). To get this kind of endorsement, the mourning family does not hesitate to pay good money to the Dalits for their services.[14] They also provide them with large quantities of arrack, for it is well known that, the more they drink, the better the Dalits drum, sing, and dance. And the better the Dalits perform, the more people will show up, thereby attesting to the deceased's wide circle of relatives and acquaintances, and the more men will commission songs proclaiming that the deceased was a great person worthy of an afterlife in heaven. A lack of savings would not stop the family from hiring the local mēḷam and treating them to quantities of alcohol. The family would pawn the wife's jewels or borrow money from in-laws or friends. They would do anything to get the Dalits to play well, so that, as one middle-aged man put it, "people say that we did well by our parents."

THE DALIT'S CRAVING FOR PRAISE

Death songs do more than serve as a source of prestige and privilege for Dalits' patrons, whether they be individual donors or the sponsoring family. The songs can also secure esteem for the singers who engage in the same behaviors as their audience. That the Dalits win any form of praise—and praise from caste Hindus at that—might surprise some scholars of Indian society. Appadurai contends, "In general, direct praise of inferiors and dependents is as uncommon as the praise of superiors is common" (1990: 99). This is consistent with my own fieldwork experiences. In the everyday public life of the South Arcot villages I know, the Dalits are usually not acknowledged and certainly not complimented. Only the big shots—the local leaders, the high-caste landlords, and the successful businessmen—get attention and respect. In the context of the funeral ritual, however, the Dalits can vie for a bit of praise alongside their high-profile patrons and providers. In fact, many singers admitted to me that the opportunity to earn acclamation is what leads them to join the mēḷam in the first place. One man recounted his first funeral singing experience: "When I was twenty, a death occurred in our village, but no one was available to sing. Since I had already acted in two village plays and drummed at many funerals, I was asked to try. I sang in rhythm to the drumbeat and everybody thought I had a good voice. That evaluation made me feel so good that I wanted to sing more." Another man told me the same thing: "I first sang at my aunt's funeral. I was complimented for it, and this gave me the incentive to sing again."

I should point out that it is not easy to enthrall a South Indian audience. In my experience Tamil people can be particularly tough critics. My consultant Janaki exemplified the Tamil people's penchant for sarcasm when she remarked, "Around here, if the singer is no good, even the dogs don't listen." The singers I met told me they were willing to work very hard to meet their audience's expectations because, once they had tasted the rewards of approval, they could no longer live without them. "I crave praise," one performer told me. "That is why I sing." When I tried to understand the basis for his craving, he replied, "When I sing well, I am the center of attention. I feel strong. People's applause energizes me." When I pointed out that he did not seem to need much positive reinforcement, since he appeared to have a high opinion of his voice, this man immediately countered, "It is not enough to have pride for one's self *[taṟ perumai]*. It is better if other people praise *[puhaḻ]* you."

Apparently it is also better if people praise you *exclusively*, for the singers I knew did not like to share audience approval. I realized this when I observed how local singers reacted to outside singers—men from nearby Dalit colonies who happened to be visiting and were willing to sing at an ongoing funeral in exchange for arrack. Suddenly the air grew tense as inside singers attempted to outdo the outsiders and vice versa. One singer complained, "It is worse than a match of cricket or football. We'll do anything to be the sole focus of attention and admiration." Perhaps unsure that I had understood him, he added, “If people happen to praise another singer, I want them to praise me more. I want to be better than him.” The same singer told me that, if he could not outshine his rivals, he would leave the funeral, offering the excuse that he was not feeling well.

With all their ambitions, desires, and tensions, Dalit performers identify with many of the same pressures and inclinations that the sponsors of their songs experience. That Dalits crave exclusive acclamation suggests that, despite their separation from and rejection by caste-Hindu men, they too value distinction and place a high premium on topping their peers. Moreover, they pursue their goals at the same time and in the same physical space as their patrons. At funerals, Dalits and caste Hindus strive for excellence side by side, even inciting one another to compete for praise. The Dalits might deliberately attempt to exploit their patrons’ rivalry by commending a man who has not even requested a song. Patrons, for their part, encourage resentment and jealousy among the Dalits by inviting outside singers to chant. Each side is skilled at bringing out both the best and the worst in the other.

The pervasive dynamics of competition and display operating on multiple levels at once lead me to suggest that the Tamil mortuary mēḷam fosters more than sentiments of social reciprocity and solidarity. At death, Dalit singers and drummers may enjoin the whole village community to assemble, but the ordering of human relations that emerges does not demonstrate cohesion and interdependence or result from ideological principles of social homogeneity and equality. On the contrary, the men who gather around the mēḷam reproduce the same values of differentiation and inequality found in caste hierarchy. They even come up with other ways of making status distinctions, according respect not merely to those who are born at the top of the caste system but also to those, including the Paṟaiyars, who perform their funeral duties well. And men are eager to play by such rules: they rush to demonstrate gratitude, largess, generosity, talent, and some proclivity for competition and overt displays of superiority. They will do anything to stand out from and prevail over others.

THE SONGS

Given all the elements that contribute to a successful funeral, my consultants most emphasized the songs. The songs, they said, beautify the drums, draw people to the funeral scene, and keep them there. The songs, they elaborated, praise the dead and absolve them of their sins. The songs, as we have just seen, are also the medium by which men gathered around the mēḷam inflate their social identities. Paradoxically, the songs' *lyrics* oppose the strategies of self-importance released by their delivery. In the dynamics of performance, the self is on prominent display. Most death songs, however, depict a social world in which the self (its pride, vanity, and pretension) is not a desired category.

Rather than commemorate the life of the deceased, most death songs recount the lives and often the deaths of characters drawn from pan-Hindu or Tamil epic, Puranic, and devotional narratives. What all these characters have in common—often in excessive abundance—is profound integrity or devotion. They are usually men who have committed themselves to living moral lives—to telling nothing but the truth, for example—or to serving God. In fact their commitment to virtue goes well beyond the norms of moral, or dharmic, conduct. It borders on the archetypal, as George Hart says of fanaticism and Indian literature in general (1995). These characters are so reliable that they never question or abandon their sense of right or wrong, even when those principles conflict with personal commitments. In fact, when the gods wish to test their integrity, these moral men "eagerly," as the songs sometimes put it, sacrifice kingdom, wives, children, and even their own lives to dharma (duty).

The Song of Ariccantiraṉ

A good example is the death song that narrates the story of King Ariccantiraṉ, who is addressed at the entrance to the cremation ground later in the ritual. This good king is known throughout Tamilnadu for speaking only the truth.[15] In the version sung to me by Vel, a Paṟaiyar man whom I discuss in the next chapter Ariccantiraṉ's problems begin when the gods convene to test his integrity. The god Brahmā asks the divine assembly, "Who will make Ariccantiraṉ lie?" and the sage Muṉivar volunteers himself with "joy" *(mahiḻcci)*. The gods laugh at him, doubting that he will succeed, and so a vexed Muṉivar leaves heaven even more determined to make the king lie. He seeks the help of a malevolent being, Saturn.

Ariccantiraṉ and his wife, Cantiramati, welcome Muṉivar and Saturn kindly when they arrive at the palace. Muṉivar conceals the true purpose of his visit. "I am just a poor Brahmin," he tells the king. "Give me what I ask without saying 'no,' and I'll praise your name." Unable to fathom stinginess or slyness, Ariccantiraṉ answers, "I'll never refuse you anything. I'll give you whatever you want with pleasure."

At this point the listeners (and readers) of this song can anticipate what is to come. Muṉivar will apply all his crafty energy to making the good king say "no," to a request, thereby causing him to lie, given his promise to refuse nothing.

But Ariccantiraṉ never forfeits his promise. When Muṉivar throws an arrow as far as he can and demands to have "whatever lies in its paths as his due," the king agrees. When Muṉivar hides his spoils, claiming that they have disappeared, Ariccantiraṉ insists on compensating for the loss. To pay off his debt, he sells his entire kingdom. When he still comes up short, he takes his wife and child to the slave market and auctions them off to a Brahmin man for thirty gold coins. (The song claims that he makes the announcement "my wife is for sale" "with joy.") Ariccantiraṉ then asks an untouchable man by the name of Vīrajāmpuhaṉ to give him some work. The man instructs Ariccantiraṉ to guard the entrance to the funeral grounds in exchange for the money and raw rice offerings placed by mourners at that threshold. The king has by this time suffered a significant loss in stature, as he now takes orders from a Paṟaiyar, the lowest of the low, and dwells in an impure setting.

However, the worst is yet to come. Frustrated by their failure to make Ariccantiraṉ rescind his promise, Muṉivar and Saturn renew their effort with increased fervor. They plot the death of Ariccantiraṉ's little boy by snakebite in the forest. This part of the song is utterly heart-wrenching, as Cantiramati (Ariccantiraṉ's wife) is forbidden by her Brahmin master to search for her little boy's body before she finishes her chores. Consequently it is not until nighttime, when "one cannot see anything," that she leaves for the forest, "running and crying all the way." When Cantiramati spots her boy's body, she covers it with kisses. Then she carries him in her arms to the funeral ground to cremate him. Still crying, she places her son on a bed of grass. Then she assembles some brush and dead wood, lifts the body onto this makeshift pyre, and lights it in the dark of night.

The fire awakens Ariccantiraṉ, who races to extinguish it. Not recognizing his wife, he lashes out, "Who are you, crazy woman? Are you a thief? Are you trying to steal from me? Don't you know you owe me three coins and raw rice?" (the standard contribution to the guardian of the funeral ground). When he finally identifies her, Ariccantiraṉ "falls into deep reflection" and "is moved to cry." The song makes it explicit, however, that "the words 'she is my wife' do not come to him." Expressing no bond with her at this terrible moment, he orders the mother of his own child to collect from her Brahmin master the money and rice offering that are his due.

Cantiramati returns to town and discovers that she stands accused of killing a child in the forest—the result of further scheming on the part of Muṉivar and Saturn. Her sentence is decapitation, to be conducted by the king himself, and it is clear that Ariccantiraṉ will have no choice but to carry out the dreadful execution. Only when Cantiramati acquiesces to the execution pleading, "Go on and cut off my head, my dear husband," does this horrific story come to a close. Up in heaven the goddess Śakti angrily scolds her husband, Siva, for "letting Muṉivar destroy this family." In response the god transforms Ariccantiraṉ's sword into a garland of flowers that falls around Cantiramati's neck. Muṉivar then admits that it is impossible to make Ariccantiraṉ lie. Siva forgives Muṉivar and takes the king his wife, and their son up to heaven.

The Song of Ciṟuttoṇṭar

Another story on the theme of sacrificing one's loved ones to a higher principle is described in the song about Ciṟruttoṇṭar, whose devotion to the god Siva was first recorded by the Tamil poet Cēkkilār in the mid–twelfth century. David Shulman warns us that Cēkkilār's stories "are usually rather grisly, rich in pathos and violent demonstrations of fanatical devotion to the god" (1993: 19).[16] This is no exaggeration, as the Ciṟruttoṇṭar described by Cēkkilār is so zealous that he does not hesitate to feed his own son to a "hungry god" (1993). Such fervent devotion continues to capture the Tamil imagination, for Cēkkilār's tale is consistent with the story that the singer Vel, an untouchable man with no formal education, chanted at South Arcot funerals in the late twentieth century.

Vel's song begins with Ciṟruttoṇṭā offering devotions to Siva so that the god will bless him and his wife with a child. When a boy is then born to the couple, Ciṟruttoṇṭā vows to feed Siva's devotees on a daily basis. This vow becomes his major preoccupation, and he eats only after he serves other Siva followers. When his son reaches the age of twelve, "the god feels like testing his servant." One day—a Friday—Siva arranges for all of his devotees to be unavailable for Ciṟruttoṇṭā's meal. Then he takes the disguise of an ascetic *(sannyasi)*, "a beggar with a bag," and posts himself near a ruined pavilion to wait for Ciṟruttoṇṭā's return home. Having found no one else to feed, Ciṟruttoṇṭā enthusiastically invites this unexpected guest to lunch. The ascetic accepts the invitation with the condition that Ciṟruttoṇṭā "promise to satisfy his wants." Once Ciṟruttoṇṭā agrees, the ascetic confesses to his unspeakable craving. He asks for "a son"—"an only son"—whose body parts the parents must willingly cut, clean, cook, and serve on banana leaves before noon. "I won't eat any later than that," he warns.

According to Vel's song, Ciṟuttoṇṭā and his wife express no hesitation to serve up their son to the ascetic. Apparently they "feel no grief whatsoever." Their one problem is that, by the time they fetch the boy from school, behead him as he naps, and cook him according to the ascetic's instructions, it is after noon—already 1:30 P.M. The old man turns down the meal. "It is too late, he says. "I lost my appetite. I don't want your food." Ciruttoṇṭā and his wife burst into tears. The song suggests, however, that they cry because the ascetic refuses to accept their "food" and not because they have killed their son in vain. They apologize repeatedly for the delay and beg the old man to eat.

He consents with one condition—that the couple joins him for lunch. As if this were not appalling enough, the ascetic adds a sardonic, "Bring your child too!" Vel's song states that at this point Ciruttoṇṭā "could not open his mouth." When the ascetic presses him, asking, "What is the matter with you? Are you mute?" Ciruttoṇṭā is afraid to say that he has killed his son. His reaction is notable in that it reveals more concern for social appearances than his personal feelings. As Vel asked in his song, "How could he tell that he had killed his own son?" In the end Ciruttoṇṭā tells the truth and the ascetic orders the couple to fetch their boy from school. The boy appears miraculously, the ascetic vanishes suddenly, and Siva blesses Ciruttoṇṭā and his family.

The Song of Rati and Maṉmataṉ

The best example of the preeminence of duty over love appears in the most popular death song in the Gingee area: the song of Rati and Maṉmataṉ, which I quoted near the beginning of this chapter. "Men love this song," the singer Vel told me; "they always request that we chant it."

The song of Rati and Maṉmataṉ is based on a Puranic story regularly staged in local village dramas.[17] In such folk dramas, Maṉmataṉ is the sex god of the Tamil pantheon. Recently married, he is full of passion for his young bride, Rati. In the eyes of the couple's fathers, who are the gods Siva and Viṣṇu, Maṉmataṉ's sexual desire is excessive and communicates the wrong message. By the gods' reasoning, if humans were to have this much sexual intercourse, they would inevitably bear too many children and there would soon be no room left on earth. To prevent this potential risk of overpopulation, these two fathers resolve to kill the sex god.

Viṣṇu himself orchestrates his son's death by advising Rati's father, Siva, to undertake a penance in the Himalayan foothills. His penance produces so much heat that the nearby world of the gods begins to burn. Only Maṉmataṉ can avert this crisis, for he alone possesses the power to stop Siva's penances. The gods send him an urgent letter requesting his help. His wife, Rati, implores him not to go because she forecasts that this is a dangerous, potentially fatal, assignment. "My father will open his third eye and you will die," she warns him. But Maṉmataṉ insists on going and, just as Rati predicts, he dies.

Many versions of this death song open with Maṉmataṉ receiving the letter, and they focus almost entirely on what the singers call "the dispute" (*vātam*, also *taṟham* in formal Tamil) between Rati and Maṉmataṉ. Here, I quote passages from the version that Arjuna's son (whose commemorative song for his father appears earlier in this chapter) sang to me one evening after working in the fields.

Arjuna's son's song begins with Maṉmataṉ's praise of Rati for her constant deference to him. Rati accepts the compliment but then speaks out in a tone that negates it: "As soon as you read the messenger's letter, you told me, 'I am going.' My husband, do not listen to what the gods say. Don't leave me! Don't go!" Still speaking sweetly to her, Maṉmataṉ counters, "We can defy anyone, but we cannot go against the gods' order. I must go. Listen to me, my beautiful lady, my garland of lilies, my jasmine scent, my beautiful forest peacock, my language of play, my friend, my darling—listen. From heaven the call of help has come. We must hear it with love. The gods need me—I am going for a good cause." His words fail to persuade Rati, who answers, "You cannot leave me. You cannot go."

Now Maṉmataṉ raises his voice. "The good king Ariccantiraṉ lost his kingdom, but his beautiful wife Cantiramati did not stop him. Likewise, don't stop me. I am going. Good-bye." Rati also grows angrier: "How many times do I have to tell you, stupid? Don't go." Then she warns, "My brainless husband, there is evil and deceit where you're going. If my father opens his third eye, you'll burn to death. Don't boast, my king. Don't brag. Don't go!" At this, Maṉmataṉ becomes incensed: "Who is your father? And why should I be afraid of him? My own father will help me." Then he calmly reasons, "My fragrant peacock, my singing bird, my source of wonder and honesty—listen to me. This life is a mass of clouds. This life is a bubble on the water. My girl, this body is imperfect and impure. Don't put your faith in this life. Don't trust it. I am leaving."

Now Rati tries yet again to dissuade him: "I am too young to be left alone. I won't eat. I won't drink. I'll think of you. Handsome Maṉmataṉ, you must not go." Still Maṉmataṉ is not moved. "Wife, you talk too much. That's enough. Don't tell me what to do. I come and go as I please." This heated exchange continues until Maṉmataṉ leaves. The song concludes with Rati lamenting his death.[18]

THE DRAMA OF DEATH AND THE COMEDY OF MEN

A Tamil high school teacher told me that "death songs are popular because they teach us a lesson." He explained, "Notions such as 'I,' 'me,' and 'mine' prevent us from reaching God. In order to free ourselves from the cycle of rebirth, we must forsake worldly concerns. We must purge ourselves of every desire. We should not be concerned about possessions *(contam)*. . . . This is what Ariccantiraṉ, Ciṟuttoṇṭā and Maṉmataṉ taught us," he added. "They taught us to give up everything without fussing or crying, because God wants us to give to him happily." The teacher concluded, "At death people are receptive to this message because they can see clearly that a life has ended and that the dead cannot take anything with them. It is a pivotal time, one in which mourners can appreciate the value of renunciation."

Inspired more by this man's own devotion to Siva than by his deep appreciation for the funeral mēḷam, his commentary is nonetheless to the point: the fundamental subject of death songs is relinquishment. The protagonists always choose to forgo personal relationships, worldly attachments, and life, and they even do so "with joy," as the songs often put it.

Over time, however, I realized that renunciation is not the key lesson commonly imparted. Most people told me that they like these songs for the opposite reason: because the characters have difficulty letting go of their loved ones and possessions. They pointed out that Ariccantiraṉ, Ciruttoṇṭā, and Maṉmataṉ are caught in situations beyond their control with no alternative but to fulfill the promises and vows or respond to the invitations that cause them to lose everything. "There is no other way," I was often told. "These men are being tested or set up to die. No one but the gods can change or prevent the course of their ordeals." In other words, the songs underscored not the characters' personal determination to confront their trials, but, according to my consultants, a certainty that fate and providence had forced the characters to do so. Moreover, although the songs indicate that Ariccantiraṉ, Ciṟuttoṇṭā, and Maṉmataṉ suffer no great qualms about sacrificing their wives and children to truth, devotion, or duty, my sources attribute to them emotional depth and even grief. The singer Vel said of his Ciṟuttoṇṭā chant, "Think of what the parents must have felt when they cut up their little boy."

In short, people like death songs because they find them tragic. A singer told me, "People like to hear sad stories, especially in this context. Mourners empathize with the characters' trials and sufferings, for they too are unable to prevent the loss of their husbands, wives, and children, and they too anguish in grief." Another singer agreed but argued that "death songs should be sad" regardless of people's preferences. This is why, he added, it is not proper for the funeral mēḷam to sing cinema songs: "Cinema is for happiness, not for death."

Comments like these never failed to confuse me. I understood that people yearn for sad songs, because tragic situations often make for captivating denouements. I also understood why dramatic scenarios were in order in unhappy circumstances like funerals. But if death songs were meant "to make people cry for both the characters and themselves," as Dalits contended, why were they delivered in an entertaining and even comical fashion? Recall that the performance of these chants is so undeniably humorous that the men and children who attend them laugh their hearts out.[19] "People love us," funeral singers often told me, "because we are fun." But why do people "love" the mēḷam's caricature of sad scenarios, and how do they manage to enjoy themselves under such morbid circumstances?

Dalit singers gave functional answers to my questions. "We must bring *tempu,* [a boost] to the funeral," they pointed out, "so that grief does not prevail." "We sing to allay *[āṟu]* mourners' grief," they also said, sometimes adding that grief is not a good thing, because it prevents the family from concentrating on the ritual proceedings. As one singer put it, "Our show *[vēṭikkai]* is meant to help the mourners focus on the ritual." The singer Vel expanded on the same notion: "We sing so that the funeral can take place. If everybody were to cry, how would the dead be buried?" When I pestered him on another occasion to clarify one more time why death singers strive to amuse their audiences, this man offered an irritated but definitive answer: "We are entertaining so that many people gather and feel jolly. Listen to me—the person is dead. There is nothing we can do about that. He is not coming back. Why should we cry? Let us bury him in a happy way with many people enjoying themselves. Is this not better than having a single person take him to the funeral grounds, grieving and crying like a cow?"

Conceivably, my method of inquiry restricted my consultants to such explanations. After all, any question that asks "Why do you . . .?" is likely to expose the investigator's puzzlement with unfamiliar behaviors—in this case, organized laughter at funerals—and invite defensive answers. Or perhaps funeral singers sensed something unnatural about their "shows" and felt the need to justify it to themselves: "What we do is good: we console mourners." In the end it was not necessary to determine whether I had misled them or they had volunteered functional explanations for behaviors they did not entirely sanction or even understand. I eventually reached the limits of their commentaries. They had nothing more to say about these songs which, although tragic, were pitched to sound comic. The discussion had been closed.

Yet my instincts told me that there was more to learn about the Dalits' comedic act. So much of it—the overdramatization of lyrics, exaggerated sobs and sighs, whistles, jokes, chuckles, profanities, lewd dance steps, and so on—could not be easily reduced to the objective of making men concentrate on their funeral duties. I am not saying that my consultants did not have a grasp of their culture. As we have just seen, they came up with profound analyses of their own practices. I am simply saying that the Dalits' exegeses fell short of thoroughly explaining their actions, that for all their apparent logic and conviction they did not articulate the full basis for their behaviors. In an attempt to probe deeper into the paradoxical dissonances between content, context, and delivery of the Tamil death songs, let us examine Bruce Kapferer's analysis of what he calls the "comic drama" of Sinhalese exorcism (1983: 207).

Kapferer notes that, in nearby Sri Lanka, possessing demons are ultimate masters of illusion. These low beings listed at the bottom of the Sinhalese cosmic hierarchy manage to persuade victims that they are frightful and powerful. When mocked into their proper place within the framework of exorcist rituals, the demons become ridiculous and eventually lose their terrorizing grip on their victims. From Kapferer's perspective, then, the puns, spoonerisms, profanities, and sexual innuendo that pepper dialogues between possessing demons and drummer-exorcists are therapeutic: they expose demons for what they really are.

Kapferer's analysis reveals that, in order to successfully suspend belief, comedy must begin by asserting belief (1983: 209, citing Handelman 1979). In other words, comedy must first construct the meaning that it aims to deconstruct. In the context of Sinhalese exorcism, for example, demons must be presented as controlling, polluting, and potentially terrifying *before* they are made fun of. Kapferer writes, "For major exorcisms to achieve their curative purpose, the nature of the cosmic order and the position of gods, human beings and demons within it must be revealed both in the truth of their experiencing *and* as objective truth" (209, his emphasis). According to Kapferer, it is the dramatic forms of the exorcism—the dialogues, for instance, that exorcists perform in everyday speech before their audience—that first objectify the demons as experienced by the patient. Comedy is the genre through which the "normal" hierarchical order or accepted truths of the Sinhalese world are then restored to "reality" (vi). Finally, on comedy's transformative potential, Kapferer remarks, "While comedy often appears to defy a rational order, and to break it up and disorganize it, comedy implicitly restores order. But it does so in a way which overthrows any limiting, 'overdetermined' or restricted perspective possible in the cultural and social world of meaning and experience. The demonic is just such a limiting perspective and [therefore] . . . an ideal target for comedy" (207). Demons, agents of disease and dysfunction, are through mockery denied their potency—that is, their power to limit, constrain, and restrict the patient undergoing exorcism.

I find Kapferer's analysis useful for interpreting the comic delivery of the Tamil funeral singer. The Dalits' jocular skits attack the message imparted by death songs. As I have suggested, this message is limiting: life is a painful ordeal that requires us to let go of material possessions, social status, intimate relationships, and life itself. The songs are the perfect medium for breaking such depressing news.

Sung in formal Tamil and full of expletives, death songs narrate in ways different from those of everyday speech, a difference further enhanced by the fact that the songs are punctuated at regular intervals, every four lines, by the pounding roll of drums. Yet the dramatic experiences they recount are accessible to all because everyone understands the lyrics. Moreover, the use of questions, answers, dialogues, and repetitions—so characteristic of the Tamil oratory style—facilitates audience comprehension. The songs, therefore, much like a play, bracket a singular reality that has the potential to become a subject of focused reflection for the audience. The songs' similarity to dramaturgical forms is particularly apparent in the Rati-Maṉmataṉ chant that unfolds almost entirely as a dialogue between the sex god and his young bride.[20]

Tamil death songs, however, do not fully voice the scenarios of loss and separation they speak about. Although I translated them from beginning to end in the previous section, they are never actually sung that way. Death songs are not perfected texts but fleeting moments of a live performance process characterized by motion and contingency. They are inscribed within constant pauses and interruptions caused by the complex dynamics, discussed above, at play in the staging of the songs.

Because they sing on demand, and because demand is high, the Dalits often skip lyrics in order to fulfill as many song requests as possible (naturally they want all the money they can get). Because they also crave praise, they do not hesitate to discontinue a chant that fails to captivate or equal the songs of their rivals. Then there is the matter of ritual momentum. When the in-laws arrive, the drummers must stop playing and formally accompany them to the household. Once all the relatives are present, the bier must be built. Meanwhile, performers take breaks to drink and smoke. Even during the final procession, when they might finally concentrate on their songs, still the singers do not sing a complete chant. As the singer Vel remarked to me, "From our village to the graveyard there is a mile—not enough time to sing a whole song." He then admitted, "I have never sung a song in its entirety."

There is simply no need to do so. Context fills in the gaps and voids of the singers' delivery. Let us not forget that the deceased lies on a cot visible to all throughout the mēḷam's performance. Let us also remember that the women of the household and neighborhood sway, moan, weep, beat their breasts and intone the sounds of expectations reduced, desires blunted, kuṟais borne—in short, sounds of loss and decline. Death (and women's lives) completes the Dalits' fragmented presentation along with the mourners, who—much like the songs' protagonists—have no choice but to lose on life and relinquish loved ones.

The only time that this context surfaces inside the mēḷam's performance is when the singer commemorates the deceased's life. Biographical songs never evolve into declaration of bereavement such as "We miss you." But in describing the deceased person as, for example, a beloved father, respected theater teacher, and dignified villager, they may intentionally invoke a mood of sorrow because, as I was told, "the praise produces more grief. It makes us miss the dead. It makes us realize how much we lost," a statement that reminds us of the role of praise in Tamil laments. Mourners may be sufficiently moved to grieve for the deceased that playfulness, evident in other songs, is here significantly muted. Although not entirely sad, the singer's delivery of biographical songs may sometimes fade to a rasp or ascend to a doleful peak. However, to my knowledge these songs do not culminate—nor do I believe they are meant to—in a communal outpouring of grief for the simple reason that they are short and quickly supplanted by the category of chants narrating the plights of legendary characters like Ariccantiraṉ.

Thus the mourners seldom have a chance to assimilate the "limiting" messages of these tragic songs (or of their context, for that matter). This is not merely because the singer's performance remains sketchy and incomplete but because he and the drummers take every opportunity to ridicule the dilemmas faced by Ariccantiraṉ, Ciṟuttoṇṭā, and Rati and Maṉmataṉ. The entire ad hoc space where the Dalits dance and sing seems bathed in a giddy stream of delight. They grin and grimace at their audience of men and children, whom they salute with exaggerated deference. They leap, hands thrown up with abandon as they tell some new gag and then, in the same breath, let out a shriek. They hiss, swear, and joke, always roaring with laughter. They dance while groping their genitals, in the highest of spirits, winking derisively at everyone. In short, the drummers and singers do everything to make fun of the proposition that life is hard and requires sacrifices, and this derision works to circumvent any power this hard moral might otherwise exert.

Now we can understand why the mēḷam is absolutely essential to the Tamil funeral. Without this band, death would be left to the crying women who, like the songs' characters, surrender to its "limiting" message. That truly would be unsatisfactory. But men's opposition to women's lamenting clusters raises a final question: why should a ritual that so mocks death give such prominence, even center stage, to the expression of sorrow, as the Tamil funeral clearly does? Maurice Bloch provides an answer in his analysis of the gender division of death among the Merina people of central Madagascar (1982).

In brief, Bloch argues that, during the funerary ceremony, Merina women create meanings of grief and pollution only so men can transcend and overcome them. To Bloch, "order," by which he means men's victory over death, "is created by the ritual, and it is created very largely through dramatic antithetical negative symbolism." He writes, "In order to deny those things associated with death [for example, decomposition, pollution, and division] emphatically and thereby 'create' the victory, the enemy must be first set up in order to be knocked down" (1982: 218). That the Merina ritual not only "sets up" death but "revels" in doing so leads Bloch to suggest that "death as disruption, rather than being a problem for the social order, as anthropologists have tended to think of it, is in fact an opportunity for dramatically creating it" (1982: 218–19).

Bloch's insight that "the positive is created by the negative" (1982: 218–19) is on parity with Kapferer's proposition that comedy springs from the assertion, even exaggeration, of limiting messages. But Bloch's analysis brings to the fore something else. Among the Merina, women enable men to "win out over death." Since the production of the positive depends on the negative, women, in their capacity as agents of death, play the "central role," or the "creative" role, in Merina funerals (218). Likewise, one could argue that at Tamil funerals women enable men to evade the inevitability or finality of death. Without women's tears, men would not laugh. Without women's antagonistic stance to the social, men would not attempt to recreate it. If women did not cling to one another, yearning to return to the past, men would not declare that notions of detachment and relinquishment are essential. Everything that men stand for—including their striving to tip the hierarchical world of the Tamil day-to-day life in their favor, even if their caste is low—appears to be predicated on their seeing and hearing women yearning for the past without consideration for performance and accomplishment.

PERFORMING WITH JOY

This is a book about Tamil funeral songs and the ways in which they address bereavement and mourning. It is also about the singers and how their songs shape their individual experiences and emotions. Chapter 2 describes how crying songs give women a language with which to speak about themselves. In the remaining section of this chapter I compare women and men's funeral songs and explore how the latter might impact the Dalits' understanding of their place and role in caste society. What do they lose or gain by singing at funerals?

Death songs are no less sad than women's crying songs. If anything, the experiences they recount are more excruciating. But there are differences between these two funeral genres. A woman's dirge does not tell a story so much as express a pervasive condition—that of kuṟai—as evidenced by the fact that the singer might be anyone (a daughter, a sister, a wife) anywhere (at home, at the market place, by the riverbank, on the road, etc.). Her mother might be dead. Her husband might be dead, too, or he might be abusing her. She might be addressing them, but then again she might speaking of someone she never knew (as when Ellamma yearned for the brother she did not have) or to God. It is hard to know, for the woman does not provide personal names. While the lament suggests a specific story, a specific comparison, it remains generic, timeless, and universal.

Whereas the lamenting woman sketches ambiguous, even cryptic, scenarios, the mēḷam singer specializes in definite and specific matters, describing a person with a proper name and clear-cut social identity (either a former member of the social community or a legendary character) who is (or was) familiar to everyone. Scholars of South Indian classical literature identify this difference as characteristic of the contrast between *akam* (interior) and *puṟam* (exterior), words the old Tamil poets employ to divide their poems into two classes (Ramanujan 1967; Blackburn and Ramanujan 1986). The akam variety consists of love poems while the puṟam group are "civic poems on war, action, kingdom, community, good and evil, death, and so on (Ramanujan 1967: 99). A. K. Ramanujan, the great translator of these two genres, noted that "akam poetry is directly about experience, not action: it is a poetry of the inner world" (103). In these poems the names of individuals are not mentioned, and the evocative associations of landscapes are more important than particular places (104). In contrast, puṟam poems are "placed in a real society and given a context of real history," as evidenced by the frequent mention of poets, kings, heroes, and places in the poems (101).

The same contrast organizes the funeral songs of contemporary Tamil men and women.[21] The women sing about the interior life *(aka vāḻkai)*, about matters of the heart (*uḷḷam*, also means "inside"). The Dalits sing about the exterior life *(puṟa vāḻkai)*, on subjects regarding conduct in the social world. The categories of akam and puṟam enacted by men and women at the Tamil funeral are not merely polarized: they are mutually exclusive and antagonistic to one another. Squatting near the threshold, women literally turn their bent backs on the public, as if alienated from society, to retreat further into their inner worlds. The Dalits, who stand on the street, face and address the community, doing everything they can to attract general attention.

The significance of such a contrast is not that women are associated with intimate matters (marriage, in particular), and men with social or political concerns, for in Tamilnadu that goes without saying.[22] This contrast does not mean that men are less self-absorbed than women. Men are just as preoccupied with themselves, but their subjectivity is constituted in the puṟam, or "outward," mode. This subjectivity is best understood in comparison to that produced by the lamenting, or akam, genre of expression.

The language of Tamil dirges may be oblique, but clearly the singer personally feels what she sings. She feels kuṟai. This feeling of deficiency *is* the whole story of her dirge. Contrary to lamenting women, the Dalits do not sing from personal grief. This is implied in the woman's saying, "The Paṟaiyar sings according to the drumbeat, and the woman according to her feelings." Further evidence is the well-known fact that the

Dalits cannot sing at the death of their own relatives. One singer told me, "When my father died, my cousins said, 'You have sung for so many people; why can't you sing for your father. What do you have to lose?' So I sang whatever came to me. But I felt too much pain. I could not bear it. The grief gave me no place to sing." This man had a similar experience at a friend's funeral. "I sang the Ariccantiraṉ song and I cried. That song is sad enough; I could not sing it then. How could I? I was in grief." In short, whereas women cannot compare unless they genuinely feel bereaved, the mēḷam singer can sing death songs only when he does *not* grieve.

Not surprisingly, then, the man is subjected to aesthetic standards that depreciate genuine emotions. His songs are worth listening to not because he suffers but because he has a "good nature." "A good singer," I was told, "is polite and willing to sing at any time." His songs are good not because they express his feelings but because "the lyrics are grammatically correct and clearly enunciated." Finally, whereas a good voice is not necessary, and may in fact be detrimental, to the lament singer, "the Dalit man should sing in tune." He should have "talent" *(tiṟamai)*, a precious gift that, according to my consultants, few people possess. "Anyone can drum," I was often told, "but few can sing." To do so, one must receive a gift from the gods, particularly Caraswati, the goddess of knowledge and the arts.

In short, the singer is appreciated not for what he feels but for how he sings. In fact, the less he identifies with his lyrics the better, for he is expected to fabricate his emotional expressions. That performance rather than experience is paramount to the success of his show is also evidenced by the fact that he has to practice his gift. Unlike women, who find the words of their dirge automatically when they feel kuṟai, the Dalit man must memorize and rehearse his lyrics.[23] In addition, he has to enjoy performing.

What is required to learn death songs is "interest," Dalit singers told me, using either this English word or a range of Tamil words that connote "sensibility" *(uṇarcci)* or "pleasure" *(ārvam)*. The singer Vel said,

"A lot of people study these songs with the hope of making money, but without understanding you cannot sing." For this reason he had never pressed his sons to join the local mēḷam. "You cannot make people do things in which they have no interest," he commented, adding for my benefit, "Would you study our songs if you did not like them?" He remarked further "When a person is attracted by an activity, and when he sees others doing it, he picks it up. At least, this is how I learned how to sing." "Interest in what exactly?" I asked. "In the work itself," Vel answered. But most of my consultants specified interest "in the art *[kalai]*." There is evidence that funeral singers are interested in art—the art of the stage in particular—in the fact that many participate regularly in village plays *(terukūttu)*. Actually, most of the singers I met had come to the mēḷam by way of village dramas and had already played in terukūttu for several years before singing at their first funerals. In other words, funeral singers have a strong predilection for the business of performance and entertainment. They like to act out.

However, what Dalits perform at funerals is simply their job *(toḻil)*. As one elderly Dalit man told me, "We sing for the money. We are common men *[potumaṉucaṉ]*." Another man's reason for singing was even more explicit: "I have no other source of income. I do not own land. My siblings do not give me food. Only my songs feed me." This man could still remember the thrill he felt upon earning his first paycheck. "I was ten years old," he told me, "when my maternal uncle took me to my first funeral, a mile away from our village. I was playing in the house, but when he came to get me I ran with him, leaving my game. I came back at nine o'clock that night. You know what I had earned? One rupee and an half. That was a lot of money in those days for a poor boy like me, with no shirt and only one pair of trousers all torn up. My maternal uncle tucked the money in my underwear. That was for me, only for me. I had earned that much by singing and dancing."

Like the lamenting women, then, the Dalits sing from a position of scarcity and deprivation. But they do not voice their wretchedness or evoke any of their personal difficulties. Save for the end of the funeral, when they press their patrons to remunerate them better, they do not even complain about their obligation to attend to death. And yet the Dalits' job is not easy. Drumming is hard work, and singing is no less stressful. It requires tremendous energy to draw and entertain people from the time when a death is first announced until the funeral—sometimes two days later. Moreover, to drum and sing at funerals is to exhibit one's untouchability and, therefore, low status for all to see. And yet every indication suggests that the Dalits enjoy accomplishing their duties, or in the normative values of Hinduism, their dharma. In this, they have something in common with the figures in death songs—Ariccantiraṉ, Ciṟuttoṇṭar, and Maṉmataṉ—who also perform their duty with zeal despite the cost. And the Dalits are like male mourners who must carry out painful obligations—the funerals of loved ones—with big grins on their faces. In times of grief, all men seem determined, even enthusiastic, to fulfill their obligations without wavering, no matter what they might feel inside.

There are genuine rewards for such dedication. If men perform well, they stand at the center of public attention, praised, elevated, and in the case of the Dalits, materially compensated. But such benefits come at an exorbitant price. For the commitment to duty requires men to not feel "from within" who they are and what they are doing. Such a requirement may account for the liberal quantities of arrack drunk on such occasions. As a drummer told me, "The alcohol makes us forget the pain in our arms, the sun, the heat." Vel agreed, saying, "The drinking loosens me up; it helps me feel less shy. It frees me and makes me sing well." And a singer, Sivamani, told me the same thing: "Without the alcohol, I would feel dull and shy; I wouldn't be able to sing."

Negating kuṟai—that paramount feeling of loss and deprivation—is no less taxing than asserting it. In fact, negation may be more costly because it entails suppressing the pain of one's circumstances. While suppression may be psychologically functional for male mourners, it prevents the Dalits from recognizing that they are exploited. Rather than sensing the pain in their arms, the heat of the sun, the burden of their untouchability, they feel good about themselves and their art. They perform with joy, striving to find their place, even if it is low, in the organic functioning of village caste society. It is as if, for the duration of the funeral, they are outside the wretched experience of their day-to-day lives. And yet it would be wrong to conclude that at funerals the Paṟaiyars always perform their duties with the same energy and enthusiasm. At the end of the ritual, they can falter.

CHAPTER FOUR

Life as a Record of Failure

By the time the funeral procession leaves a South Arcot village, the mood of the day has changed. The expectant tension that had previously filled the air is now gone. The strained ceremonial displays of kinship, the chaotic unfolding of commemorative rituals, disputes over money, women's wails, the deafening sounds of the funeral band, the commotion of lifting the corpse onto the bier, the boisterous clamor of the funeral procession moving down the main street of the village—all are now things of the past.

As the drumming ends in the afternoon, an awkward, almost restless quiet descends upon the small group of men who accompany the deceased to the grave. There is a weary edge to their movements, the suggestion of emotional and physical fatigue. Most have not eaten since the night before, and the euphoric effects of the alcohol have faded. Led by those carrying the bier, the men walk in a single file to the riverbank that borders most South Arcot cremation grounds. Dazed by the mid-afternoon sun, the men do not look up to see the dunes, pebbly wastes, and rocky ridges that fuse in a vast expanse of grayness devoid of life for miles. Nor do they seem to notice the stunted black shapes of trees and the reeds that crunch when touched or the crows that circle low in the sky.

The entrance to a South Arcot cremation ground is usually marked by a stone *(kal)*—often an uncarved, pointed rock smeared with turmeric and vermilion powders—that is said to represent the good king Ariccantiraṉ.[1] At this spot, also called the "middle stone" because it is between the worlds of the living and the dead, the men, refocused by a sense of purpose, stop to place the bier on the ground with the corpse's head pointed toward the village.[2] This part of the ritual calls for the Dalits to petition *(viṇṇappam paṇṇa)* the king to open the gates to the afterlife, so that the soul of the deceased can depart to the afterworld.[3]

After an offering of raw rice at the four corners of the entrance to the cremation grounds, the Dalit petitioner and his escort *(tuṇai)* step forward in a matter-of-fact, almost mechanical, manner. The petitioner makes his address conscientiously, without instrumental accompaniment. Although he does not read it, he speaks in formal Tamil rather than everyday speech. His delivery is fast and loud—even energetic—but his rhythms are monotonous. The exaggerated emphasis on the last words of his sentences, punctuated by his escort's nasal exclamations of "Ein!" become predictable. Unlike the dirges and death songs that moved people to cry or laugh earlier in the day, the petition arouses no discernible reaction. Silence usually prevails from beginning to end.

When it is over, ten to fifteen minutes later, the village barber instructs the chief mourner (usually the deceased's son) to offer ceremonial coins and a camphor flame for Ariccantiraṉ. Now that the king, the gatekeeper of the funeral grounds, has received his due, the men of the family lift the bier and turn it so that the corpse's head is pointed toward the cemetery. At this point a member of the assembly often says, "There is no going back; the dead are not wanted among the living." The men then proceed to the riverbank, where they bury or cremate the body.[4]

This ritual suggests belief in an existence after death, a belief that, as one man framed it, "when we die, only our bodies come to an end." Although they refused to link the end of physical being with physical decay,[5] my consultants hesitated to speculate on forms of the afterlife—often countering my investigation with the pragmatic question "Who knows what really happens after death?"[6] They often invoked, however, representations of a last judgment. "While the Dalits make the petition," I was told, "the good and bad deeds of the deceased are counted." Many added that this bookkeeping is done in the presence of Ariccantiraṉ, because the king is the embodiment of truth: "He never told a lie. That's why at the end of life we are judged before him." And I was told that the final ledger of people's deeds is a kind of prestation. As one man explained, "When we reach the middle stone, we must give Ariccantiraṉ his due. He is blocking the path. If you want to go to the other side, you must pay. The record of our lives is a kind of payment. If it is done, Ariccantiraṉ will open the gates."

What is paradoxical, however, is that much of the petition to Ariccantiraṉ is not directly concerned with gate opening, final judgment, or the afterlife. For the most part, the petition unfolds in the form of what ethnographers typically classify as an origin myth about death.[7] Since death in the Tamil Hindu world is inextricably related to untouchability, the petition goes back to the beginning of the Paṟaiyars' specialization in funeral duties.

Indeed, the petition is really the story *(katai)*, as the Dalits themselves put it, of Vīrajāmpuhaṉ, the first Paṟaiyar man. The Dalits I met said that Vīrajāmpuhaṉ was "our ancestor," "our man," often adding that his name means "the brave Paṟaiyar" or "courageous drummer."[8] On the surface, such an impersonal, almost generic, designation is a little surprising. One expects the hero of a story—especially an *ancestral* hero—to be a little more distinctive. However, the purpose of telling this story is to incite Vīrajāmpuhaṉ himself to reveal the details of his life: who he is, where he comes from, and what he does. In short, the story asks him to tell what he knows about himself.

What is additionally puzzling about this story is that the Dalits have a hard time telling it. "Sometimes," the petitioner named Vel told me, "the desire *[ārvam]* to tell the story is there and sometimes it is not. I lose interest. At my brother's wife's funeral, for example, all I was able to utter was the first line of the petition. For half an hour, I tried to speak but no words came out of my mouth. I could not even open it, so I simply folded my arms in respect and left. Many times I have had such experiences. All of a sudden the story will stop coming out, and I'll have trouble breathing. I'll feel drowsy as if something were lifting me up or blocking *[aṭai]* me." The petitioner Sivamani reported similar symptoms. "I feel like I am being lifted up," he told me. "I have chest pains and difficulty breathing." The son of another petitioner told me that these sensations had led his father to faint on more than one occasion.

These men explained that it was the job of the escort to prevent or stop these symptoms: "He rubs our chests or taps our backs so that we can breathe." Such gestures, I was also told, "break the block; they ease us up and calm us down." A petitioner claimed that they gave him "voice." Yet another one did not feel that such assistance always helped him. "Sometimes," he lamented, "I am in such a state of shock that I simply can't go on. I feel as though I have completely forgotten the story."

This chapter examines the story of Vīrajāmpuhan̲, focusing on its varying and sometimes conflicting versions and meanings.[9] I explore the reasons why this particular life story is so difficult to recite at the entrance to the funeral ground and, in doing so, return to two themes raised in previous chapters. The first is that the advent of death in Tamil culture is decisively linked with the origin of social divisions and the formation of a sense of self that feels disconnected from, and rejected by, others. The second is that such a sense of self is insistently constructed through narrative. Here, however, the feelings and sensations experienced by the Dalits during their narration suggest that the process is neither cathartic nor elevating, as is the case (at least partly) in dirges and death songs, but restrictive and downgrading.

FIELDWORK WITH PETITIONERS

In my efforts to understand the meanings invested in the petition, I worked with the same four men who assisted my research on the mēḷam, for they were also funeral singers. These men had learned to make the petition after they had already mastered a repertoire of death songs, usually when they were in their forties, for the purpose of earning extra income. I spent as much time with these men as I did with the four criers of dirges introduced in chapter 2. I usually met them "on their turf," for it is inappropriate for a Tamil man to visit a woman unrelated to him, especially one living, as I did, alone in a middle-class neighborhood. On the rare occasions when they came to my rented house, Dalit men were stiff and timid and our conversations awkward. In their homes or work places, our rapport could not have been more different. Gone were the uncomfortable silences and thin exchanges. My male consultants relaxed, revealing loquacious, sometimes ebullient, personalities. Despite the fact that I was a foreigner and a woman, they did not seem to mind talking to me about their lives.

These men's reminiscences of earlier times were not so different from those of the lamenting women I interviewed. They too idealized their parents, particularly their fathers, and their maternal uncles. They too evoked the traumatic first years of married life, but from the perspective of spurned husbands. And they too complained about spouses, particularly the wives who had betrayed them. If I do not transcribe their confidences it is because they do not add much to our understanding of death songs and petitions. The connection between men's lives and these two genres is first and foremost socioeconomic. As I have already indicated, at deaths Dalit men sing and petition because this is part of their caste ritual work and their main source of cash. Their low standing in the social hierarchy rather than any personal feelings for parents or spouses prompts them to perform at village funerals.

In actuality my male consultants and I seldom discussed their social status. The few times that I did raise the subject, I encountered their resignation and justification. To the question of how they felt about their lowly condition, for example, men replied that they were not angry, because the great god Siva had fated them to be Paṟaiyars. As one petitioner told me, "God created me in this caste. I have no resentment *[kuṟai]* about that. Who I am today is god's creation and design." Another man stated, "We the Paṟaiyars are *patiyal* [slaves], 'the ones who work for food.' God gave us the work but neither the money nor the comfort. We cannot complain about this." I never tried to find out whether these men actually meant what they said, because I sensed that the subject of their caste identity was problematic, even embarrassing to them. "The absence of pride in being a Paraiyar," is also noted by Deliège, writing about the Ramnad district. As he specifies, "The caste represents shame which has to be hidden as much as possible" (1997: 127).

And yet the four men I worked with were willing to describe and discuss the very activities that define them as Paṟaiyars: drumming, singing, and petitioning at funerals. Perhaps this happened because they knew I did not subscribe to the values of purity and impurity that underlie caste hierarchy (I ate their food, I sat in their houses, I touched their drums). And perhaps my curiosity flattered them, heartening them to express their own interest in their art. My questions also gave these men a chance to articulate a positive image of their work and themselves, as when, for example, they explained that mourners needed their services. However, our conversations also brought up some of the negative side of their work.

The first petitioner I met was Sivamani, a good-looking widower in his midforties who lived near the village where I resided in the early 1990s. Aside from the income he earned from his funeral songs and petitions, Sivamani made his living as a part-time cattle broker. He also raised peacocks (sacred birds in South India), which he sold to rich devotees at the nearby Tiruvaṇṇāmalai temple.[10] When I first visited him, he agreed to answer any questions I might have about his funeral duties. He showed me his drums and, without my asking, began to recite passages of the petition. He punctuated his tirades with inquisitive gazes to see whether I appreciated his delivery.

Our association was not easy. My friends in the village disapproved of it, warning me that Sivamani was a womanizer and a thief. But Sivamani gave me valuable information. He was the first to demonstrate that the petition cannot be grasped in isolation from the exegeses and social experiences of the performers. When I asked him for comments on any aspect of his Vīrajāmpuhaṉ story, he offered a whole spectrum of meanings for it. He also raised a number of provocative points on the relation between what he narrated and what he felt at the entrance to the village funeral grounds, some of which I explore below. It is fair to say that without Sivamani I might never have perceived the extent to which the various meanings of the funeral petition emerge during the performance. I also might never have pursued other petitioners to gather their opinions on matters concerning the Vīrajāmpuhaṉ story.

Sivamani introduced me to Vel, the most important voice of this chapter. Our first meeting occurred more than ten years ago at a funeral in Vel's colony, seventeen kilometers west of Gingee. Vel was drunk at the time and paid little attention to me. Nor did I pay him much attention at first, for I was distracted by the ongoing wails of the crying women. But then he transfixed me by evoking passionately, song after song, the struggles and ordeals typical in death chants. His charisma and skills were such that, on that day, male mourners—people from his colony—paid him a lot of money just to hear him sing.

Vel was much more than a talented performer. A small man who could not have weighed more than a hundred pounds, and who always wore the same torn shirt and ragged cloth around his waist and never seemed to trim his flowing gray beard, Vel was a lively speaker as well. Like Sivamani, he loved to expound on the petition, but he differed in the fact that he took the origin scenarios of his story at face value. There was no question in his mind that these scenarios had once taken place, and he would get feisty whenever Sivamani questioned their authenticity. Since the two inevitably engaged in hermeneutic debates that resulted in rancor on both sides, I began to visit Vel alone. On the cement floor of his one-room house, or more often at his work post—the irrigation pump he operated in the fields of a Chettiar landowner—he would recite and interpret his version of the petition in the language that best suited his imagination.

Arjuna, the third petitioner with whom I worked in 1990, was related to Janaki, one of the women discussed in chapter 2. Unlike other petitioners, Arjuna was educated: he had studied up to the fifth standard, the equivalent of a high school education. Because his father had refused to let him take a teaching position outside their ancestral village near Tiruvaṇṇāmalai, he worked instead as an agricultural laborer, sometimes (like Sivamani) supplementing his wages by selling cattle at the Gingee market. In his midtwenties, to fulfill his literary aspirations, he had joined a local drama troupe and his village's funeral band. Although I never heard Arjuna sing, I recorded his version of the petition, which he had learned from a book or, more precisely, a leaflet he had purchased from a bookstall in Madras City. In contrast, Sivamani and Vel who were illiterate, had slowly memorized the story by listening to and repeating it.

These three men—Sivamani, Vel, and Arjuna—gave me an introduction to the petition that would lure me back to Tamilnadu in 1999. On my return I was not able to reconnect with all of them. Sivamani had remarried, and his young wife had just given birth to his fourth daughter. He had begun a new job as village policeman and was in the midst of building a large cement house. We met a couple of times, but it was clear that Sivamani was too busy to assist my ethnographic research. Arjuna had passed away a year earlier. In order to fill in the blanks our past collaboration, I sought out his two sons, one of whom praised his father's life in the eulogy I quoted in chapter 2, but they seldom had the time to elucidate what their father had tried to communicate to me nine years earlier. Only Vel was free to resume work with me on a regular basis. Despite the fact that his large brown eyes had become so nearsighted that they appeared empty and unfocused as they stared at my face, Vel had lost neither his voice nor his spirit. He still sang for anyone who would listen. As he was no longer able to operate the irrigation pumps, we met in his new government-subsidized house, tirelessly discussing the content of his petition and its impact on him until I left the field seven months later.

I also worked with one new petitioner, Ettyan, a sixty-year-old man with a broad face, who resided a few miles east of Gingee. His was one of the most out-of-the-way and desolate colonies I had ever seen. Any efforts the government was making to improve the living conditions of the Dalits had bypassed this place. The poorest of my consultants, Ettyan was also the most alone, living with neither a wife nor children but instead with his eighty-year-old mother. At first I was disappointed by his rendition of the petition. His delivery of the Vīrajāmpuhan̲ story was dull and his exegeses vague and thin. I soon realized, however, that, although uninspired and sometimes hazy, Ettyan's version was just as rich as the others. Less consistent, his explications nonetheless completed the commentaries I had previously recorded.[11]

THE STORY OF VĪRAJĀMPUHAN̲

This tale lacks many of the devices familiar in Western narratives. Instead it fits George Hart's description of the old Tamil love poems as "conversations of the people involved in a story" (1995: 168; also see Blackburn 1996: 14). In all versions of this story, the main conversation takes place between Vīrajāmpuhan̲ and the god Brahmā (or Siva), who calls upon the hero in order to solve the problem of overpopulation. When Vīrajāmpuhan̲ appears before the god, however, Brahmā does not immediately instruct him about his mission. In Vel's version, especially, instead of getting right to the point of his summons, the god first asks Vīrajāmpuhan̲ to state who he is, where he comes from, and what he knows about the world. In no apparent hurry—as if he were interviewing a job candidate—the god proceeds to question Vīrajāmpuhan̲, who patiently submits to the interrogation.

In all versions, only when Brahmā knows something about Vīrajāmpuhan̲ does he instruct him about his mission. "The earth goddess [or the primordial serpent, Āticēshan̲] can no longer support the weight of the world, because the ripe fruits [*paḻam;* also means 'a very old person'] cling to it. Go and proclaim by beat of drum *[paṟaicāṟṟa]* the fall of the ripe fruits."[12]

The hero departs, only to bungle his job as he beats the fall of both the ripe *and* the unripe fruits (but see Arjuna's version in appendix A). Then he returns to Brahmā to announce that from now on he will make his living as a funeral attendant. In most versions, the god's reaction to Vīrajāmpuhan̲'s explanation is not exactly what one would expect. Dropping the subject altogether, as if the Paṟaiyar were entitled to make death his business, Brahmā returns to the question of exactly who Vīrajāmpuhaṉ is and what he knows of the world. Again, Vīrajāmpuhaṉ humbly submits to this interrogation, relating, for example, how he was born and what he knows of moral patterns of behavior and their consequences. In Vel's version, Brahmā enjoys Vīrajāmpuhaṉ's answers so much—"You speak well," he keeps telling him—that the dialogue between the god and hero seems never-ending. But eventually this conversation links up with its ritual context, as Vīrajāmpuhaṉ petitions King Ariccantiraṉ, "to please open the door *[katavai tiṟa]* and give the way *[vaḻiya viṭu]*" to the deceased, on behalf of whom, of course, this whole story is told (but see Arjuna's version in appendix A).

With the exception of framing conventions—a standard preliminary invocation to the god Ganesh and the final petition to Ariccantiraṉ (or sometimes the goddess Kālī)[13]—all four versions of this story that I recorded follow a different sequential order. Nor do they give the same emphasis or interpretation to the standard episodes narrated by Vel (see appendix A). Yet a survey of the different ways in which my four narrators shaped the organization and the discourse of their stories points to the same thing. The request that King Ariccantiraṉ open the gates of the afterlife for a dead person is essentially a petition for the brave Paṟaiyar to tell who he is—what he eats, what he does, and what he knows. The result is often a candid and even naive self-presentation on the part of our hero. On this level of basic personal disclosures—and, as we will also see, their existential consequences—the petition works best as a story. What do these four versions of the petition, and their interpretations by Sivamani, Vel, Arjuna and Ettyan, say about Vīrajāmpuhaṉ, his origin, and his destiny?[14]

The Firstborn

In all four versions that I recorded, Vīrajāmpuhaṉ relates that he is the firstborn. This attribute seems to supersede all other distinctive markers of identity, including political status. Vīrajāmpuhan̲ may be, as Arjuna once explained to me, "a great man" *(periyavar)*. He may rule over the East, which is according to Vel, the most powerful direction because it is where the sun, moon, and stars rise. He may also be a bit full of himself, as we can infer from the condition he places upon his visit to the god: he will come if Brahmā gives him his royal white elephant. He is not political, however, and he does not seem to strive for power or even for personal favors. These traits—and the importance given to his role as firstborn—are most evident in Ettyan's version of the story. When Brahmā asks Vīrajāmpuhan̲ which country he rules, the latter answers, "I don't govern any country; I am not anyone's king. I am the eldest. I am the firstborn. I am the one with the sacred thread on his back. I am the Par̲aiyan̲ with the conch." The only claim that Vīrajāmpuhan̲ makes is for precedence (*mutalmei*, primacy) in the world, a claim that apparently entitles him to carry symbols of superiority of the upper castes, such as the sacred thread and the conch.

The specifics of his birth vary from one petition to another, but Vīrajāmpuhan̲ consistently speaks of divine origin. In Vel's version, the hero reveals that he emerged from the womb of Pārvati (the great Hindu goddess). In two others he claims to be Siva's first son. My four consultants each told me that Vīrajāmpuhan̲ did not merely issue from the gods but instead was "like a god," which explains why he has a conch—a divine emblem—on his head.

Yet Vīrajāmpuhan̲ is not exactly a deity. Unlike true deities, who function principally to create life, his function has more of a regenerative nature. In three versions of the narrative, the Par̲aiyar tells how, at the beginning of time, the world was destroyed and how *he* was instrumental—indeed indispensable—in its re-creation, for *he* alone possessed the essential regenerative ingredient: the only lump *(uṇṭai)* of mud left on earth.[15] Thus, the firstborn symbolizes the possibility of renewed life rather than life-giving itself.

For my four narrators the firstborn derives his re-creative powers from his connection with water. According to Arjuna, this connection goes way back. "At birth," he once told me, "Vīrajāmpuhaṉ was so hot that his father, Siva, immersed him in water." Later in life, the firstborn still dips in water whenever he gets hot. In Vel's version, for example, when the earth catches on fire, Vīrajāmpuhaṉ takes the last lump of unburned soil and runs to the seashore. Arjuna's description of this episode is even more to the point: "While the North, the South, and the West are in flames, the 'water-dipped Vīrajāmpuhaṉ' comes out of the ocean. On the shore he takes the last handful of unburned sand from the shore and goes back into the ocean to hide, so that the gods are unable to re-create the world without the one in the water." In Ettyan's version it is a "flood" or, more accurately, "an ocean swelling with waves" that threatens to devastate the earth. But here too Vīrajāmpuhaṉ prevents total destruction, because he "takes the last lump of dry earth, slips into a gourd and floats in the waves."[16] The Paṟaiyar's affinity with water is reflected in real life. In the South Arcot district many Dalit men are, like Vel, in charge of irrigating the fields of their villages' landlords.

Vīrajāmpuhaṉ's relationship with culture is more complicated. Clearly there would be no culture without him, for in saving the world from destruction, he makes possible the formation of social practices. In fact, he requires that marriage—a social institution par excellence—be the essential condition for the re creation of the world. In Vel's version, for example, he surrenders the last lump of soil to the one god who will marry Vīrajāmpuhaṉ's daughter. And yet the firstborn's notion of marriage is not entirely cultural. In all versions of the petition, Vīrajāmpuhaṉ weds his daughter to Siva, his own father. Even if my reading of this arrangement is too literal, the fact remains that the Vīrajāmpuhaṉ of Ettyan's version explicitly commits incest. In this version, Vīrajāmpuhaṉ takes his daughter with him in the gourd. While floating in the water, they conceive three girls, whom Vīrajāmpuhaṉ later marries to the three gods, Brahmā, Siva, and Viṣṇu.

There is also evidence that the firstborn does not know his society's basic rules of conduct. In two versions of the narrative, he volunteers the information that he once "dried" and "feasted" on a "share" of dead cow "morning and night for three days." As if this revelation were not enough, his intimate knowledge of the practical uses *(putumai)* of a dead cow's body parts—horns can be made into combs; skin can be made into parasols, bridles for horses, muzzles for cattle, sandals for people, and so on—exposes him as the disposer of its carcass. How can Vīrajāmpuhan̲, the elder of all castes, not know that eating beef and removing carrion are impure and, as the Tamils put it, "disgusting" activities in Hindu society?

Here we may surmise that the fundamental element of being "firstborn"—that is, having been born *first,* before all others—contributes to Vīrajāmpuhan̲'s cultural ignorance. The firstborn was fated to live alone, without the company of siblings, without the guidance of other men and women, without a heritage handed down to him. He had to work out his own morality and truth. We may wonder about the exact cause of his estrangement, but the fact remains that the Par̲aiyar is "unclean," defiling, and therefore "untouchable" *(tīṇṭā).* And since, in the Hindu world, impurity is inevitably associated with lower status, he is an inferior as well (Dumont 1980). This firstborn may be the conduit for more life, and he may have saved the world from total disaster, but he is fundamentally a subaltern, someone who must toil for others. This fits with my consultants' description of senior kinship roles in contemporary Tamil families. The firstborn son, they argued, is the "sufferer": "If the father dies, he is expected to provide for his mother and younger siblings. They'll ask him to give everything he owns, even his share of the inheritance, but they won't credit him for his generosity." There is therefore something poignant about Vīrajāmpuhan̲'s claim that he "comes first, even before the Brahmin, in all ceremonial occasions of life." Despite his seniority and his privileges, the firstborn—like the elder son described by my consultants—is a subordinate, someone that can be exploited.

The Drummer

In two versions of this story, it is precisely when Virajampuhan identifies himself as a beef-eater and handler of animal wastes and corpses that

Brahmā entrusts him with the inauspicious and polluting task of proclaiming by drumbeat "the fall of the ripe fruits." Understandably, my Dalit narrators were reluctant to confirm this equation. Ettyan, for example, told me that Vīrajāmpuhaṉ was chosen because "Brahmā thought well of him." Others contended that "other people did not have the power to drum." Sivamani admitted that considerations of superiority *(mēlmai)* and inferiority *(tāḻmai)* might have been at play. "Brahmā was the boss," he explained. "As for Vīrajāmpuhaṉ—he was just a slave. He had to obey Brahmā's orders." Only Vel had no qualms about articulating what made Vīrajāmpuhaṉ particularly suitable for his assignment. As he told me, "Paṟaiyaṉ is the untouchable, the lowest of the low, the name of those who beat the drum. Vīrajāmpuhaṉ was the only one who could do this work; he was a worker."

Asked why Brahmā provokes Vīrajāmpuhaṉ to say that he is a beef-eater, as if the god did not already know, my narrators answered, "Brahmā wants to make sure that the firstborn does not lie." As Sivamani explained to me, "Brahmā wants to test Vīrajāmpuhaṉ. He wants to know whether his servant is telling the truth."[17] Brahmā may have good reasons to test his servant, for according to Vel, in an older version of this story Vīrajāmpuhaṉ attempts to conceal the fact that he eats beef, an omission that prompts the god to say, "Don't hide, Paṟaiyā!" In Arjuna's variant the reference to his nonvegetarian diet is entirely suppressed. But in most of the versions I recorded, Vīrajāmpuhaṉ is fairly candid about his diet and his occupation. I surmise that he tells the truth about himself because he does not understand the full implications: the Paṟaiyar does not seem to know that he is an untouchable. Recall the beginning of the story, when he does not behave like the servant he is. "Tell Brahmā to send me his royal white elephant," he says proudly to the God's messenger as if, Vel commented, "he thinks of himself as equal to the god." In all versions he also appears before Brahmā adorned in silk, a luxurious cloth that inferiors do not wear.

The Paṟaiyar may lack a sense of where he stands in caste society, but he knows his line of work. In all versions, Vīrajāmpuhaṉ agrees to his assigned role on one condition. "Swami, I have a request," he says, using the same word *(viṇṇappam)* that describes the narration of this story at the entrance to the funeral ground. "If I must broadcast the fall of ripe fruit in cities and hell, you must give me five *kalams* [a measure of thirty-six liters] of marijuana, ten kalams of alcohol, and your royal elephant." According to my narrators, these demands reflect Virajampuhan's grasp of what he will need to carry out his mission effectively. "Virajampuhan has to go around and broadcast news by beat of drum," they explained. "This is hard work. The elephant would make his rounds easier. The alcohol and marijuana would give him a boost [my narrators used this English word] and remove his shyness."

The Angry Man

My narrators often stressed that Vīrajāmpuhaṉ's line of work is not only tiring but also dangerous and, therefore, demands bravery, as indicated by the fact that the epithet *vīram* (courage) is prefixed to his name. "Vīrajāmpuhaṉ must be courageous," Vel reasoned, "because he is on the road. As he goes through villages, he maybe robbed." From Vel's perspective the fact that the Paṟaiyar is not the bearer of good news, but rather the herald of death, increases the likelihood that he will "be beaten, even killed." Vel concluded, "There are liabilities, even dangers, to his work."

Indeed, the drummer runs into trouble. Not right away, for according to Vel's version, "throughout the first ten streets of the neighborhood, Vīrajāmpuhaṉ dutifully proclaims. 'The ripe fruit must fall! The old people must die!'" His problems begin on the eleventh street, the street of the artisan caste *(Kammāḷa)*. There he sees some women singing and dancing. Distracted, he drops his drum (or, in some versions, his drumstick) on the ground. The women dash to hand it back to him. Vīrajāmpuhaṉ catches the drum with his left foot. The women feel insulted. "What is this?" they say. "We gave him the drum with our right hands and he received it with his left foot!" They throw stones at him, and one hits his forehead. Vīrajāmpuhaṉ sees his blood dripping on the ground.

Angrily he lashes out, "May the universe fall apart! May heaven and earth come to an end! May this world crumble to pieces! May Siva's throne shake! May all kings run in fear!" These are a mad man's words, words that lack power of their own to destroy the world. But then Vīrajāmpuhaṉ issues a curse that will become reality because he drums it out: "May the flowers *[pū]* fall [*utir;* also means "die"]! May the budding fruits *[piñcu]* fall! May the unripe fruits *[kāy]* fall! May the ripe fruits *[paḻam and kaṉi]* fall!" The firstborn has just proclaimed that death will be with us at all stages of existence. His broadcast is especially harsh because it is expressed through metaphors of growth and maturation. The unborn babies (flowers), the children (tender fruits), the adults (unripe fruits), and the old people (ripe fruits) will all have to die. Jāmpuhaṉ even curses "the six-month babies to scream and fall" (also see Arjuna's version of this episode in appendix A).

In his study of mythologies of death, the Romanian historian of religions Mircea Eliade found that "among archaic societies, most of the myths explain Death as an absurd accident and/or as the consequence of a stupid choice made by the first ancestors" (1977: 13–14). Reviewing a number of these myths, he concludes, "Seldom do we encounter a more appropriate illustration of the absurdity of Death. One has the impression that he is reading a page of a French existentialist author" (14).

The Tamil funeral petition seems to corroborate Eliade's insight that the appearance of death "is so hopelessly incomprehensible that a ridiculous explanation is more convincing because it is ridiculously absurd" (1977: 14). In fact my narrators concurred that the whole episode on the artisan street made no sense. Certainly Vīrajāmpuhaṉ commits an infraction; but the women go too far. "The girls should have forgiven Vīrajāmpuhaṉ," Vel lamented. "They should not have stoned him." Sivamani agreed: "If they had excused him, Vīrajāmpuhaṉ would have never cast his command *(kaṭṭaḷai)*." Vel best captured the sheer "absurdity" of these events when he attempted to justify Vīrajāmpuhaṉ's reaction. When I suggested that Vīrajāmpuhaṉ's death curse seemed excessive, even disproportionate to his injury, he replied, "Vīrajāmpuhaṉ had been hit by a stone. He was bleeding and confused. He was angry and drunk. He did not know what he was saying." To say that untimely death entered the Tamil world because a man was disoriented and "did not know was he was saying"—this is the kind of explanation for death that Eliade describes as absurd.

In my opinion, the most absurd aspect of this episode is Vīrajāmpuhaṉ's failure to realize that receiving an object with the left side of the body—or worse still, the left foot—is offensive to Hindus, especially when the givers are, as in this case, high-caste women. Once again the firstborn is ignorant of caste etiquette, of behaviors pertaining to purity and impurity. His ignorance is particularly apparent once he has been appointed to move about and communicate in an unfamiliar world. Perhaps this is why Vīrajāmpuhaṉ's job is considered "dangerous." Because he does not know the appropriate codes of conduct, the firstborn is liable—almost guaranteed—to misbehave.

I suspect that his transgressions are considered painful not only because they entail physical punishment but also because they reveal to him who he is. During the bruising encounter with the artisan women, Vīrajāmpuhaṉ becomes aware of himself for the first time and fulfills his destiny of becoming a man conscious of his own estrangement and untouchability (but see Arjuna's version in appendix A). This is why he gets angry. He has not simply been stoned; he has been hit with the realization of his standing in caste society. He is a worker who performs degrading services while other castes (the artisans, in particular) do valued work (craftsmanship) and establish the codes of behavior. Naturally, once conscious of this injustice, Vīrajāmpuhaṉ tries to retaliate or, as Sivamani put it, "take command." The firstborn does not have the power to change the social rules, for he does not make them, but he does have control over life and death. And so with an eye-for-an-eye mentality, he drums out words that will make everyone "fall." Thus, in this Tamil story, the appearance of death is not all that absurd. It is born from the anger of having discovered that one is a "pariah" (but see Arjuna's version in appendix A).

The Rational Man

By the time he is asked by Brahmā to account for his terrible broadcast, Vel explained, "Vīrajāmpuhaṉ is sober and no longer angry." This may explain why he does not say to the god, "Some caste people made me feel bad about myself, so I cursed them with untimely death." Rather than revisit this painful episode, he rationalizes his curse on the grounds that he needs to make a living.[18] He seems haunted by the desire to find a niche in the world he has just discovered. In Vel's version of the story, Vīrajāmpuhaṉ states this outright: "Before there was nothing. Now there is a world, a sky, an earth, boundaries, and enclosures *[kōllai]*. I need to work." In Ettyan's version, Vīrajāmpuhaṉ reasons, "I have no means of making a living," implying that death will provide him with one. Indeed the Paṟaiyar (or in Ettyan's version, his wife) sees the potential for returns in this new venture: "For a big corpse there will be big money; for a small corpse there will be small money." In Sivamani's version, he says, "With the young dying, with death being a daily matter, I'll make a proper living."[19]

Although his reasoning is practical, I think Vīrajāmpuhaṉ has set very low goals for himself in choosing an occupation that is inauspicious, polluted, and certain to exclude him from caste society. Ironically, even the pay for this occupation is not good. As he announces, "I will get mouth rice, change for burning the corpse, change for burying the corpse, the coins that are put at the four corners of the middle stone, new cloth, a piece of loincloth, and the six coins for Ariccantiraṉ. All this will be my due *[contam]* now." When I proposed to Vel that Vīrajāmpuhaṉ might have chosen a more lucrative line of work, he replied, "Vīrajāmpuhaṉ does not have the brain to wish nice things." The comment confirmed my impression that the firstborn does not know how to get along in society. He is ignorant not only of the behaviors despised by caste Hindus (beef eating, alcohol, consumption, left-hand etiquette, removal of dead animals, etc.) but also of the advantages of social life (material gain, possession, and the like). Yet perhaps the Paṟaiyar is smarter than Vel assumed. Once Vīrajāmpuhaṉ knows where he stands in the world of "boundaries," or differences, that he has just discovered, maybe he also realizes that he can take on only the impure and low-paid tasks. This may explain why he seems resigned to make death his business.

The Learned Man

My consultants offered many explanations of why the god does not reprimand Vīrajāmpuhaṉ for his transgression: "Brahmā understands that Vīrajāmpuhaṉ needs to make a living." "If Brahmā had gotten angry, Vīrajāmpuhaṉ would have quit his job, and so who would have done the work?" They also brought to my attention the fact that Vīrajāmpuhaṉ had done a great service to the world: "Brahmā realized that Vīrajāmpuhaṉ had done the right thing. The death of only the old people was never going to solve the overpopulation problem." "There is wisdom to what the Paṟaiyar drummed. If no one were to die, life would be a nightmare. There wouldn't be any room left to walk on earth. Households would be overcrowded. And where would we get the money to build bigger houses?" Everyone seemed to agree that Vīrajāmpuhaṉ had saved the world from the calamity of unchecked demographic expansion.[20]

There is other evidence that Vīrajāmpuhaṉ is wise and knows things about the world that no one else knows. "He is the firstborn," Arjuna told me in an attempt to explain. "He knows everything." "Vīrajāmpuhaṉ," Sivamani specified, "is not merely *Paṟaiyar* but *paṟaicāṟṟakkūṭiyavar*," which means "the one who knows everything."

What does the Paṟaiyar know? In all versions of this story, he demonstrates that he specializes in beginnings and endings. He knows how the world was re-created, how the cow was born, and how he—the first man—was conceived. He also knows what happens at the end of life, particularly to cattle and human beings, whose corpses he disposes of. His professional occupation grants him a particular domain of expertise that becomes his specific contribution to culture.

Human beings, Vīrajāmpuhaṉ declares, continue to live after death.

The nature of their postlife existence depends on who they were and what they did while alive, so that human beings are actually responsible for their own fate.[21] Good people go to heaven (or, in some versions, reach liberation from transmigration), and bad people go to hell. Vīrajāmpuhaṉ does not cast himself as the final arbiter, but he does decree specific standards of good and evil or, in other words, what actions qualify the dead for either realm in the afterlife. Not surprisingly, his list of sins and virtues neglects to include behaviors that in caste society are considered either "impure" or "pure." Nowhere does Vīrajāmpuhaṉ state that those who handle corpses, eat beef, and drink alcohol will go to hell. Nor does he determine that those who avoid defiling tasks and adhere to a strict vegetarian diet will go to heaven. Instead, in Vel's version, he explains in one breath that those who raise dangerous dogs, kick cows with their feet, hit their mothers with the backs of their hands, hurt their brothers' feelings, or cheat on wages and measurements will be thrown into pits of snakes, lizards, and leeches. As for those who betray their kinsmen, cast an evil eye on fruit trees, dwell upon already settled disputes, remove boundary stones to plow the land of others, fail to perform consecration ceremonies, and commit murder, they will be tied to a red-hot pole and pushed into a river of fire.[22] Conversely, he says, those who do not commit these actions will reach God. Vīrajāmpuhaṉ invokes a code of morality that does not seem to be specifically Hindu. Injunctions such as "do not hurt your kin, cheat, plunder, or murder" resonate cross-culturally if not universally. They sound almost like Christian commandments.

The Petitioner

Only at the very end does this narrative (at least in three of the versions recorded) take on its ritual meaning, when Vīrajāmpuhaṉ requests that King Ariccantiraṉ, the guardian of the cremation grounds, open the gates to the afterlife for the deceased person (on whose behalf this story is told, of course). By the end, the firstborn has fulfilled his destiny: he is a drummer, a funeral servant, a man who petitions for his living (but see Arjuna's version in appendix A). Although permanently associated with—in fact, dependent upon—endings, the firstborn does not lose his unique connection with beginnings or, rather, "re-beginnings." After all, he once saved the world from destruction by supplying the last lump of unburned earth to the gods. Now once again he saves human beings from complete extinction by petitioning for their postlife existence. His other funeral duties are also reminiscent of his participation in the re-creation of the world. The Paṟaiyar cremates the dead and supplies the ashes to mourners, who then immerse the ashes in water—a river or the sea—to facilitate the souls' passage to the world of the ancestors. In his occupation, then, as in earlier history, the Paṟaiyar continues to supply the necessary ingredient—what is left of the old form of life—for the renewal of the Hindu world and its inhabitants.

DALIT MYTHS OF ORIGIN

Robert Deliège has suggested that, for many Indian low castes, the myth of origin is a "rationalization of the caste's inferior status." "This rationalization," he explains, "is not presented as the fruit of divine will, or as a defect inherent to the members of the caste. Quite on the contrary, the lowness of the caste always appears as the result of a mistake, a joke, wickedness or deceit." According to Deliège's generalization, "The pattern is always the same: at the outset, the caste was honourable, but through the artlessness of its members, or through the craftiness of others, its status gradually sank lower until it became what it is today" (1997: 128). Based on his own ethnographic research among Tamil Paṟaiyars, as well as that of Michael Moffatt (1979), Deliège gives specific examples of this pattern that often express a brotherly relationship between the Paṟaiyars and another caste (the Reddiars or Brahmins). In all these myths, the Paṟaiyars are the elder brothers and, through a "piece of bad luck" or "the fruit of an injustice," become inferior to the other caste. To Deliège this pattern suggests that untouchables' origin myths contest both the divine legality and the fairness of the caste system (Deliege 1997: 129).

Deliège is quick to add, however, that such myths do not represent a fundamental search for a new caste status. Unlike certain Tamil low castes (the Nadars for example), who have used myth to improve their social positions, "the Paṟaiyars do not have these ambitions for social advancement. . . . [Their] myths . . . do not in fact aim at giving the reasons for social ascent. They are actually a record of failure" (135).

The Vīrajāmpuhaṉ story—a kind of Paṟaiyar "myth of origin"—confirms much of Deliège's analysis.[23] As we have just seen, this story relates how the firstborn—the elder of all castes and the savior of the world—became a poor funeral worker (but see Arjuna's version in appendix A). It is worth noting that god does not force Vīrajāmpuhaṉ to drum and petition for his living. In fact, as Deliège writes of other Paṟaiyar myths, "God does not impose anything" (1997: 129). Although god selects Vīrajāmpuhaṉ for the job of broadcasting the fall of the unripe fruit, the Paṟaiyar himself confirms that he is the right candidate: he eats beef, he disposes of dead cows, he knows what is needed to drum. Nor does god pressure Vīrajāmpuhaṉ to make death his profession. In fact, death for god is only a solution to an urgent problem, the overpopulation of earth, not a perfected scheme. Recall that Brahmā makes no provision for the disposal of the timely dead. It is the Paṟaiyar (or, in Arjuna's version, his wife) who systematizes death by casting its curse upon everyone and appointing himself its attendant. But, much as in the myths analyzed by Deliège, Vīrajāmpuhaṉ's downfall is not entirely his own doing. It results from an unfortunate mishap and the ensuing consequences. It is because Vīrajāmpuhaṉ is stoned for picking up with his left foot the drum handed to him with "right" intentions that he ultimately brings about both death and his untouchability (but see Arjuna's version in appendix A).

Since it reads as a "record of failure," this story could be interpreted as one more example of the kind of rationalizing imagination that Deliège imputes to the Paṟaiyars. My feeling, however, is that there are dangers in reading a myth of origin, as he does, as a "form of self-representation" (1997: 127). For one thing, it is difficult to assess whether, and if so to what degree, the narratives people tell about themselves express who they think they really are. The claim that myths of origin encapsulate a people's sense of themselves is especially hard to sustain when, as Deliège himself indicates, they do not widely circulate. He writes, "I have no wish to make the reader believe that the myths occupy an important place in this society; it is in fact quite the reverse. Many villagers do not know this myth nor any other. The Paṟaiyars work hard and have little time to do with literature." Deliège further adds, "The story of the caste is not of much concern to these practical people" (136).

Much the same is true of the Vīrajāmpuhaṉ story. Only the Paṟaiyar men who are paid to petition for the dead know it. Others, and this includes most funeral drummers and singers, do not. That this myth falls in the category of esoteric rather than popular knowledge is also evidenced by the temporal and spatial parameters of its telling. The story of Vīrajāmpuhaṉ is recited at no other time than when the funeral procession reaches the entrance to the cremation ground, it is recited at no other place. Before reading it as a strict expression of a general caste consciousness, then, we should ask ourselves why this story is told at the place where the souls of the dead are believed to depart from society, rather than anywhere else? In other words, we should explore the connection of this origin myth with its ritual setting.

TEXT IN CONTEXT

While in the field, I witnessed the recitation of the Vīrajāmpuhaṉ story on three separate occasions without understanding this connection. Only when I listened to petitioners' explanations that feelings sometimes prevent them from telling this story, did I begin to appreciate its relation to the time, place, and function (as a petition to permit a dead person to proceed to the afterworld) of its narration. Petitioners' testimonies acquire critical significance when we look at the distinctive forms of experience typically associated with South Indian performances.

Scholars of South Indian performance have documented that actors playing in folk theater sometimes experience a state called in most vernaculars *āvēcam* (de Bruin 1998b; Hiltebeitel 1988). These scholars have shown that this Sanskrit word refers to the actor's complete identification with his character (de Bruin 1998b: 28).[24] Hence we have the category āvēcam, which literally glosses as ā, meaning "without," and vēcam, referring to the "role" or "covering" (costume, makeup, etc.) that actors put on to play their parts. A survey of this literature also suggests that this merging of actors with their roles tends to occur during highly charged and, more specifically, sacrilegious scenes. Alt Hiltebeitel's research on the Tamil folk performances of the pan-Hindu epic the Mahābhārata, for example, documents how the actor playing an evil fellow named Duḥśāsana experiences āvēcam when he attempts to disrobe the goddess Draupadī (1988: 269–77).

My own field research in the South Arcot district adds to these findings the observation that āvēcam is an inclusive term for a range of experiences in which a person is taken over by a powerful emotion. As one man told me, "Āvēcam means that you are not in control of your emotions. Emotions control you." He added, "You are then not in your usual state; . . . [you are] not yourself, nor even aware of what is happening to you, because āvēcam comes without a person's knowledge." Others described āvēcam as an "explosion," a state in which "your heart simply bursts out," and this explains why in common parlance the word *āvēcam* also refers to vehement speech, such as one hears from Tamil politicians. Everyone agreed that emotions of anger or outrage trigger the state of āvēcam. I was told much the same as what Hiltebeitel was told: "Avecam first builds up as a feeling of being overcome with 'anger' *[kōpam]*" (1988: 275). An example is the person no longer able to endure an abusive relationship, who thus reacts or, rather, overreacts, because āvēcam translates as an uncontrollable urge to behave violently. This is why it is considered "a dangerous state." "It may lead you to kill," an actor once told me.

Like the scholars cited above, I discovered that this highly emotional state is often triggered by acting in or witnessing scenarios involving the ritual desecration of revered people, places, or ideas. The son of the petitioner, Arjuna, poignantly illustrated this to me. I say *poignantly* because his testimony related violent incidents that took place at the funeral of his own father. According to the son, a big fight erupted between his father's and mother's kin, and a heavy brick was thrown at one of his maternal uncles, who was knocked to the ground. "When I saw this," Arjuna's son told me, "I experienced āvēcam. I had never before been that angry. All I could think was, 'How do they dare behave like this at my father's funeral?' I could not control myself: I ran to beat the man who had thrown the brick. The police came and arrested people from both sides. They forbade us to drum and sing, ordering that my father's body be buried immediately. I felt very bad about that too. My father had sung for so many people, and no one was there to sing for him."

I have spent some time on the subject of āvēcam to show that it surfaces in many Tamil performances (theater, public speaking) and rituals (festivals, funerals). It also occurs in sacrificial contexts, which is not surprising, because, as I have shown elsewhere, Tamil sacrifice involves both dramaturgical and sacrilegious dynamics (Nabokov 2000). We must then ask if 'petitioners,' who after all recite a dramatic story, ever feel āvēcam at the entrance to the cremation grounds?

"It is possible," Ettyan conceded. "There is a place for anger in that story." Nor did Sivamani rule out the probability. "If a petitioner is to experience a state of āvēcam," he suggested, "it would be at the point when Vīrajāmpuhaṉ announces the fall of the flowers and immature fruits." He thus confirmed the notion that āvēcam translates as an outburst of tremendous destructive energy that results from having endured—Vīrajāmpuhaṉ had just been struck by a stone—or witnessed an act of violence. But the petitioners, who were familiar with the state of āvēcam, for they often acted in religious plays of high emotional intensity, told me that, in reality, during the narration of the Vīrajāmpuhaṉ story they feel no āvēcam, or that āvēcam is a "more abiding state" than what they have experienced at other times. In fact, they enter a state contrary to that of āvēcam. Rather than feel compelled to act out the Vīrajāmpuhaṉ story, they actually struggle to tell it. Incapacitated and in a state of shock, they are unable to speak or even breathe.

The difficulty with which petitioners explained these feelings to me further demonstrated their inhibitions. Their commentaries seemed impromptu and confused. Sivamani argued that chest pains and breathing problems were the natural outcome of the performance. "It is because we must speak loudly and energetically," he told me, "that we are hindered." According to Arjuna's son, the explanation lay "in the story itself." When I asked him to elaborate, he was unclear, finally blurting out, "Perhaps the evil spirits hanging around the cremation ground create the obstacles. They hinder us because we are telling the truth, the true story of Vīrajāmpuhaṉ." Ettyan claimed that the deities opposed him by "lifting him up" or "by poking him in the heel," but he could not, or would not, tell me why.

For all their ambiguities, these statements nonetheless point toward the same thing: telling the truth, the true story of Vīrajāmpuhaṉ, is not easy. On this point the telling merges with the tale, for contemporary petitioners are not alone with their trouble in telling the truth about Vīrajāmpuhaṉ. The firstborn himself has difficulties revealing who he really is. He forgets his own genealogy or deletes certain problematic biographical facts. "How can I disclose my mother's and father's names?" Vīrajāmpuhaṉ asks in Sivamani's version. The god immediately replies, "If your birth is true, you ought to remember." Recall also that, in an earlier version of this story, according to Vel, Vīrajāmpuhaṉ tries to conceal from Brahmā the fact that he kept a share of the cow for himself, an omission that prompts the god to say, "Don't hide, Paṟaiyā!"[25]

In this story telling the truth is important. According to my narrators, Brahmā's interrogation of the firstborn is a "test," "a way of making sure that the Paṟaiyar does not lie." Moreover, this interrogation is enacted before King Ariccantiraṉ, who symbolizes absolute integrity. And yet, despite the high value put on honesty, the rest of this story warrants Vīrajāmpuhaṉ's hesitations and deletions. Recall that telling the truth only causes trouble for the firstborn His disclosures about his beef-eating and his practical knowledge of the cow's carcass typecast him in a dangerous, nonlucrative, and despised role and occupation. But the story does more than simply say that you are what you eat and what you do, and that there is no escape. The story appears to assert that any factual revelations about the self are dangerous because they lead to the rupture of social (that is, sibling) ties and therefore to one's demise.

Ultimately, I believe, the petitioners experience difficulties during their performances because they feel the burden of this complex process of telling the truth about one's self. They may not feel āvēcam, but they nonetheless identify with Vīrajāmpuhaṉ's predicament. Because the Paṟaiyar's story is their origin story as well, they may also feel their own inhibitions while trying to recount his downfall. This is evidenced by the fact that, according to their own admissions, petitioners do hide certain details. Vel, for example, admitted that he occasionally neglected to reveal that Vīrajāmpuhaṉ cooked and ate a cow. When asked why, he immediately replied, "So as not to shame the Dalits." "Not that there is disgrace in eating beef," he continued. "In the old days the celestial bodies themselves used to do it. But times have changed. Nowadays it is considered to be disgusting."[26] It is clear, then, that petitioners might not be comfortable with telling the true story of their ancestor. But there are additional layers to an explanation of their difficulties.

The story of Vīrajāmpuhaṉ is a petition to Ariccantiraṉ to open the gates to the afterlife, and the petition entails some form of judgment or assessment. At that moment, in front of the middle stone, my consultants told me, a dead person's good and bad deeds are "added up." One's life is reviewed from beginning to end, and all actions are accounted for. Like Vīrajāmpuhaṉ, the dead are "tested," or interrogated. They too must answer truthfully, and their answers determine their final destiny. Essentially, good people go to heaven and bad people go to hell. But all of them must depart, or "fall," from society. This process of interrogation, judgment, separation, and demise occurs for every person who dies, although we do not hear the individual's unique story. We hear only the story of Vīrajāmpuhaṉ, who, as firstborn, goes first in everything. However, Vīrajāmpuhaṉ's experience—especially his exclusion from society, relegation to a death-related occupation and ultimate undoing—seem inclusive of all experiences to follow.

I suspect that the petitioners also feel the uneasiness they imagine the dead person to feel when faced with the final question: "Who are you?" My suspicion is not based solely on personal intuition, however. While the petitioners never claimed to empathize with the dead to the point of experiencing forces (demonic or otherwise) that inhibit the petitioners from telling who they are loudly, clearly, and candidly, certain signs indicate that, in their bodies, text and context unite. All of their performance-related symptoms—breathing problems, faintness, chest pain, feelings of levitation—suggest identification with the dead and their ascent to the afterworld.

A MISSING AUDIENCE

To the degree that it describes a decline, a life with a downward trajectory, the Vīrajāmpuhaṉ story appears to confirm Deliège's analysis of the untouchables' myth of origin. But rather than strictly rationalizing the Dalits' downfall, this narrative speaks to the ubiquity and inevitability of "falling" in one's life. Like so many other of life's tasks that are relegated to untouchables because of their impurity, danger, or unpleasantness, it falls to the Dalit petitioners to tell, and hear, the hard truth about life that death announces at the middle stone: everyone, and not merely the untouchables, is doomed to part with society. I say *to hear* for, in the end, I must issue a word of caution about this word *story* used by my consultants to refer to the funeral petition. The word inherently connotes an expectation that someone is listening and responding to its narration. Charlotte Linde refers to this notion of expectation when she describes telling a story as a "relational act," a phrase that necessarily implicates an audience (1993: 112–13). Storytelling is usually such an act in Tamilnadu, where listeners often react strongly to a story world. As far as I can tell, though, the Vīrajāmpuhan̲ story does not engage its human audience, for nobody listens to it.[27]

To answer my inquiry about what the Dalits recite at the entrance to the cremation ground, caste Hindus invariably respond, "The story of Ariccantiran̲." The response is interesting because, although the life story of Ariccantiran̲ intersects with that of Vīrajāmpuhan̲, it is a completely different narrative. As noted in chapter 3, Ariccantiran̲ is not a Paraiyar but a king, and he consistently tells the truth. Practically no one can identify Vīrajāmpuhan̲ or recall his dialogue with Brahmā, his grim assignment, his curse, and so on. And I do not refer only to women and children, who do not in any case follow the funeral procession to the cremation ground, but also men—men old enough (over the age of forty to have attended many funerals.

Even the two other specialists in Tamil funerals—the village washerman and the barber—do not seem to know his story. The washermen I spoke to sought to justify their ignorance by stating that, since there is no work for them to do at the middle stone, they take off for a smoke or a rest under a tree.[28] But the barbers, who must stay for the ten- to fifteen-minute duration of the petition to contribute to the ritual both before and after it, cannot reconstruct the story either. "I listen to it, but I don't remember it" is the usual answer. For their part, the mourners justify their indifference to the Dalits' narration on the grounds that, by the time they reach the middle stone, they are exhausted, or that the Dalits speak too fast.

That no one listens should not surprise us. For all its dramatic import, the Vīrajāmpuhan̲ narrative is not meant to entertain a human audience. It solicits the gods. This is why I believe it is delivered loud, fast, and somewhat solemnly, in the way inferiors supplicate superiors. And this is why mourners and ritual specialists remember only the final formulaic address to Ariccantiran̲, sometimes repeating it verbatim: "Please open the door and give the way!" They know this story is not for them.

But there are additional reasons why the story does not capture the attention of human beings at the entrance to a Tamil cremation ground. Although not a myth in the Lévi-Straussian sense of the word, this story offers a model for speaking about one's life that is not particularly compelling, for three reasons. First of all, one must say everything, for one cannot (or should not) hide anything from the gods. Second, one must pay the price for one's transgressions, no matter what their cause, whether ignorance, accident, intense anger, or something else. And finally, the price is high, as it involves a rupture in social relations. Quite simply, in this case telling one's story is not curative as is postulated by most Western therapeutic theories, or even palliative as seems to be the case in the Tamil lamenting tradition. Here it leads to further ostracism and alienation. No wonder it takes courage and the help of an escort to say it. Nor is it surprising that the tribulations of those who must leave life do not captivate the living. Rather than hear that life is "a record of failure," the living remove the dead from society and get back home as quickly as possible.

CHAPTER FIVE

Between Performance and Experience

I have shown that Tamil funeral discourses—crying songs, death songs, and petitions—transcend their immediate context. They reach out of the circumstances of their production—the mortuary ritual—and into the less circumscribed world of day-to-day experience and its inherent social and personal predicaments. Women and men do not simply perform some abstract or highly symbolic scenarios: they perform life, their own lives, the situations that deplete them, energize them, block them, and so on.

Yet we should not conclude that what is performed at Tamil funerals is unrelated to immediate context. If not always death, then irrevocable loss and separation provide the main themes of Tamil dirges, songs, and petitions. Women bemoan the deprivations and disjunctions they suffer at life transitions and in their daily lives, in particular comparing marriage to a kind of death, a sudden sharp end to their flourishing. Men buy songs that narrate the sad stories of those who would rather part from loved ones forever than fail to exhibit virtue. Untouchables recount the original split between the firstborn and his younger siblings, between men, in other words, who were once of the same kind.

What is odd, of course, is that all these discourses remain without audiences. For the most part, women do not listen to each other's laments.

Nor do they hear what the mēḷam singer is saying, and this despite the fact that the man shouts out his lyrics loudly and clearly. This was underscored when my consultant Ellamma, who by her own count had attended "over a thousand funerals," proved to be unfamiliar with the basic plot of the Rati and Maṉmataṉ song, the most famous death chant in the Gingee region. She justified her ignorance by saying, "There is no connection between us [women] and the mēḷam. We are separated; we don't listen to the [Dalit] singer." For their part, men do not pay heed to women's crying songs, but neither do they listen to the death songs meant for them. It is well known that men focus less on the singer's lyrics than on his public acknowledgements of their names and donations. Later, at the entrance to the funeral ground, when the competition for recognition is over, one might expect men to concentrate on what is said. But here they pay so little attention to the Dalits' petition that they do not know it any better than do the women, who are not allowed to attend and thus have no opportunity to hear it at all.

One possible explanation for these neglected discourses is that no one gives a damn about what others are saying. Indeed, as I have tried to suggest, at the Tamil funeral, attendees care only about themselves (their own feelings of depletion, their own cravings for praise, etc.). But conceivably, people may use death to produce and reproduce the distinctions most fundamental to their society. In other words, here content, reception, and function seem to fit together. Funeral discourses are not merely about separation, nor are they simply unattended: they work to recreate the "natural" differences between women, men, and untouchables. They do so by zooming in on, indeed enlarging and magnifying, the qualities and attributes that in the day-to-day world validate these differences. Women display emotionality, men preoccupation for "exterior" appearances, untouchables impurity. The purpose of these discourses is not simply for men and women to perform these basic (and allegedly intrinsic) differences, but for them to feel these differences intimately. Boiling emotions, intense cravings or blockages, and experiences of isolation or self-absorption are part of the fundamental process and form by which Tamil categories and social distinctions are rendered as natural and incontestable. In other words, they are part of the process by which Tamil women and men culturally order themselves.

Such pervasive symbolism of differentiation—and its root in prevailing day-to-day experiences of inequality, discrimination, and exclusion—now prevents me from idealizing the Tamil funeral. I say *now* because at first I did romanticize the subject of my research. After I saw the ritual that I describe in the introduction, I came home tired but exhilarated and told my neighbors that, were I to pass away in the field, I wished to be buried according to local custom—with women crying and men drumming, drinking, dancing, and petitioning for my afterlife. To me it seemed that this, rather than the subdued—if not anesthetized—ceremony of American mortuary rites, was the right way to leave this world. I have waited until these final pages to disclose my initial reaction to dirges, death songs, and the Vīrajāmpuhaṉ story because in retrospect I am not so proud of it. The research for this book and its writing taught me that these three genres are replete with grim experiences, grimmer than I first suspected. We may appreciate them for their poetic beauty and utter originality, but we should never forget they are rooted in inexorable and intimately felt predicaments of hardship.

I learned this from talking with my consultants. They pointed out to me how their funeral discourses led them to experience and reexperience the traumatic events (marriage, separation from home, etc.) and strivings (the urge to be best, in particular) that come with their gender and social roles. Yet, as I have also tried to suggest in this book, there are limits to the exegetical culture of Tamil funeral discourses. By this I am not suggesting that the women and men I worked with did not know, or could not articulate, what they were doing or feeling. On the contrary, my consultants were bright, verbal, and eloquent. Even those singers or petitioners who could not (or would not) ascribe any logic to their lyrics or mode of delivery were eventually able to hint at what "blocked" them. Despite being carefully considered, however, women's and men's comments on and explanations of their funeral songs and petitions never added up to what we could call a critical analysis. At the very least, singers and petitioners did not seem to grasp that their conceptions of, and participation in, lamenting, singing, and petitioning limited them. Here were women and men who generally could identify the root causes of the feelings of frustration, deprivation, and hindrance that permeated their songs and petitions, but who fell short of seeing that these very genres reproduced their social and personal experiences of marginalization and hardship. If anything, both the women and the untouchables told me that their songs gave them relief from their problems, for instance, or gained them full attention.

Does this mean that I suffer from the all-too-common anthropological syndrome of assuming that somehow I know better than these people? Before I am found guilty, I would like to point out that throughout this book I have tried to modulate my voice. In so doing I have tried to show my wholehearted enthusiasm for research and narrative techniques that let the consultants speak for themselves. I conversed with, rather than observed, the Tamil women and men who participated in my research, and I quoted more often than I paraphrased them. But assuming that such so-called experimental forms of ethnography are (or should be, or can be) free from the anthropologist's interpretation is simplistic, even dangerous. Any form of writing is an act of authority (a word with links to *authorship* that run much deeper than mere etymology). The thing therefore is not to aim at suppressing the writer's interpretation, for I do not think we can, but to make explicit where the author is coming from.

In my case I can not help concluding that Tamil funeral discourses are not liberating for the participants. To be sure, since they are formulated during the liminal phase of a ritual, they offer, in the Turnerian sense of these words, a space to critique society. Women, for example, deplore the marriage practices (notably, the patrilocal rule of residency) that cut them off from their natal homes. But their protests inhibit a full reproof of the patriarchal ideology. This is especially true when the women's intent is to move others to pity them: in this process of persuading others of the truth of their laments, women cannot avoid formulating and even reproducing certain stereotypes. In yearning for circumstances of the past to continue in the present, for example, they seem to reify the cultural proposition that women are more attached to the world of things and relationships than men are. It is true that women rarely dare crying out dirges before an audience. Most cry at home or in the privacy of the crying clusters in order to cool off the burning sensation caused by feelings of kuṟai. But in doing so, they work themselves into a state that, although cathartic, embodies the stereotypic characterization of women as more emotional, weaker, and less controlled than men.[1] Jonathan Parry's contention—that, at North Indian funerals, men's "stoicism" and women's "ostentatious grief" "become part of a process by which hierarchical relations between the sexes are reasserted and their legitimacy 'proved,'"—certainly applies to South Indian funerals as well (1994: 157–58). That Tamil women's mourning roles work against them is also suggested in their motions—they pull their hair, beat their mouths, beat their chests, and undertake other self-mutilating behaviors—all of which add up to "an attack on oneself," as Maurice Bloch discerned among Merina mourners (1982: 214–15).

The language of crying songs therefore seems to be what Arjun Appadurai calls, in reference to other Indian women's songs, both "commentatorial" and "constitutional" (1991: 470). That is, it represents—and here I slightly modify Appadurai's meaning—a discourse about women that reproduces encompassing conceptions of female roles and identities. The constitutionality of this discourse is particularly evidenced when women speak of their own lives. As I argue in chapter 2, women like Ellamma and Archana actually come to live the sad truth of their comparisons: namely, that to be is to wane.

The most limiting thing about the practice of crying songs is not that women speak a language which ultimately creates more dependency and yearning, but that crying songs isolate women from each other. For all the clusters, embraces, and touching, women do not really "share grief." They cry, just as they say, for themselves, for no higher purpose than to be *individually* pitied, soothed, praised for forbearance, or relieved of their kuṟai. Despite the fact that many Tamil women make the same comparisons in their laments, lamenting clusters do not foster the sense that women "stand united in our common plight." To the contrary, the clusters only heighten a woman's own feelings of deprivation and lack of a better present.

But then again, death *is* divisive, and no one knows this better than the Dalits, who in life as in myth intimately experience how their funeral duties set them off as untouchables. What I have tried to show in this book is that these duties—drumming, singing, and petitioning—are not simply imposed on them by the higher castes, or by God, for that matter. The Dalits themselves come up with complex and surprising discourses of meaning and feeling that keep them at their profession. Instead of disliking the very work that defines them as the lowest of the low, they value, and indeed cherish, it.

To the men who assisted my research, drumming and singing at funerals are not entirely reducible to material conditions or economic necessities. These activities are rooted in God's gift: the Paṟaiyars have been chosen to drum and sing. Singing is not an unskilled specialization but an art requiring a certain disposition and talent. Moreover, singing is not merely a caste chore but a personal vocation. It demands what my consultants called the "interest" to learn and entertain. Finally, singing and petitioning are valuable, indeed indispensable, services that constitute the Paṟaiyars' unique contribution to society. As the petitioner Sivamani proudly told me, "The dead derive benefits from my work; they get praised and go to heaven." "As for the living," he added, "they are distracted from their grief, and they learn what's right and wrong."

To say that the Paṟaiyars prize the very job that keeps them at the bottom of society is not to say that they do not use it for their own ends. Since they are needed at funerals, and since they and only they can handle death, they command authority for the moment. As one man put it, "At funerals we the Paṟaiyars get to boss the mourners." Singers stalk the bereaved family with requests for monetary gifts or payment, and their demands can be aggressive or even antagonistic. They also get to allocate praise, thereby arbitrating the status of the very men who in day-to-day life order them around. While fulfilling their patrons' ambitions and aspirations, they also get to gratify their own craving for exclusive attention and homage. The funeral ritual is one of the few public events in which the untouchables can actually reproduce for their own benefit the esteem and deference highly regarded by Tamil men. When untouchable men sing well at death rites, everyone, including the rich and the powerful, praises them.

And yet ironically, to sing well the untouchables must drink large quantities of alcohol. They drink, as they say, to work themselves into the state of high-keyed enthusiasm necessary for their performance. They require a boost in order to joke, whistle, jump up and down, lewdly dance—and do whatever else they do to mock death. And apparently, they drink to forget that these behaviors make them Paṟaiyars. So it is no wonder that at the entrance to the funeral ground, when the alcohol wears off, these men hesitate to declare outright who they are. In the end, the Dalits might get their "fifteen minutes of fame," but they also come to perform, experience, and, therefore, reproduce the limitations associated with their social identity as outcastes.

CHANGING EXPERIENCES, CHANGING PERFORMANCES

"In this life nothing ever remains the same," a Tamil man once told me. Indeed the mortuary discourses described in this book are changing or, more exactly, disappearing. At death, Tamil women from the Gingee area continue to cry in cluster formations, but they compare less and less in their crying songs. Men seldom march through the village to the beat of the mēḷam's drums or the shrill of death songs. They still stop at the entrance to the funeral ground, but only to offer camphor to the good king Ariccantiraṉ, for "nowadays," as one village headman told me, "the Dalits no longer make the petition."

Funeral discourses are waning because gender and social experiences are different than they were. This is not my own explanation: my consultants themselves identified the causes of their songs' demise. The women I worked with reasoned, "Nowadays, girls go to school; they have neither the time nor the interest to learn our songs." "In the old days," they added, "women had more kuṟai. They could not choose their husbands, and they would eat only what their mother-in-laws gave them. Nowadays women marry whomever they want, and they eat what they want. They are not afraid of anyone." One woman reiterated this point: "Nowadays women don't feel the need to lament, because they have power [*tairiyam:* literally boldness; guts], they have control over their lives, [and] they can do whatever they want."[2]

Some of the Dalits I met invoked similar arguments: they no longer drum or sing at times of death because their lives are changing. And this is undeniably the case. Although not eradicated, untouchability is now illegal in India. Children are provided access to all government schools. In classrooms they are not segregated. Untouchables are also given some compensatory preference in institutions of higher education. The same scheme of preference has provided them access to public employment. Some untouchables are becoming lawyers and doctors. They are freely admitted into public hospitals. They can travel on the train with people of any caste background (Mendelsohn and Vicziany 1998: 39–40). Their lot has especially improved in cities where, because less visible than in villages, untouchables can eat and worship wherever they wish. But even in rural communities, they are gaining rights. Untouchables are increasingly granted access to the wells from which the higher castes draw water.[3]

All these changes have made the Dalits more self-conscious and assertive. This is especially apparent in the South Arcot district of Tamilnadu, where young untouchables are increasingly standing up for their newly acquired rights.[4] They refuse to be called "Paṟaiyar," and they retaliate against those who do not show them respect. They also feel confident that they now call the shots. A twenty-eight-year-old Dalit bank clerk told me, "We have been oppressed for a long time. We have worked very hard in the sun and in the rain, while others stay in the shade. If we start to act violently, what will they [caste Hindus] do? Now they are afraid of us; now we are all educated." Young people such as this one naturally decline to assume their traditional caste occupations, as also noted by Deliège in his account of the Ramnad district: "The Paraiyars have freed themselves from most of their obligations. They no longer perform tasks of scavenging and knackery which were incumbent on them in the past. They no longer play drums at funerals, nor do they dig the graves of the high castes" (1997: 165; also see Racine 1996: 200, 212).

Indeed, the young Dalits I met vehemently refused to carry on their elders' chores. One of them told me, "The name *Paṟaiyaṉ* means one who beats the drum, carries the funeral bier, sings death songs, and obeys his master; but we don't like this name anymore. We don't want to beat the drums, nor do we want to work at funerals in exchange for 'mouth rice' [the raw rice offered to the deceased]. Nowadays, we tell the mourning family, 'Dump the rice in the river or take it home; we don't want it.' We are equal to the other castes, we deserve better than the food of the dead." This young man, who happened to be the son of the singer who helped me transcribe the Rati and Maṉmataṉ chant, was terribly ashamed of his father.[5] "When my father sings at a funeral," he told me, "people say, 'He is just a Paṟaiyaṉ!' I don't like people to think that we are cheap [he used the English word here]. I hate death songs. My father should not sing them. I go to college. People should respect me. How can my friends respect me if my father sings and dances at funerals?"

Caste Hindus' reactions to the young Dalits' repudiation of their funeral duties have evolved over time. When a young Dalit in the village in which I resided in 1990 declined to drum at death rites, the dominant landowning castes retaliated by denying all the residents of the nearby colony the right to graze animals on their fields. But when I returned to Tamilnadu ten years later, I got the sense that most caste Hindus were resigned to the fact that the mēḷam was a thing of the past. One village headman told me, "The people in Tamilnadu feel that they live in a time of big change. The old economy [the *mērai* or *jajmānī* system] is gone even in the big people's houses. We do not think that traditions should change, but there is nothing we can do about it. The government is against tradition. In the old days, village life depended on the cooperation of all the castes. Now the police tell us, 'Don't force the Dalits to work; let them go.' In the old days Dalits did what was demanded of them. Now they are educated and no longer want to do the work. We cannot stop them from growing up and seeking better jobs. Of course we feel bad that our culture is dying, but the Dalits don't."

It is not exactly true, however, to say that all young Dalits have defected from the funeral. A few are replacing the mēḷam with what they call the "band." Strictly instrumental, the band models itself after Western military musical ensembles of the sort that one can still hear on Sunday afternoons on the main pier of the nearby town of Pondicherry, formally a former French territory. Save for two handheld rattles that are clearly home made, the musicians play the same clarinets, big brass drums, and barrel drums and are dressed in white uniforms. And in these outfits the master, as band leaders call themselves, and his drum masters (a term that refers not only to percussionists but to all instrumentalists) perform their new social experience.

Sober and clean looking, these men exhibit an attitude of formal expertise that the old drummers, with their tattered clothes, drunken clamors, and burlesque acts, never had. The masters neither dance nor joke; they simply play their instruments with an air of prim professionalism. What resounds is not the old rhythmic, and yet unmelodious, pitch of death songs but the tunes of famous tragic Tamil films. There are no lyrics, no dialogues, no voices. Gone are the loud, racy repartees of the old drummers, and gone are the vociferous bids for songs, for few mourners commission the master to play sad cinema music.

To me this, and *not* the old mēḷam's performance, constitutes the ultimate show of untouchable resistance. No longer acting out their impurity, the Dalits display their aspirations and recent achievements. They are the masters, cloning the foreign forms of leadership that once controlled their superiors. And so they rule not by amusing, flattering, or petitioning, but by tiring people out. For with the disappearance of comedy sketches and competitive punches, what remains is the stark reality or "limiting perspective" of death and grief. One indication that the absence of fun and strife in men's confrontation with life's finality might be upsetting is that nowadays, as everyone agrees, male mourners drink much more than in the past. And what is perhaps even more ironic is that the Dalits charge a lot to recast death as morbid business. In 1999, I was told that, in general, bands charge the hefty sum of two thousand rupees, twice what mēḷams used to cost.

In all likelihood, then, the men introduced in this book represent the last generation of funeral drummers, singers, and petitioners. Caught between the past and the present, they swing back and forth between polarized definitions of their funeral discourses. On the one hand, they still love their art, but, on the other hand, they have come to doubt and even disclaim it. And as the following final testimonies suggest, this process can be painful.

When asked how he felt about the changing perspectives and practices just described, the father of the Dalit youth quoted above answered, "My son tells me not to sing at funerals, but I go anyway" [he laughed]. Then he added more seriously, "I believe in the message of Dalit emancipation. But drumming is our duty, our work. We cannot stop doing what we have learned to do. We cannot stop doing what our forefathers did. Till my death, I will sing. I like to sing. I cannot sit still when there is an opportunity for me to do so. How can I turn down a man who calls on me to sing for his dead father or mother? The very fact that he calls me is a mark of respect. He needs me.[6] Besides, the higher castes appreciate our songs. This appreciation feels good because we know at that moment that they respect us. I even made a friend from a superior caste, a teacher, a landlord, through this line of work. After he heard me, we had some very close moments; like you, Isabelle, he asked me a lot of questions. There is nothing wrong about this work." Yet when I asked him on another occasion what he had learned about himself from his singing, this man replied, "I have learned good and bad things about myself. I have learned that I have the power to move people, that I am talented. And I have learned that my children despise me for dancing at funerals." My favorite singer, Vel, who is nearly blind, expressed similar feelings. "All my life," he once bitterly remarked, "I was hooked on these songs. I liked to drink and sing, and I liked the money. But now people have spoiled it for me. They don't understand the value and beauty of these songs. And so now I feel bad about my work."

These men did not seem to mind that death songs were vanishing. As Vel told me, "No one is interested in learning them. So I don't mind if they go. I won't regret the loss." Women had similar reactions about their dirges. "Why should I care that the songs disappear?" one of them exclaimed. "I am singing, people are hearing me; that is enough." Nor were women particularly interested in the result of my research. As my consultant Janaki bluntly put it, "You should publish our songs, but if you don't, don't worry about it. We have memorized them, and there are plenty of books about them." Ellamma was the only one who genuinely wanted me to print her repertoire and explanations. She insisted on it. The reason was somewhat predictable: she hoped that my readers would feel sorry for her. But once, when it was my turn to lament that I did not see the point in recording dirges young Tamil women looked down on, she too replied, "Let the crying songs die, then, let them go. Why should we cry over their loss?"

APPENDIX A

A COMPARISON OF THE FOUR ABRIDGED VERSIONS OF THE VĪRAJĀMPUHAṈ STORY

VEL'S VERSION

Vel's story begins with Vīrajāmpuhaṉ humbly requesting that his guru, the god Ganesh, listen to his petition. His address is standard; in Tamilnadu, Ganesh, the remover of obstacles and the embodiment of success in undertakings, is always invoked prior to a performance and ritual.

With this obligatory preamble out of the way, Vīrajāmpuhaṉ then proclaims that each of the world's four directions is associated with a particular kingdom (*tuṟai*, or literally, "harbor."): "In the South lies the kingdom of the chief angel, Tēvēntiraṉ. In the North lies the kingdom of the king Vellārāyan. In the west lies the kingdom of the god Īsvaraṉ [Siva], who has no equal, and in the East lies his own kingdom, the kingdom of Vīrajāmpuhaṉ."

The god Brahmā must be listening to this declaration, for he now asks Vīrajāmpuhaṉ to describe the wonders *(aticayam)* of his kingdom. Vīrajāmpuhaṉ replies, explaining that the sun, the moon, and the twenty-seven stars were all born in the East. He also reveals that the creator *(karttaṉ)*, the god Murukaṉ, the universe, the sky, the five Pandavas (heroes of the great Hindu epic, the Mahābhārata), the priests *(Vaḷḷuvars)*,[1] the shepherds, the washermen, the barbers, the potters, and the carpenters also come from his kingdom.

(Although there is no indication that Vīrajāmpuhaṉ disappears, it is clear from what happens next that we are privy to a conversation he does not hear. This is a crucial shift, for what follows is the central explanation for Brahmā's interest in the Paṟaiyar.)

Turning to the sage Vacuteva, the four-faced Brahmā announces a crisis: "The earth goddess who was born in the underworld *[nakalōkam]* can no longer support the weight of the world, because the ripe fruits cling to it. Go and get Vīrajāmpuhaṉ right away, and tell him that I want him to proclaim by beat of drum the fall of the ripe fruits."

Vacuteva goes to the North, but Vīrajāmpuhaṉ is not there. He goes to the East, the West, and the South, but Vīrajāmpuhaṉ is not there. He searches around the four worlds, but Vīrajāmpuhaṉ is nowhere to be found. Anxious, the saint reports back to Brahmā. "My lord," he laments, "I have gone around the four worlds, but I did not find Vīrajāmpuhaṉ."

"I'll tell you where to find him," Brahma replies. "He is in the underworld. In that world, there are four thousand streets. One of these streets has a thousand houses. This is where Vīrajāmpuhaṉ lives. He'll be in the street of the doves, where the peacocks dance and the cuckoos sing. He'll be leaning on a golden pillar, surrounded by dancing peacocks and hundreds of dancing women. One thousand young girls will be offering him incense and betel on a silver tray. That'll be him—Vīrajāmpuhaṉ. Bring him back quickly."

Upon hearing these words, Vacuteva departs for the underworld. He navigates through the four thousand streets and finally reaches Vīrajāmpuhaṉ's alley. Somewhat afraid to enter, he calls out from the eastern entrance, "Is Vīrajāmpuhaṉ here? Who is Vīrajāmpuhaṉ?" At first, Vīrajāmpuhaṉ does not hear him. Then, motioning to the women to be quiet, he comes out.

When he learns that Brahmā wants to see him immediately, Vīrajāmpuhaṉ replies, "Tell the god to send me his royal white elephant." Brahmā agrees to this request, and Vīrajāmpuhaṉ prepares himself for his visit. Selecting the best-smelling flowers of ninety varieties, he places them on his head and at his waist. Washing his feet with rosewater, he dries them with a silk cloth. Once ready, he mounts the white elephant and heads for Brahmā's place.

As soon as Vīrajāmpuhaṉ sees the god, he joins his hands before his closed mouth in a gesture of respect.

"Swami, please tell me why you called me."
"Is that you Vīrajāmpuhaṉ?"
"Yes, it is me alright."
"Tell me about yourself."

"I am the firstborn," Vīrajāmpuhaṉ answers; "I am the one who wears the sacred thread on my back. I am the Paṟaiyar with the conch. I am the elder of all castes. I am the one who took the king Ariccantiraṉ as a slave." Then Jāmpuhaṉ volunteers more information about himself. "On the west side of town," he explains, "there is a banyan tree. Underneath that banyan tree, lies an anthill. From the insides of that anthill, a black cow was born. From the guts of that cow, Pārvati [the god Siva's wife] was born. From the stomach of Pārvati, the Paṟaiyaṉ was born. He tied the black cow's legs and cut its neck and body into eight even shares."

As Brahmā presses him to reveal "who got these eight shares of the cow," Vīrajāmpuhaṉ replies, "The sun, Venus, the moon, Cahatēvaṉ [the youngest of the five Pandavas brothers of the Mahābhārata], the sky goddess, the earth goddess, Kālī who protects the village, and myself." When Brahmā asks, "What did you do with your own share?" the Paṟaiyar answers, "I dried it and feasted on it morning and night for three days."

Brahmā next wants to know about the practical use of the cow's bodily parts and fluids. "What is the use *[putumai]* of the head?" "What is the use of the horns?" and so on, he keeps asking. Vīrajāmpuhaṉ's detailed answers reveal that, although he eats beef, he reveres living cattle and attributes protective spiritual powers to them. His answers also suggest that he knows how to handle and process the cow's waste and carcass.

He teaches the god that placing a cow's head in a rice field immediately stops the afflictions caused by the evil eye. Horns can be made into combs and small tips for women to apply eye makeup *[mai]*. The skin can be fashioned into parasols, bridles for horses, muzzles for cattle, sandals for people, and leather ropes for drawing well water. The concretion, or bezoar stone, inside a cow's stomach has healing properties. When placed in a betel leaf and crushed, its secretion curtails children's convulsions. The liver can serve as a grinding stone for sharpening the goldsmith's knives and precious stones. The cow's urine is sprinkled on new temples and houses to prevent their destruction or deterioration. The four legs of the cow can be used to build the thrones of the sages and deities and of Siva and Pārvati.

At the end of this systematic exposition, Brahmā instructs Jāmpuhaṉ of his mission: "The earth goddess can no longer support the weight of the world, because there are too many living people. Go and beat the drum for the ripe fruit!" Vīrajāmpuhaṉ agrees to his assigned role on one condition. "Swami, I have a request," he says, using the same word *(viṇṇappam)* that describes the narration of this story at the entrance to the funeral ground. "If I must broadcast the fall of ripe fruit in cities and hell, you must give me five *kalams* [a measure of thirty-six liters] of marijuana, ten kalams of alcohol, your royal elephant, twelve musical instruments, and eighteen kinds of weapons."

Brahma agrees to these demands. Vīrajāmpuhan̲ grinds the marijuana and the alcohol in an oil-maker's press with the help of a bullock. Dividing the mixture into three lumps, he feeds two to his elephant and swallows the third one himself. Then he mounts the elephant and leaves with his silver drum.

Throughout the first ten streets of the neighborhood, Vīrajāmpuhan̲ dutifully proclaims, "The ripe fruit must fall! The old people must die!" On the eleventh street, the street of the artisan caste, he sees some women singing and dancing. Distracted, he drops his drum on the ground. The women dash to pick it up and hand it back to him. Vīrajāmpuhan̲ catches the drum with his left foot. The women feel insulted: "What is this? We gave him the drum with our right hands and he received it with his left foot!" They throw stones at him, and one hits his forehead. Vīrajāmpuhan̲ sees his blood dripping on the ground. Angrily he lashes out: "May the universe fall apart! May heaven and earth come to an end! May this world crumble to pieces! May Siva's throne shake! May all kings run in fear!" These are a madman's words, words that lack power of their own to destroy the world. But then Jāmpuhan̲ issues a curse that will turn into reality because he drums it out: "May the flowers fall! May the tender fruits fall! May the unripe fruits fall! May the ripe fruits fall!"

As soon as the god learns about this terrible announcement, he demands to see Jāmpuhan̲ right away. Vīrajāmpuhan̲ calmly requests permission to explain why he disobeyed orders. "My lord, please listen to me. If I beat the drum for the unripe and the tender ones, I will be able to make a living. Please hear me out. Before, there was nothing. Now there is a world, a sky, an earth, boundaries, and enclosures. I need to work. For a big corpse, there will be big money. For a small corpse, there will be small money. I will get mouth rice, change for burning the corpse, change for burying the corpse, the coins that are put at the four corners of the middle stone, new cloth, a piece of loin cloth, and the six coins for Ariccantiran̲. All this will be my due now."

At this point Brahmā returns to the question of exactly who Vīrajāmpuhan̲ is. "You told me," the god says, " 'I am the firstborn. I am the one with the sacred thread. I am the Par̲aiyar with the conch. I am the elder of all castes.' How can this be? In this earth, there are so many gods and sages; how can you be the firstborn?"

Once again Vīrajāmpuhan̲ politely requests that the god listen to him. "Long ago," he begins, "the fire goddess [Akkin̲i or Agni tēvi] cursed the earth goddess [Pūmi tēvi] to turn into ash. For nineteen days the earth went up in flames. In the South, the North, and the West everything was burning. The East, where Vīrajāmpuhan̲ ruled, was beginning to blaze as well. When the last bamboo grove caught on fire, Vīrajāmpuhaṉ ran to the earth goddess, who agreed to give him the last lump *[uṇṭai]* of unburned mud on earth. He took it, put his daughter Kaṅkābāvaṉi on his shoulders, and went to the seashore."

Meanwhile the three gods—Brahmā, Visnu, and Siva—needed unburned mud in order to reconstruct the world. When they learned that Vīrajāmpuhaṉ had what was left of it, they pushed on to the seashore. Vīrajāmpuhaṉ greeted them politely but put a condition on giving them his lump. "Ayyō, swamis," he lamented, "that one lump of mud contains the whole world. I'll give it only to the one who'll marry my daughter."

Siva agreed to his demand. In exchange for the unburned mud, he put Kaṅkābavāṉi on his head (meaning, he married her). "Now tell me who is the mightiest?" bragged Vīrajāmpuhaṉ. "You are indeed a very clever fellow," Siva replied. "From now on you'll be the first in this world."

Brahmā enjoyed Jāmpuhaṉ's story. "You speak well," he tells him. "Now tell me, what are virtues and what are sins." (This request is startling. Does Brahmā, the creator of the world, not know what is good and what is bad? And how can Jāmpuhaṉ—a beef eater, a remover of dead cows, and a funeral drummer—have this kind of wisdom? Jāmpuhaṉ's answer, however, suggests that he does know something about moral patterns of behavior and their consequences.)

He begins by listing many specific cases of wickedness, explaining in one breath that those who raise dangerous dogs, kick cows with their feet, hit their mothers with the backs of their hands, hurt their brothers' feelings, cheat on wages and measurements, betray their kinsmen, cast an evil eye on fruit trees, dwell on already settled disputes, remove boundary stones to plow the land of others, fail to perform consecration ceremonies, and commit murder will all be cursed. He warns that the people who do such things will be thrown into pits of snakes, lizards, and leeches or else tied to red hot poles and pushed into a river of fire. Conversely, he says, those who don't commit these actions will reach god. A palanquin will come to get them, after which they will go around Īsvaraṉ (the god Siva) three times and reach the blissful state of *motcam* (or release from the cycle of births and rebirths).

The dialogue between the god and the hero seems never-ending. Brahmā now wants Jāmpuhaṉ to tell him the story of his mother's birth. Vīrajāmpuhaṉ begins to relate how his mother was born on the cremation grounds of Kārūr Karuma, but we do not get to hear the rest. At this point the story links up with its ritual context, as Vīrajāmpuhaṉ petitions King Ariccantiraṉ "to please open the door and give the way!"

SIVAMANI'S VERSION

The original Tamil for this story can be found in appendix B.

In this version of the story, the narrator, Sivamani, rather than the main character, Vīrajāmpuhaṉ, appears to request the god (most likely Ganesh) to listen to him. Then out of the blue comes the declaration that Vīrajāmpuhaṉ was born when the world was created: "[Vīrajāmpuhaṉ] was born first, he wore the sacred thread around his back, he had the conch and the horse. He was the eldest for all castes. He was Vīrajāmpuhaṉ. He told everyone that he was superior to all castes." This version goes on to relate that, upon hearing Vīrajāmpuhaṉ profess his precedence in the world, the god Brahmā ran to inform him that he must beat the drum for the ripe fruit. Here, however, Vīrajāmpuhaṉ puts no condition on accepting the god's assignment; Brahmā himself enjoins the courageous drummer to ingest large quantities of alcohol and marijuana and ride on a white elephant.

The episode that follows, which tells about the street of the artisans, is virtually identical to that narrated by Vel. So is the god's reaction to Vīrajāmpuhaṉ's explanation that the fall of the unripe fruit will allow him to make a proper living. Brahmā then interrogates Vīrajāmpuhaṉ on the subject of the origin of things, such as the four directions, celestials, temples, and so on. He also wants to know what Vīrajāmpuhaṉ did with his share of a calf that died three days after its birth. The Paṟaiyar's detailed description of the practical uses of the cow's bodily parts and fluids is consistent with Vel's version. His list of actions that constitute sins, however, is somewhat different: "Those who do not feed injured calves; do not provide for their mothers; rape other men's wives; put thorns on the path, sharp needles in bathing tanks, snakes on sleeping mats . . . will go to hell. They will be pushed into a snake's pit and in a lizard's pit. They . . . will be reborn as dogs, and people will throw stones at them. They will be crying on the streets. That's what is in store for them." Charity is the only virtue *(puṇṇiyam)* mentioned in this version. As Vīrajāmpuhaṉ declares, "Those who build rest houses, large water tanks, feed the poor, and make donations of gold will go to heaven. A chariot of flowers will pick them up and take them to the fourth stage [union with the god]."

At this point in the story, the god asks Vīrajāmpuhaṉ to state his parents' names. When the hero falters, the god warns him that, "if his birth is true, he ought to remember." Vīrajāmpuhaṉ identifies his parents and makes his petition: "I brought a new corpse. Yamā, make space! Kālīammā, open the doors! King Ariccantiraṉ give me the way! For the dead man to reach heaven, for all those present to go home, turn the bier around! Beat the drums! Take the corpse! Kōvinta! Kōvinta!"

ETTYAN'S VERSION

The third version of this story is unique on a number of points. First it adds a sequence of actions not found in the other three, beginning with the statement that, prior to leaving for his mission, "Vīrajāmpuhaṉ digs [*aṭi*, which also means 'beat,' as in 'beat the drum'] two holes. He puts the sun in one hole and closes it; he puts the moon in the other and closes it too. Then the world goes dark." The rest of Ettyan's version is familiar. Intoxicating himself and his elephant, the Paṟaiyar goes off to drum the fall of the ripe fruit.

When later, on the artisan street, he is stoned by the girls for picking up his drumstick with his left foot, Vīrajāmpuhaṉ gets angry but does not curse the unripe fruit to fall. Some time later, still drunk, he reports to Brahmā that he has in fact drummed the fall of both old and young human beings. But he provides no rational for his curse, so that in this version the association of untimely death and the Paṟaiyar's need to make a living is entirely missing. Like in the two previous versions, however, Brahmā proceeds to drill the hero; "Please tell me what is right from wrong? "How did the species appear?" "What is the use of the dead cow?" "What is the origin of the other things on earth?" At this point the story most diverges from the two summarized earlier. The following is a literal translation of its next sequence:

> Before, when Jāmpuhaṉ was the guardian of the funeral grounds, his wife, Vīravaḷḷi, would bring him food and clean cloth every morning and every night. Jāmpuhaṉ had only one daughter. One day Vīravaḷḷi was not feeling well, and she sent the girl to feed her father. He had planted the seed of a gourd that had produced only one fruit *[kāy].* That fruit had matured, and he had made a hole in it, emptying it of its content, so as to keep only the shell. When his daughter, Mañjaḷāvati, brought him his meal, the ocean was swelling with waves. Waves as high as sixty-two feet high rolled on, and Jāmpuhaṉ thought, "My daughter, my wife, and myself are going to die." Then he told himself, "I must protect my daughter." He put her in the gourd, took a handful of earth in his right hand and slipped into the gourd as well. When the waves came rolling in, this gourd floated in the water.

Worried that the flood will end the world, the three gods (Visnu, Siva, and Brahmā) set out to search for Vīrajāmpuhaṉ. Vīrajāmpuhaṉ agrees to surrender the lump of earth on condition that the three gods marry the three girls he has procreated with his daughter while they were floating in the gourd. At this the gods reply, "That is why we came; give us your girls, give us the earth!" After the weddings, the three gods, Siva, Visnu, and Brahmā, give the lump of earth to Sakti, "who scatters it on the water, so as to dry the earth. Eight hundred thousand species, male and female, from the elephant to the ant [appear?: the verb is missing from Ettyan's account]." We are also told that, "since the species are still not differentiated enough, the three gods take more earth from Pārvati's anthill and remake them, with Brahmā giving life, Siva defining the categories, and Visnu creating. . . . In this way," this version goes, "the three gods create the human beings, the seventy-four worlds, and the fifty-six countries."

The rest of Ettyan's version is not clear. What transpires is that, after the original creation, human beings fight among themselves and begin to die as a result of their enmity. Moreover, at this point the three gods decide to create a separate ontological category for human beings, so that women and men can be delivered from the cycle of births and deaths *(mukti motcam)*. But Ettyan's sentences trail off, and his grammatical structure is not sound, making the story hard to follow.

The end is even more cryptic, but apparently Jāmpuhaṉ declares that, since he has been incestuous, since he had sex with his daughter, "he ought to be called 'Vīra' rather than 'Vīrajāmpuhaṉ.' . . . It is thus in the capacity of Vīra [which also means 'hero,'];" this story tells us, "that [the Paṟaiyar] employs the virtuous king, Ariccantiraṉ, and tells him his life story." The good king either forgives him or Jāmpuhaṉ's sins are absolved; some words are missing from the account. In any case, "Vīra [then] asks to be sent to the entrance of the cremation grounds and be given four coins, mouth rice, and the other usual funeral prestations." He also requests "that the gate to the goddess Kālīkā, who [in this version] also happens to be his mother, be opened." Then, we are told, "Ariccantiraṉ opens the gate, the path to Kālīkā." The story finishes with these words: "All men on earth came to the cemetery, gave him [Jāmpuhaṉ] money for wood, mouth rice, cloth, and so on, saying he needed to be given *motcam*."

ARJUNA'S VERSION

This telling of the story is the most singular in that several key episodes are either missing or given an entirely different twist. Its idiosyncrasies may result from the fact that, unlike the other three petitioners, Arjuna learned the story not by hearing it but from a leaflet that he had purchased from a bookstall in Madras City.

His version begins with the usual petition "Swami, I am going to address the people of this world; please listen to me!" Then Vīrajāmpuhaṉ declares, "In this world there are eight thousand forms of life *[yōṉi]* that crawl, twelve thousand that fly, and four thousand that walk. Among those that walk are people from villages and people from the world. There are also many low castes: washermen that bleach clothes, and healers that treat wounds. In the forest there are many kinds of beings that live in termite hills. In the termite hill there was once a black cobra. [It bit the black cow (Arjuna actually forgot this line)]. The cow died and reached eternal bliss in Siva's world."

Out of nowhere the god Siva (and not Brahmā) next asks Jāmpuhaṉ about the use of the dead cow. The Paṟaiyar provides the usual answers, but in this version he neither kills the cow nor eats its meat.

When Āticēshaṉ, the primordial serpent, complains that he can no longer support the weight of the earth on its head, the god then calls for Vīrajāmpuhaṉ, who dutifully reports to him. "Spitting out his chewing betel [a gesture of respect], he washes the god's feet with rosewater, dries them with a silk cloth, and asks, 'Swami, would you be kind enough to tell me why you called me, your slave?'" His subsequent request for the white elephant, however, does not sit well with the god. "Brahmā thinks to himself, 'The man who now asks for my white elephant may ask me later for my wife.' For a split second his face registers a look of weariness."

What is unique to Arjuna's version is that Vīrajāmpuhaṉ puts one more condition on his departure: he must ask his wife's permission. Her response will change the denouement of this story: "When she learns that he is about to drum the fall of the ripe fruit, Pātāla Laksmi cries out, 'You fool, how are you going to make a living like this? This is what you should say, "May the ripe fruit fall, may the green fruits fall, may the flowers fall, may the tender ones fall, may the six-month embryos fall with a tremor! For a little corpse, a little money; for a big corpse, a lot of money!" Go with this goal in mind; go with the sole intention of making your living!'"

Since the Paṟaiyar departs with the intention of broadcasting the death of the young, his conduct on the artisan street produces different consequences. Once there, he drops his drumstick on the ground. ["The stick fell down when children hit it with a stone," Arjuna explained.] A woman hands it back to him with her right hand, and he takes it with his left foot. But instead of getting angry, the woman is concerned that Vīrajāmpuhaṉ might have hurt himself, so she asks a young woman from the oil-pressing caste to massage his foot with oil.

Arjuna himself had a badly mutilated left foot with all toes missing, which brings up the question of whether he might not have projected his own injury and fantasies about care onto the story. This conjecture is supported by the fact that his narration of this whole episode is completely at odds with the other three versions, and by the fact that, while telling it, Arjun was diffident, even inaudible at times.

Jāmpuhaṉ's recitation of sins and virtues in this version is typical, but the conclusion is nothing like the others: "The gods brought six conches so as to blow them, but none resounded. Then Vīrajāmpuhaṉ asked his wife to bring him his own conch. She cleaned it and adorned it with a dot of vermilion and flowers. It is said that, at the moment Vīrajāmpuhaṉ blew his conch, all seven conches resounded at once and in unison."

Another narrator of this story, Sivamani, disputed the veracity of this particular ending, arguing that, although Jāmpuhaṉ was born with the conch, he did not have the power to blow it. He added that, since the conch was of no use to him, the firstborn had given it to the Paṇṭāram (a Saivite village priest), who, outside this story, blows it at funerals of the members of high castes (Brahmins and Ācāris). Sivamani's comment helped me realize that the Vīrajāmpuhaṉ of Arjuna's version is somewhat "Sanskritized": he neither kills, nor eats beef, nor petitions for the dead, and his function as funeral drummer is very much downplayed. In fact, by the end of the story that function is subsumed by his exclusive expertise with an instrument that is the symbolic opposite to the drum: he blows the conch. Since Arjuna passed away before I returned to the field in 2000, I could not confirm whether his depiction of the firstborn as an incorporated Hindu man-god is the product of his own wishful thinking or that of the leaflet he bought in Madras.

APPENDIX B

THE STORY OF VĪRAJĀMPUHAṈ IN TAMIL

Sivamani's Version

வீரஜாமுகன் கதை

தொழுதேன் குன்னாமல் அடிபணிந்தேன்
நின்னக்கால் பரவி நெடுங்கால் பரவி
தேவாடியே திருவடியே என்மாதா தக்கலோகமே.
சாமிகுருவே சாமி குருவே அடியேன் என்
விண்ணப்பம் கூறுகிறேன் கேளுமய்யா
பூமிதோனி பூலோக தோனி விலவுதோனி வெள்ளான தோனி
அப்பொ முந்திப் பிறந்தவனாம் முதுகுநூல் பூனூல் தரித்தவனாம்
சங்கும் புரவி தரித்தவனாம் சாதியெல்லாம் பெரியவன்
வீர ஜாமுகனான்.
ஜாதிஎல்லாம் பெரியவன் வீரஜாமுகன் நான் என்று
வீரஜாமுகன் தெரிவித்தானாம்
சொன்னதை பிரமதேவன் கேட்டு ஓடிவந்து
வீரஜாமுகா முந்தி பிறந்தேன் முந்தி பிறந்தேன் என்கின்றாயே
தொன்னூறு காலத்தில் பழுத்த பழமானது
உரிகட்டி வைத்திருக்கும் ஆதிசேஷனுக்கும் இந்த
பூமா தேவிக்கும் பூமிபாரம் பொறுக்க முடியாது

ஐகலச் சாராயம் ஆறுகல ஆவனி ஏழுகல கஞ்சா
இதுஎல்லாம் எடுத்து நீ சாப்பிட்டு விட்டு
வெங்கல பேரிகை எடுத்து வெள்ளையானை முதுகில் வைத்து
பழம் உதிர பழம் உதிர என்று
பறைசாற்றும் பிள்ளாய் என்று
தெரிவித்தாராம் வீரஜாமுகனிடத்திலே.

பிரமதேவன் கூப்பிட்டு வீரஜாமுகனிடத்திலே
வீரஜாமுகா! ஐங்கலச் சாராயம் ஆறுகல ஆவனி

ஏழுகல கஞ்சா இதுயெல்லாம் நீ எடுத்து சாப்பிட்டுவிட்டு
உன் வெள்ளை யானையின் முதுவில் வைத்து
பழமுதிர பழமுதிர என்று பறைசாற்றும் பிள்ளாய் என்று
தெரிவித்தாராம் வீரஜாமுகனிடத்திலே.
வீரஜாமுகன் அதை கேட்டு ஓடிவந்து
உங்கல சாராயம் ஆறுகல ஆவனி
ஏழுகல கஞ்சா இதுஎல்லாம் எடுத்து சாப்பிட்டு விட்டு
வெங்கல பேரி எடுத்து வெள்ளையானை முதுவில் வைத்து
பழமுதிர பழமுதிர என்று கார் ஊர கம்மாள தெருவில் போய்
பொற்பறை சாத்திக் கொண்டே வந்தானாம்.

அப்படி வீரஜாமுகனானவன் பிரமதேவன் சொல்லை தள்ளாமல் படிக்கு
ஐங்ல சாராயத்தையும் ஆறுகல ஆவனியையும்
ஏழுகல கஞ்சாவையும் எடுத்து சாப்பிட்டுவிட்டு
வெங்கல பேரி எடுத்து வெள்ளையானை முதுவில் வைத்து
கார் ஊர கம்மாளத் தெருவில் போய் பறைசாற்றும் போது
வீரஜாமுகன் கையில் இருந்த வெள்ளிப் பிரம்பானது
தவறி கீழே விழுந்து விட்டதாம்.
அப்போது கார் ஊர கம்மாளப் பெண்கள்
தங்கக் குடம் எடுத்து பட்டு உடுத்தி (பல் துலக்கி)

தண்ணி குடத்தை எடுத்துக் கொண்டு
ஜலத்துக்குப் போகும் போது
வெள்ளிப் பிரம்பானது கீழே இருக்கவும்
அதை எடுத்து வீரஜாமுகன் கையில் கொடுக்க
வீரஜாமுகனானவன் மதிப்பு கொடுக்காமல்
இடது காலால் வாங்கி வலது கையினால்
பறைசாத்தி விட்டானாம்.

அப்படி சாத்துகின்ற காலத்திலே
காறூற கம்மாள பெண்கள் கண்டு
அடே வீரஜாமுகா!
பெண்கள் கையினால் கொடுக்கும் பிரம்பை
காலால் வாங்கி நீயும் கையினால் பொற்பறை
சாத்தி விட்டாயா? என்று கோபம் பிரவேசித்து
எங்களை நீ மதிக்கவில்லை என்று
கல்லையும் கட்டியும் வாரி வாரி அடித்தார்களாம்.

அந்த கல்லானது வீரஜாமுகனின் நெற்றியில் பட்டு
ஒரு குண்டுமணி இரத்தம் சிந்திவிட்டதாம்.
இந்தக் கல்லால் அடிபட்ட உடனே வீரஜாமுகன்
நெற்றியில் இருந்து குண்டுமணி இரத்தம் கீழே சிந்தவும்
உடனே வீரஜாமுகனுக்கு கோபமானது அதிகமாக
பிரவேசித்து விட்டதாம்.
உடனே வீரஜாமுகன் என்ன செய்தானாம்
தன்னுடைய கோபத்தையும் பாராமல் படிக்கு
காய் உதிர கனி உதிர பூவுதிர பிஞ்சுதிர
ஆறுமாசத்து பிண்டம் அலரி விழ என்று சொல்லி
பொற்பறை சாத்தி விட்டானாம் வீரஜாமுகன்

உடனே பிரமதேவன் கேட்டு பிரமதேவன்
ஓடி வந்தாராம்.
அடே வீரஜாமுகா!
நான் ஒரு வன்னமாகப் பறை சாற்றச் சொன்னேன்
பழமுதிர, காய் உதிர, பிஞ்சுதிர என்று நீ பறைசாத்தி விட்டாய்.
நான் சொன்ன பறை

பழுத்த பழம்தான் விழ வேண்டும் என்று நான்
பொற்பறை சாத்தச் சொன்னேன்
என் சொல்லைத் தவறி நீ ஏன் இப்படி சாத்திவிட்டாய்?
என்று கேட்டாராம் பிரமதேவன் வீரஜாமுகனை.

அப்போது வீரஜாமுகன் தெரிவித்தானாம்.
சுவாமி! என்னுடைய பிழைப்புக்குப் போதாது என்று
நான் பொற்பறை சாத்திவிட்டேன்.
என்னுடைய பொழப்புக்குத்தான் இப்படி சாத்தினேன்
உங்களுடைய சொல்லை கட்டுமீறி நான் சாத்தவில்லை என்று தெரிவித்தானாம்.
அப்போது வீரஜாமுகன் சொன்னதை பிரமதேவன் கேட்டு
வீரஜாமுகா உன்னுடைய பிழைப்பு என்று
சொல்கின்றாயே அது என்ன பிழைப்பு என்று
நன்றாக அறிந்து சொல்லும் பிள்ளாய் என்று கேட்டாராம்.

அப்போது வீரஜாமுகன் தெரிவித்தானாம்.
நூறுவருஷம் சென்று ஒரு பழம் செத்தால்
எனக்கு ஜீவனம் செய்ய முடியாது
என் பிள்ளைகளையும் காப்பாத்த முடியாது
குடும்பத்தையும் நடத்த முடியாது
நாள் ஒன்றுக்கு ஒவ்வொரு பிரேதம் செத்தால்
கால் பணமும் காப்படி அரிசி, முழ துண்டு
வாய்க்கரிசி ரோம சோறு
இதுகளெல்லாம் எனக்கு தினமும் கிடைக்கும்
என்னுடைய குடும்பம் நன்றாக நடக்கும்
என்று தெரிவித்தானாம் வீரஜாமுகன்.
உடனே வீரஜாமுகன் சொன்னதை பிரமதேவன் கேட்டு
வீரஜாமுகா!

மிந்தி பிறந்தேன் மிந்தி பிறந்தேன் என்று சொல்கின்றாயே
ஊறுதோணி உலகதோணி விலவுதோணி
வெள்ளான தோணி என்று தெரிவித்தாயே
அந்த தோணி வழியாக யார் யார் பிறந்தது என்று
நன்றாக அறிந்து சொல்லும் பிள்ளாய் என்று கேட்டாராம்.
ஆனால் சுவாமி
தங்களுக்கு கீழ்ப்பட்டு நானும் இப்போது நான்
தெரிவிக்கின்றேன்.
நன்றாக கேட்டுக் கொள்ளுங்கள் என்று தெரிவித்தானாம்
வீரஜாமுகன்.
அப்படியாக பிரமதேவன் சொல்லும் பிள்ளாய் என்று கட்டளையிட்டாராம்.
வடக்கு துறையிலே வாசுதேவன் பிறந்தான்
தெற்கு துறையிலே தேவேந்திரன் பிறந்தான்
மேற்கு துறை காறை வெள்ளான துறை
கிழக்கு துறை என்துறை என்துறை என் று தெரிவித்தானாம்
வீரஜாமுகன்.
உடனே பிரமதேவன் ஓடிவந்து வீரஜாமுகா!
கிழக்குத்துறை உன்துறை என்று தெரிவித்தாயே
அந்த துறையில் யார் யார் பிறந்தது அதை எனக்கு
நன்றாக அறிந்து சொல்லும்
நானும் கவனமாக கேட்க வேண்டும் என்று
தெரிவித்தாராம்.
ஆனால் அப்போது வீரஜாமுகன்
சுவாமி! தங்களுடைய வார்த்தைக்கு நான்
தக்க பதில் சொல்கிறேன்
நீங்கள் நன்றாகக் கேளுங்கள் என்று தெரிவித்தாளாம்
வீரஜாமுகன்.

கிழக்குத் துறையிலே வெள்ளி பிறந்தான் வேந்தன் பிறந்தான்
முப்பத்து முக்கோடி முனிவரும் பிறந்தார்கள்
நாற்பத்து நாலாயிரம் ரிஷிகள் பிறந்தார்கள்
செம்பு பிறந்தது மாணிக்கம் பிறந்தது
வைடூரியம் பிறந்தது இவை எல்லாம் என்னுடைய
சீப்புப் பிலாவிலே பிறந்தது சாமி என்று தெரிவித்தானாம்
வீரஜாமுகன்.

வீரஜாமுகா! இவை எல்லாம் உன்னுடைய சீப்புப்
பிலாவிலே இருந்து பிறந்தது என்று தெரிவித்தாய் அல்லவா
வடக்குத்துறை வாசுதேவன் துறை என்று சொன்னாயே
அந்தத் துறையில் யார் யார் பிறந்தது
அதையும் எனக்கு நன்றாக அறிந்து சொல்லும் பிள்ளாய்
என்று கேட்டாராம்.
ஆனால் சுவாமி என்துறையை நீயும் நன்றாக கேட்டுக் கொண்டாய்.
வடக்குத் துறைபற்றி விவரமாக சொல்கிறேன் நீங்களும் கேட்டுக் கொள்ளுங்கள்
என்று தெரிவித்தானாம் வீரஜாமுகன்.
சங்கு பிறந்தது சாணார கன்னி பிறந்தாள்
லிங்கம் பிறந்தது தப்பு பிறந்தது
குருபூஜை, அறுபூஜை, சிவபூஜை
இது எல்லாம் பிறந்தது இன்னும்
வடக்க போன வாலி திரும்பவில்லை என்று
தெரிவித்தானாம் வீரஜாமுகன்.

உடனே வீரஜாமுகன் சொன்னதை பிரமதேவன் கேட்டு
வீரஜாமுகா! வடக்கு துறை பற்றி
நன்றாக தெரிவித்து விட்டாய்

தெற்குத்துறை தேவேந்திரன்துறை என்று
தெரிவித்தாயே
அந்தத் துறையில் யார் யார் பிறந்தது அதை எனக்கு
நன்றாக அறிந்து சொல்லும் பிள்ளாய் என்று கேட்டாராம்.
ஆனால் சாமி நானும் இப்போ உனக்கு சொல்லதான்
அடிமைபட்டவனாய் இருக்கிறேன்.
நீங்களும் நன்றாக கேட்டுக் கொள்ளுங்கள் என்றானாம்
வீரஜாமுகன்.
அப்போது வீரஜாமுகன் தெரிவித்தானாம்
இந்திர ஜாலம் மந்திர ஜாலம் கொச்சி மலையாளம்
இப்பேர்பட்ட சகலமும் பிறந்தது சாமி
இன்னமும் சிலவார்த்தைகள் நன்றாக சொல்கிறேன்
கேளும் சுவாமி என்று தெரிவித்தானாம்.
அனுமார் பிறந்ததும், இலங்கை அழிந்ததும்
சீதா தேவியை சிறையில் எடுத்ததும்
விபூஷணர்க்கு பட்டாபிஷேகம் சூட்டினார்கள் சுவாமி
என்று தெரிவித்தானாம் வீரஜாமுகன்.
இதுகளெல்லாம் நன்றாகத் தெரிவித்து விட்டாய்
பிள்ளாய் இன்னமும் எனக்கு நன்றாகத் தெரிவிக்க
வேண்டும் பிள்ளாய் என்று தெரிவித்தாராம்
அப்போது வீரஜாமுகன் தெரிவித்தானாம்
மேற்குத்துறை காற வெள்ளாளன் துறை என்று தெரிவித்தாயே
அதையும் எனக்கு நன்றாகச் சொல்லும் பிள்ளாய்
என்று கேட்டாராம்.

இந்திரஜாலம் மந்திரஜாலம் மாயாஜாலம் சகலமும் அத்துறையில் பிறந்தது என்று தெரிவித்துவிட்டானாம் வீரஜாமுகன்.

வீரஜாமுகா! நான்கு துறையும் நன்றாக அறிந்து சொன்னாய்
கேட்டுக் கொண்டேன்.
இன்னமும் சகலத்தில் தோணியில் ஆலயங்கள் பிறந்ததை எனக்கு இப்போ சொல்ல வேண்டும்.
சுவாமி! ஆலயங்கள் பிறந்ததை நான் சொல்ல வேண்டுமானால் இப்போது சொல்கிறேன் என்று
தெரிவித்தானாம்.
சுவாமி நானும் ஒவ்வொரு ஆலயத்தையும் நன்றாக பேர்களைச் சொல்கிறேன்
நீயும் மௌனமாக இருந்து கேட்டுக் கொள் என்று
தெரிவித்தானாம் வீரஜாமுகன்.

அப்போது வீரஜாமுகன் சொன்னதை பிரமதேவன் கேட்டு நல்லது வீரஜாமுகா!
சீக்கிரம் சொல்லு என்று தெரிவித்தாராம்.
ஊருக்குத் தெற்கே காளியம்மன் கோவில்
ஊருக்கு வடபுறம் ஈஸ்வரன் கோவில்
ஊருக்கு கிழக்கே பெருமாள் கோவில் தோணி
ஊருக்கு மேற்கே ஆலய விருச்சிகம் தோணி சுவாமி
என்று தெரிவித்தானாம் வீரஜாமுகன்.
வீரஜாமுகா! ஊருக்கு மேற்கே ஆலய விருட்சதோனி என்று சொல்கிறாயே
அந்தத் தோணியில் யார் பிறந்தது அதை எனக்கு நன்றாகச் சொல்லும்
பிள்ளாய் என்று கேட்டாராம்.
சுவாமி ஊருக்கு மேற்காலே விருச்சிக தோணி
ஆலய விருச்சத்திலே ஐந்து கண் புற்றுக் கண்
ஐந்து கண் புத்துக் கண்ணிலே காராம் பசு பிறந்தது
காராம் பசு வயித்திலே ஒர் கன்று பிறந்தது சுவாமி
என்று தெரிவித்தானாம் வீரஜாமுகன்.
வீரஜாமுகா! காராம் பசு வயித்திலே கன்று பிறந்தது என்று தெரிவித்தாயே.

அந்த கன்றாவது எச்செயலானது? என்று தெரிவித்தாராம் வீரஜாமுகனிடத்திலே பிரமதேவன்.

சுவாமி! அதனுடைய கன்றின் இளமை நான் அறிந்து சொல்கின்றேன் கேளும்

சுவாமி என்று தெரிவித்தானாம் வீரஜாமுகன்.

கன்று பிறந்து மூன்று நாள் சென்று சிவலோக பதவி அடைந்துவிட்டது சுவாமி

என்று தெரிவித்தானாம் வீரஜாமுகன்.

வீரஜாமுகா! கன்று பிறந்த மூன்று நாள் சென்று இறந்துவிட்டதா?

என்று கேட்டராம் பிரமதேவன்.

ஆமாம் சுவாமி என்று தெரிவித்தானாம் வீரஜாமுகன்.

வீரஜாமுகா! கன்று இறந்துவிட்டதே அதை நீ என்ன செய்தாய்?

என்று கேட்டாராம்.

சுவாமி! இறந்த கன்றானது எடுத்து நானும் அறுத்து

ஆகாய வாணிக்கு ஒரு பங்கு, பூமாதேவிக்கு ஒரு பங்கு,

சுக்கிரனுக்கு ஒரு பங்கு, சூரியனுக்கு ஒரு பங்கு,

ஈஸ்வரர்க்கு ஒரு பங்கு இப்படியாக ஏழு பாகத்திலே ஒரு பாகம்

எனது சுவாமி என்று தெரிவித்தானாம் வீரஜாமுகன்.

பிள்ளாய்! ஏழு பாகத்திலே ஒரு பாகத்தை எடுத்து நீ என்ன செய்தாய்?

என்று கேட்டாராம் பிரமதேவன், வீரஜாமுகனை.

சுவாமி! எனக்கு வந்த மாமிசத்தை நானே எடுத்து சமைத்து

புசித்துவிட்டேன் என்றானாம் வீரஜாமுகன்.

வீரஜாமுகா! இதை எல்லாம் நீ நன்றாக அறிந்துச் சொன்னாய்

என்று நானும் கேட்டுக் கொண்டேன்.

அதனுடைய தோலானது எதற்காகும் என்று கேட்டாராம் பிரமதேவன்

முன்னூறு குதிரைக்கு மோக்கரையாகும்.

நானூறு குதிரைக்கு நாற்காலியாகும் (நகைப் பானுக்கும்)

மீதி தோலானது சுவாமி தேருக்கு வடமாகும் என்று

தெரிவித்தானாம் வீரஜாமுகன்.

வீரஜாமுகா!

அதனுடைய தோல் விவரத்தையும் சொல்லி விட்டாய்.

அதையும் நன்றாக நான் கேட்டுக் கொண்டேன்.

அதனுடைய கொம்பானது எதற்கு ஆகும் என்று கேட்டாராம்.

அதனுடைய கொம்பானது ஆடும் பொம்மையாகும்

பாடும் பொம்மையாகும், வாரிட சீப்பாகும்

சிகாரக் கோலாகும் தேவேந்திரனுடைய பெண்களுக்கு

வாரிடக் கோலாகும் என்று தெரிவித்தானாம் வீரஜாமுகன்.

அதனுடைய கொம்பின் பெருமையும் தெரிவித்து விட்டாய்

அதை நானும் கற்றுக் கொண்டேன்.

அதனுடைய (சாணியானது) எதற்காகும் என்று கேட்டாராம் பிரமதேவன்.

சாமி! அதனுடைய சாணியானது எடுத்து தண்ணீர் விட்டு பெசஞ்சி

உண்டையாகச் செய்து அக்கினி தேவனை பிரவேசம்

பண்ணி அது சாமி விபூதி பட்டையாகும் சாமி என்று

தெரிவித்தானாம் வீரஜாமுகன்.

ஆனால் வீரஜாமுகா! அதனுடைய சாணியுடைய அற்புதத்தை நானும் கற்றக் கொண்டேன்.

அதனுடைய கோமியமானது எதற்காகும் என்று கேட்டாராம்.

அதனுடைய கோமியமானது சாமி இப்போது தெரிவிக்கிறேன் கேட்டுக் கொள்ளுங்கள்

என்று தெரிவித்தானாம் வீரஜாமுகன்.

அதனுடைய கோமியமானது பாழடைந்த மனைகளுக்கும் , கன்னிப்பெண்கள் கயிறு வாங்குவதற்கும், புதுமனை கட்டுவதற்கும், அந்த கோமியத்தை வாரி வீசி வந்தமானா மேலே ஒரு குண்டுமணி மேல பட்டா அந்த பாவ புண்ணியம் விமோசனமாயிடும் என்று தெரிவித்தானாம் வீரஜாமுகன்.

வீரஜாமுகா !
அதனுடைய கோமியத்தினுடைய பெருமையை நானும் கற்றுக் கொண்டேன்.
அதனுடைய கோரோஜனமானது எதற்கு ஆகும் என்று கேட்டாராம்
வீரஜாமுகனை பிரம்மதேவன்.

சுவாமி அதனுடைய கோரோஜனமானது
சிவனுடைய பதிக்கு எமனோடே வாதாடிக் கொண்டு இருக்கும் போது
இந்த உயிரானது ஊசலாடும் போது அந்த கோரோஜனத்தை எடுத்து,
ஒரு உரை உரைத்து பாலில் இதமாக வாயில் விட்டால் அந்த தீர்மதேவதையானவள்
ஒரு ஐந்து நிமிடம் காத்துக் கொண்டிருப்பாள் என்று தெரிவித்தானாம் வீரஜாமுகன்.
உடனே வீரஜாமுகன் சொன்னதை பிரம்மதேவன் கேட்டுக் கொண்டு வீரஜாமுகா!
இதுகளெல்லாம் நீ நன்றாக அறிந்து சொல்லிவிட்டாய்.
அதனுடைய வாலானது எதற்காகும் அறிந்து சொல்லும் பிள்ளாய் என்று கேட்டாராம்.
சுவாமி அதனுடைய வாலானது
காஞ்சிபுரம் காமாட்சி அம்மனுக்கு
வெண்சாமரமாக வீசலாம் என்று தெரிவித்தானாம் வீரஜாமுகன்.

வீரஜாமுகா! இவைகளெல்லாம் நீ
நன்றாக அறிந்து சொல்லிவிட்டாய் எனக்கு பாவத்தை கொஞ்சம் நன்றாக
அறிந்து சொல்லும் பிள்ளாய் என்று கேட்டாராம்.

சுவாமி நான் பாவத்தை உங்களிடத்திலே சொல்ல நான்
கடமைப் பட்டவனாய் இருக்கிறேன்.

உங்கள் கேள்விக்கு தக்கபதில் சொல்கிறேன் நீங்கள் கேட்டுக் கொள்ளுங்கள்
என்று தெரிவித்தானாம் வீரஜாமுகன்.

அடிபட்ட கன்றுக்கு பால் விடாதவனும்,
பெத்த தாய்க்கு சோறுபோடதவனும்
பிறர் மனைவியை கற்பழித்தவனும்
நடக்கிற வழியிலே முள்ளை நாட்டி வைத்தவனும்
குளிக்கிற குளத்திலே கூர் ஊசியை நாட்டி வைத்தவனும்
படுக்கிற பாயிலே பாம்பை விட்டவனும் இப்பேர்பட்டவனுக்கு
நரகத்துக்குச் சமமாகக் கடவது என்று தெரிவித்தானாம் வீரஜாமுகன்.

இன்னும் நன்றாக அறிந்து சொல்லும் பிள்ளாய் என்று கேட்டாராம்.
ஆனால் சாமி நான் நன்றாக அறிந்து சொல்கிறேன் கேள் என்று தெரிவித்தானாம்.

ஊருக்கு கலகம் பண்ணுபவனும்
மண்ணதிர நடந்தவனும் காய்ச்ச மரத்தை கண் எடுத்து பார்த்தவனும்
வாழ்கிற குடியிலே தீ இட்டவனும் இப்பேர் பட்டவனுக்கு
(பாம்புக் குழி பல்லிக்குழி) என்று தெரிவித்தானாம் வீரஜாமுகன்.

வீரஜாமுகா! இன்னமும் குறை இல்லாமல் நன்றாக அறிந்து சொல்
என்று கேட்டாராம்.

அப்போது வீரஜாமுகன் தெரிவித்தானாம் (இட்ட பயிரில் மாட்டை விட்டவனும்)

பங்காளிக்கு பங்கு கொடுக்காதவனும், குறை மரக்கா இட்டவனும், கூலியை
குறைத்தவனும் (அங்காடி கூடை) அதிரவிலை இட்டவனும் நரகத்திற்குக் கடவது
என்று தெரிவித்தானாம்.

ஏழுகடலுக்கு அந்தாண்ட போய் திருப்பாற் கடலுக்குப் போய்
நாயா பிறந்து நடுத்தெருவில் ஓலமிட்டு கண்டவர்கள் இவனைக் கல்லால்

இப்பேர்பட்ட சகலமும் செய்தவனுக்கு இப்பேர்பட்ட தண்டனை என்று
தெரிவித்தானாம் வீரஜாமுகன்.

வீரஜாமுகா! இதுகளெல்லாம் நீ நன்றாக அறிந்துச் சொன்னாய் அந்த
புண்ணியத்தை கொஞ்சம் அறிந்துச் சொல்ல வேண்டும் என்று கேட்டாராம்.

ஆனால் சுவாமி நானும் இப்போது புண்ணியத்தை அறிந்து சொல்கிறேன் கேளும்
என்று தெரிவித்தானாம் வீரஜாமுகன்.

சத்திரம் சாவடி ஏரிகள் குளங்கள் வீடுகள் அன்னதானம் சொர்ணதானம் இப்பேர்பட்ட
தானங்கள் செய்தவருக்கு தெய்வலோகத்திலிருந்து ஒரு பூந்தேர் வரும்.
அந்த பூந்தேர் மேல் ஏறிக் கொண்டு ஜாலோக ஜாமிப்ப ஜாருச்ச இப்படி சொன்ன
நான்காம்பதி யடைய வேண்டும் அன்னதானம் கோதானம் வஸ்திர தானம் செய்தவர்களுக்கு
நான்காம் பதிக்கு முக்தி மோட்சம் அடைய வேண்டும் சுவாமி என்று தெரிவித்தானாம்
வீரஜாமுகன்.

ஆனால் வீரஜாமுகா! முக்தி மோட்சம் நான்காம்பதி என்று சொல்கின்றாயே
உனக்கு நன்றாகத் தெரியுமா? என்று கேட்டாராம்.
அந்தப் பாவத்தை நீக்கி புண்ணியத்தை செய்தவருக்கு கர்த்தனுடைய காலடி
சேர வேண்டும். சுவாமி எனக்குத் தெரிந்தமட்டும் அடியேன் சொன்னேன் கேட்டுக்
கொள்ளுங்கள் என்று தெரிவித்து விட்டானாம்.

வீரஜாமுகா! நீ சொன்னதெல்லாம் நானும் ஒத்துக் கொண்டேன். உன்னுடைய
தாய் பேரும், தகப்பன் பேரும் நீயும் விபரமாகச் சொல்ல வேண்டும் என்று
கேட்டாராம். அப்போது வீரஜாமுகன் தெரிவித்தானாம்.

என்னுடைய தாய் பேரும், தகப்பன் பேரும் எப்படி நான் சுவாமி தெரிவிக்க
வேண்டும். நீ உண்மையாக பிறந்து ஜனனமாகி இருந்தால் உன்னுடைய தகப்பன் பேரும்
தாய் பேரும் உனக்கு நன்றாக நாவில் வரும் என்று தெரிவித்தாராம்.

அப்போது வீரஜாமுகன் தெரிவித்தானாம்.
என்னுடைய தகப்பன் ஆதிசிவன் என்னுடைய தாயானவள் காரூர கம்மாள பறைச்சி
நான் அடியேன் சொல்வது பொய்யும் மெய்யுமானால் காஞ்சிபுரம் காமாட்சியம்மன்
கோவில் ஆயிரம் பொற் கதவு ஆயிரம் பொற்கதவில் திறந்து பார்த்தால்
அரை கதவு, அரை கதவில் செப்பூசியால் சிலையாக நாட்டி வைத்திருக்கும்.
அதை எழுதியதை நீ எண்ணற படித்து எழுத்தற கற்றுக் கொண்டால் அடியேன்
வணக்கம் சுவாமி என்று தெரிவித்தானாம் வீரஜாமுகன்.

வீரஜாமுகன் சொன்னதெல்லாம் பிரம்மதேவன் உண்மை என்று ஏற்றுக் கொண்டு
சந்தோசப்பட்டுக் கொண்டு விட்டாராம். உடனே வீரஜாமுகன் தெரிவித்தானாம்.
புதுவும் சிசுவும் புதுரகம் கொண்டு வந்தேன், எமனே எடம் விடு, காளியம்மா
கதவத் திற, அரிச்சந்திர மகாராஜா வழிய விடு, செத்த பிணம் சிவலோகம்
போய்ச் சேர இருந்தவர்கள் இருப்பிடம் போய்ச் சேர மின்னும் பின்னுமா தேரை
திருப்புங்கள் அடியுங்கள் மோளத்தை எடுங்கள் சவத்தை. கோவிந்தா! கோவிந்தா!!

NOTES

INTRODUCTION

1. Other ethnographers have recorded similar gender patterning in the behavior of Indian mourners (Das 1986; Parry 1994). In the northern city of Banaras, for instance, according to Jonathan Parry, "Women weep. They refuse to bow to the inevitable separation of death. . . . They try to hang on to the corpse. But however deep their personal anguish, the close male mourners are enjoined to show restraint, to accept what is inevitable, and to get on with the serious business of begetting an ancestor." Parry also noted how the more distant male mourners are free to express the same emotions and behaviors that I recorded in Tamilnadu: "While the women wail, the young men dance in a burlesque of female sexuality—gyrating hips, upturned thumbs held in front of the chest to suggest breasts, and sometimes a woman's shawl draped over the head and with mock allurement half across the face" (1994: 155).

2. Although cremation is the preferred method of disposal, most South Arcot villagers, especially the untouchables, bury their dead. A burial is a cheaper substitute for cremation.

3. The joyous celebration of death—the boisterous singing, erotic dancing, and decorated bier—is characteristic only of the funeral procession of an old person who has lived a full and complete life—one who has died a "timely death." The funerals of those who have died in their prime by accident, murder, or sickness are sober and mournful occasions. In such instances, as Jonathan Parry says of mourners in North India, "The sharp gender division in the expression of grief

is likely to be somewhat muted" (1994: 155). The untouchables do not joke or make reveling gestures, and men can also shed tears.

4. Derived from Sanskrit, *Dalit* is a word in the Marathi language of western India that, according to Oliver Mendelsohn and Marika Vicziany, means "ground" or "broken or reduced to pieces generally" (1998: 3–4). Throughout India this term is increasingly used to refer to all untouchables regardless of caste and locality. In most of Tamilnadu, it is fast replacing the categories Harijan, which means "children of God" in Hindi, Āti Drāvida, which means original Dravidian in Tamil, and the old caste names (Paṟaiyar, Paḷḷar, etc.).

5. Although the Tamils may refer to dirges as "crying songs," they seldom use the verb *chant* to describe the act of lamenting. Instead they use the verb *cry (aḻu)*.

6. Sixteen days after the actual burial or cremation of the polluting corpse, the prototypical Hindu funeral adds a second, crucial ceremony, known in Tamil as *karumāti*, which dispatches the departed *(preta)* to the hereafter as an honored ancestor *(pir)*. This ceremony climaxes with a feast that concludes mourning and death pollution. For excellent descriptions of Tamil funerals and their symbolism, see Moreno 1981; and Good 1991: 132–54. On Telugu death rites, see Tapper 1987: 145–58. For a lucid and concise discussion about the value of death and its place in the literary traditions of Hinduism, see Bowker 1991. Also see Schombucher and Zoller's 1999 anthology on the meanings of death in South Asia.

7. For a focused discussion on the differential symbolic functions of men and women, kin and affines, and close and distant mourners at urban Punjabi funerals, see Das 1986.

8. This distancing of mortuary duties from daily life is in line with the French anthropologist Robert Hertz's brilliant suggestion that, at funerals, social facts, cosmological representations, and ritual behaviors mirror one another (1960).

9. The turn to performance has also persuaded scholars of South Asian texts to pay attention to context. But these scholars often reject or modify the notion of context advanced by performative theorists. Stuart Blackburn, for example, proposes a "text-centered" analysis of the South Indian bow song tradition (1988). Blackburn explains his method: "A text-centered approach to performance . . . starts with the narrative outside its enactment. It consciously rejects the claim that the meaning of a text lies only in performance, that the text is inseparable from its telling" (xviii). In her research on North Indian women's narratives, Rachel Meyer argues, "A concept of context should stretch to include the interstices among multiple performance frames where meaning exists in the spaces

traced out between different contexts, rather than residing in any one of them" (2000: 159–60). And in his conclusion to a volume on South Asian expressive traditions, Arjun Appadurai suggests that "the prevailing sense of context [in much recent folklore] tends to be relatively small-scale and confined to a variety of immediate and intricate micro-features of performances. . . . What the South Asian material contained in this volume invites us to do is to move toward somewhat larger-scale ideas of context, in which broader ideological frameworks, historical currents, and social formations are brought into the conceptualization of context" (1991: 469–70).

10. For example, those found in Bauman 1986; and Briggs 1988.

11. For this reason, perhaps, the meaning of the root word for *Paṟaiyar* is often translated as "drum" (Clarke 1998: 121). But according to my Dalit consultants, *paṟai* means "information by beating the drum" and refers neither to a generic nor a specific drum. Josiane Racine similarly notes that "l'étymologie de *paṟai* renvoie secondairement à la notion de tambour, et prioritairement au concept de parole, de déclaration, de proclamation" (1996: 208, citing Burrow and Emeneau 1984: 359; and Tamil Lexicon 1982: 2563). That drumming is primarily associated with informing is also evidenced by the fact that the main Tamil word for beating drums, *paṟaicāṟṟa*, means "to announce requests, orders, services, and news." The genre of funeral petitions analyzed in chapter 4 suggests that the first drummer, Vīrajāmpuhaṉ, was a news broadcaster. Nowadays the Dalits still drum out public announcements of various sorts, the coming of a festival, for example, or the schedule of a local election or other governmental notices.

12. Anthropologists working in North India have referred to this system of remuneration as *jajmānī*, but in the South Arcot district of Tamilnadu it is known as mērai. *Mērai*, I was told, referred to the payments made by the castes that owned land to the castes that were attached to them by a relation of hereditary services. Such prestations were not all alike: they varied according to the services rendered. In the village where I conducted my dissertation research, for example, the carpenter who made and maintained the agricultural tools of the landowning castes used to receive a larger yield of the harvest than the potter who supplied clay vessels to the same castes. According to members of landowning castes, mērai was a benevolent system, "a way of providing work and an income to people who did not have land."

Some of my consultants even invoked notions of philanthropy. Describing the customary remuneration of the barber and the washerman, a Chettiar man for example, told me, "Everyday we used to give food to them; it was a way to help them, a form of charity *[utavi]*." This man acknowledged that such "charity" was not entirely altruistic, since it conferred on the donors benefits both in this world and the other. The families who kept service relations were "respected," and those who did not "lost their good names" and were treated like outcastes. And since, in Hinduism, giving alms on a daily basis is a way to acquire religious merit, "they also went to heaven." Yet this man and others emphasized that such worldly and otherworldly privileges were costly, even burdensome, because relationships with service castes entailed financial responsibilities and obligations that had to be met "in both good and bad times."

13. In this particular village, as elsewhere in rural South Arcot, there is no Brahmin family. The majority of the population consists of a large spectrum of non-Brahmin castes of varying status and power, with Dalit castes making up 20 percent of the population (also see Racine 1996: 201).

14. Drumming is considered an impure activity because it requires touching the skin of dead cows or goats.

15. Many ethnographers have long stressed the emotional pain incurred in Hindu women upon marriage and transition to their marital kin (for example, see Lamb 2000: 209–12). For an exception to this scholarship, see Nishimura 1998. For a different exploration of Hindu marriage, see Harlan and Courtright 1995.

16. For ethnographic and theoretical interpretations of South Indian kinship and marriage practices, see Trawick 1990; Kapadia 1995: 13–67.

17. My method is also inspired by the teachings of Alan Dundes, the great folklorist and my professor at the University of California, Berkeley. As early as 1966, Dundes argued that *"folklorists must actively seek to elicit the meaning of folklore from the folk"* (1966: 507, emphasis in original). For a wonderful application of his "oral literary criticism" approach to North Indian women's songs, see Narayan 1986, 1995, and 1997. Such an approach is especially useful since, as I note in chapters 1 and 2, everything in Tamil lament is left ambiguous, so that the question of who is speaking to whom, and who is feeling what toward who, can be answered only by the singer. This is consistent with Margaret Trawick's suggestion that "intentional ambiguity" is intrinsic to Indian culture and especially Tamil poetry (1988b). For a study that uses performers' interpretations to guide the analysis, see Blackburn's 2001 collection of Tamil folktales.

18. See Ram 1991; Das 1990; Raheja and Gold 1994; Trawick 1988a; Kumar 1994.

19. Moffatt writes, "In their definition of their own identity and its lowness in *toRil* [service] and myth, then, the Harijans of Endavur are in fundamental consensus with the higher castes. They define themselves as low for the same rea-

sons as higher castes do, and they agree with the evaluation that persons with their characteristics should be low" (1979: 129). Also see McGilvray 1983.

20. See Berreman 1971; Mencher 1974; Freeman 1979; Kapadia 1995; Mosse 1999.

21. This phrase was coined by James Scott (1985) to describe poor Malay villagers' opposition to their own subordination.

CHAPTER ONE

1. Women continue to lament in clusters until, as one woman put it, "the men put the body in the pit," which may not take place until all close male relatives reach the household, one or two days later. Then women in the family weep every day at a certain hour for a period of thirty days.

2. For scholarship on Tamil lament, see Venugopal 1982; Egnor 1986; Trawick 1988a; Ramaswamy 1994.

3. That the Tamil genre of crying songs requires deep emotional involvement will not surprise scholars of lament. In the Cretan village where she conducted fieldwork Anna Caraveli discovered that "the consensus regarding the definition of a lament is that it is a song for the dead, produced when one is immersed in and inspired by pain *[ponos]*. A lament performed by someone who is emotionally disengaged might be considered for its poetic merit but is not a true lament" (1986: 172; also see Danforth 1982: 141–52; Seremetakis 1991: 116–20; Honko 1980; Grima 1992).

4. Such definitions seem to suggest that a man's kuṟai refers more to his financial and respect-related worries than to his internal state of grief or sorrow.

5. This is evidenced by the fact that laments often begin with the dative form of the personal pronoun "I" *(eṉakku)*. In her study of Tamil laments, Margaret Egnor also notes, "The first-person pronoun is repeated again and again" (1986: 303).

6. Anna Caraveli-Chaves also notes that lament poetry in Crete "bridges" or mediates between important contrasting realms of existence: life and death, past and present, and so on (1980).

7. For another example of the ways in which a lament tradition may question, contradict, and even oppose religious meanings, see Seremetakis 1991.

8. For another recorded version of this dirge, see Egnor 1986: 305.

9. While researching the meanings of marriage for young girls in the village of Mangaldihi, in West Bengal, Sarah Lamb recorded similar associations. She

writes, "The young brides who spoke to me anticipated the pain of cutting so many ties with their natal families, homes, and friends with dread, not comprehending how they would ever survive such an ordeal. These conversations were similar to those I had with older people about the separations at death" (2000: 209).

10. Loring Danforth also notes that, in mainland Greece, marriage is an important metaphor for death (1982: 74–115). He observes that the Greek orthodox funeral (and its metaphor as wedding) "establishes an analogy between departure from the world of the living for the grave, on one hand, and a departure from one's home and family of origin for the home of one's affines, on the other" (89).

11. Trawick suggests that "daughters are more anxious about the break in mother-daughter continuity than are mothers." As she explains, "The mother stays in the place she was, and she may have other children to console her, but the daughter has no other mothers. So a daughter may feel herself to be shattered by her marriage. Conversely, a return to the mother's home may be felt by the daughter as a reuniting of herself, with herself" (1990:167). Trawick concludes that "mothers do not value daughters as highly as daughters value mothers" (169).

12. The use of comparisons or implied comparisons between a scene in nature, for instance, and an emotional landscape is not merely typical of laments, but is the key characteristic of Tamil classical poetry (see Ramanujan 1967; Cutler 1987).

13. For scholarship on the special bond between a Tamil sister and brother, particularly an elder brother, see Peterson 1988; Trawick 1990; Nuckolls 1993; Nabokov 2000.

14. In their laments (as in day-to-day life), Tamil women do not address their husbands by their first names. They use the word for "king" or the names of heroes, such as Bīma or Arjuna of the pan-Hindu epic the *Mahābhārata;* the allusion here, in addition to comparing the husband to Bīma and Arjuna, perhaps indicates that the "silver book" is the epic.

15. For a study that contrasts the experiences of Indian women widowed in youth with those widowed after menopause, see Lamb 2000. For a different perspective on Indian widows, see Yuko Nishimura's research on gender, kinship, and property rights among the Nagarattar, a prominent mercantile Tamil caste residing in Chettinadu (1998: 292–312).

16. Such dirges are delivered at the actual widow-making ceremony, on the final day of mourning.

17. Raheja and Gold 1994; Trawick 1988a, 1991; Das 1990. Benedicte Grima, however, argues that Paxtun women's expression of grief and lamentation is not a channel for protest (1992: 132).

18. For a similar interpretation of Greek laments, see Caraveli 1986; Seremetakis 1991.

19. Ramanujan defined *countersystem* as "an alternative way of looking at thing." As he explained, "Genders are genres. The world of women is not the world of men" (1991: 53).

20. The notion of "making people cry for you" also explains the peculiar language of Tamil laments. Tamil dirges are replete with metaphors, or rather metonyms. In this respect they compare with laments from all over the world. Of the Baltic-Finnish tradition, for example, Aili Nenola-Kallio writes, "The most striking feature in Karelian laments is that usually nothing is called by its everyday name; instead people, places, situations, animals and things all have their special metaphorical lament names" (1980: 42–43; also see Danforth 1982: 72–115, passim; and Honko 1980). In an attempt to account for the abundance of tropes in Greek lament, Loring Danforth reminds us that "metaphors establish relationships between things that were thought to be unrelated . . . forc[ing] us to see things in a different light" (1982: 82). Drawing on James Fernandez's 1986 argument that metaphors specifically help us to grapple with "inchoate experiences," Danforth logically concludes that death "would seem to be a particularly suitable subject for metaphor" (83). Indeed, death would seem to be the one experience that is the least comprehensible for human beings. I do not believe, however, that the wealth of nature and agriculture imagery in Tamil lament (birds, river, plants, rain, citrus fruits, trees, creepers, bull carts, crops, etc.) works merely to "make sense" of death. Rather than being explanatory, such images are rhetorical. They aim to persuade, which is also how Fernandez characterizes the mission of tropes in general. Specifically they make the case that the lamenting woman's kuṟai is true. However, Danforth does not conclude that metaphors in Greek laments work to make death more intelligible to mourners. To him, metaphoric relationships between the process of exhumation and the wedding ritual, for example, or between traveling abroad and journeying to the afterworld, attempt to overcome the contradiction between life and death. Because his analysis is inspired by the structuralism of Claude Lévi-Strauss, for whom culture never quite functions to solve anything, Danforth does not find such attempts entirely successful. He writes, "In the end, however, no complete resolution is possible" (1982: 95). For an analysis of the role of persuasion in Tamil folklore, see Venugopal 1985.

21. Loring Danforth also notes that in mainland Greece, death places the bereaved in a state associated with heat and lack of water: "Death burns. Women in mourning are commonly referred to as burned by death" (1982: 107). And he adds, "Finally, the emotions aroused by death (grief, pain, and anxiety) are all associated with heat, fire, and flames, and people who experience these emotions are said to be withered or consumed" (108). To rid themselves of such emotions, women in mourning visit the graveyard and cry. Danforth indicates that such crying is cooling (144).

CHAPTER TWO

I borrow this chapter's title from William Blake's collection of poems (1794) and from Norman Cutler's 1987 book on Tamil devotional poetry.

1. Not every scholar appreciates the extent to which formulaic poetry can be personal, if not autobiographical, and creative, even self-recreative. This is how, for example, Murray Emeneau, a well-known linguist, characterized Toda (a tribe-like caste in the Nilgiri hills of South India) lament (1971: 109–405). He writes, "The poet is not expected to search for originality of verbal expression or for originality in his statements about himself and his fellows and their place in their universe, which for the Toda is essentially his culture. . . . The poet's verbal originality seems to lie in the expertness of the choice which he makes from the stock of traditional formulas and combinations of formulas in setpieces, when he wishes to allude to any particular event or situation" (xlvi–xlvii).

2. Women's personal narratives illuminate not merely the course of a life over time but also the impact of gender roles on women's lives. This is because the story is rarely told without reference to the dynamics of gender. As the editors of a recent feminist anthology argue, "Women's personal narratives are, among other things, stories of how women negotiate their 'exceptional' gender status both in their daily lives and over the course of a lifetime. They assume that one can understand the life only if one takes into account gender roles and gender expectations. Whether she has accepted the norms or defied them, a woman's life can never be written taking gender for granted" (Personal Narratives Group 1989: 5).

3. For an extensive consideration of the relationship between experience and narrative, see Bruner 1991; Mattingly and Garro 2000; Mattingly 1998; Cavarero 1997; Rosenwald and Ochberg 1992.

4. For a fascinating psychological study of childhood and early family dynamics in India, see Kakar 1981.

5. According to my Tamil consultants, a diet consisting of hot foods (such as meat, fish, onions, and garlic) excites sexual passions and worldly attachments. This is why widows (who are forbidden to remarry) and ascetics (who seek to remain celibate and renounce material possessions and relationships) exclude from their diets any hot foods. For similar notions of bodily heating and sexuality in the Indian state of Bengal, see Lamb 2000: 126, 216.

6. This confirms Margaret Egnor's observation that crying songs "are sung spontaneously, in solitary places, and not for the purpose of entertainment" (1986: 303).

7. Women seem to be willing, however, to share their lives with female anthropologists; see, for example, Racine 1996; Trawick 1991, 1997; Nabokov 2000.

8. The Indian psychologist Sudhir Kakar validates my impression when he writes that the Indian lifelong yearning for the confirming presence of the "good (M) Other" is not viewed the same way in most Western cultures, in which such longing and the distress it may cause are often held to be "childish" and "regressive" (1981: 85).

9. Sarah Lamb also notes that, in the Bengali village where she conducted fieldwork, marriage is the most formative experience for women. She writes, "For girls in Mangaldihi, it was through marriage that they became most marked and that the ties of their personhood were substantially unmade and remade" (2000: 209). Benedicte Grima also found that, for Paxtun women, hardship begins with marriage: "Most women agreed, upon my asking, that the time before marriage was one of happiness" (1992: 127).

10. Sudhir Kakar argues that "an Indian child tends to experience his mother almost totally as a 'good mother.'" He specifies, however, that the "idealized image of the 'good mother' is largely a male construction" (1981: 83). As my female consultants' laments and testimonies suggest, however, Indian women too may "sentimentalize" or even "adore" their mothers throughout the course of their lives.

11. In her beautiful work on the Bedouin discourse of self and sentiment, Lila Abu-Lughod (1986) argues that two ideologies exist, each used for different types of discourse, and each with its own models of experience. She juxtaposes the poetic discourse of self and sentiment, on the one hand, and the ordinary discourse of honor and modesty, on the other. My fieldwork also suggests a radical difference between the poetic language of the inner life and the presentation of the self in day-to-day life. The former encourages, even requires, the outpouring of rage and outrage; the latter inhibits the unearthing of such emotions.

12. Unlike the Paxtun men studied by Benedicte Grima (1992: 61, 158), Tamil

men did not reprimand women for lamenting at funerals. Nor did they make fun of them. Much like Paxtun men, however, Tamil men viewed the lamenting mode of expression as a loss of control in a person, which may explain why they saw it as inappropriate behavior for them.

CHAPTER THREE

1. The paṟaimēḷam plays principally at village goddesses' festivals and the funerals of caste Hindus, with the exception of Brahmins and artisans (Ācāris), who do not use the mortuary services (drumming, singing, bier building, etc.) provided by untouchables (also see Moffatt 1979: 113). The paṟaimēḷam does not usually play at auspicious rites of passage celebrated in the village *(ūr)*. For marriage and young girls' coming of age ceremonies, caste Hindus recruit the more prestigious tavul-nadeswaram band of their barber *(ampaṭṭar)* caste. The *tavul* is a double-ended, barrel-shaped drum played with the hand and with a stick. The *nadeswaram* is a large double-reeded wind instrument. Both are more difficult to master than the paṟaimēḷam drums. Among untouchable castes, however, *paṟai* drummers play at all auspicious rites of passage (also see Moffatt 1979: 199–200). On happy occasions, such as marriage, they play "good" beats.

The paṟaimēḷam near Gingee generally consists of one or two singers and four drummers. The numerical composition of this band, however, is variable. In the nearby village of Karani, Josiane Racine reports, the local paṟaimēḷam comprises eight members (1996: 205). Of the North Arcot village of Endavur, Michael Moffatt notes that the *paṟai* band "generally consists of five drummers, four playing parai and one playing satti [pot]" (1979: 198).

2. Although my previous research confirms that drumming in general is intended to keep low and malevolent spirits away (Nabokov 2000), my consultants never told me that the funeral mēḷam functions to "bid and contain the spirit of the dead," as Clarke found in the Chengelput district (1998: 117; also see Moffatt 1979: 113). Like Josiane Racine (1996: 209), I found that, in the South Arcot district, it is up to non-untouchable drummers (players of the *pampai* and *uṭukkai*) to exorcise the spirits of the dead, especially the maleficent spirits *(pēys)* of humans who have died in childbirth, by suicide, or by accident (Nabokov 2000).

3. The Dalits, however, are exempted from drumming, even forbidden to drum, in times of deadly epidemics, suicide, and murder. In such circumstances the family is in a hurry to bury or cremate the dead in order to prevent the risks of contagion or of a police investigation. Nor do the Dalits drum at funerals of

children or adolescents under the age of fifteen, because, as I was told, "The death of a child is a private not a public affair." Moreover, children are considered to be innocent. Since they have not committed sins, their souls do not need to be praised by the mēḷam singer and his audience (I discuss this later in the text).

4. The barber (ampaṭṭar) presides over all funerary rites (the feeding of the corpse, the breaking of the water pot at the cremation ground, etc.). The washerman provides ritual cloth, ignites commemorative torches, and assists the barber (also see Brubaker 1979).

5. The body of the tōṟikaṭṭai drum is made out of the wood of a jack tree that is coated with tin. Cow skin covers the two extremities. It is played with one stick and one hand. Usually there is one tōṟikaṭṭai drummer per mēḷam.

6. This is small clay pot covered at the rim with goatskin that is glued with a thick paste made of tamarind. It is played with two sticks. It is considered the "lowest" of the three drums. It is heavy and difficult to play. Ideally, a mēḷam requires three pot drummers.

7. This drum is made of three pieces of tamarind wood that have been bent and joined into a circular frame and covered on one side with calfskin. It is played with both hands. Usually there is one palahai drummer at a funeral mēḷam. While the tōṟikaṭṭai and caṭṭi players remain stationary, the palahai drummer executes various dance steps. For further description of these drums, see (Moffatt 1979: 112).

8. Although most people cannot name the distinctive beats *(tāḷams)* played by the Dalits on various ceremonial occasions, they can usually differentiate between "auspicious" and "inauspicious" beats. They immediately recognize the *cāvu mēḷam* (here, "death beat"). However, the drummers actually begin, if only for a minute or two, not with the death beat but with the marriage beat *(kaliyāṇa mēḷam)*. I was given two main reasons for this. First, in whatever the Dalits undertake, whether good or bad, "there should be auspiciousness." Second, the Dalits cannot suddenly announce a death: "It would be too much of a shock. They need to prepare people." For further description of the Paṟaiyars' drum beats, see Moffatt 1979: 199; McGilvray 1983: 103; Clarke 1998: 112–18.

9. Josiane Racine notes that funeral singers sometimes take the opportunity to "take revenge," if only implicitly, against the dead who once exploited and dominated them (1996: 206). The Paṟaiyar singers with whom I worked never confirmed that they intersperse their lyrics of praise with innuendoes.

10. For an excellent discussion of the poetics and politics of praise in Tamil culture, see Ramaswamy 1998: 80–85.

11. For a social history of the role and place of patrons in another South Indian

performing art, see Zarrilli's study of Kathakali, the distinctive dance-drama of Kerala (2000: 17–38).

12. The importance of the patron's generosity, and the praise of the yajamāna and the gift itself, was integral in song culture far back into Vedic times too.

13. Moreover, women tend to request folk songs *(nāṭṭuppuṟa pāṭal)* narrating the stories of women in dire straits. A favorite is the song about "the good little sister" *(nallataṅkāḷ katai)* who, having experienced a devastating drought, drowns herself and her seven children after her prosperous sister-in-law refuses to give her and her family food, hospitality, and protection.

14. In 1999, a family spent on average two thousand five hundred rupees for a funeral: one thousand rupees on the mēḷam, five hundred rupees on the barber and the washerman, five hundred rupees on ritual essentials such as garlands of flowers and new clothes *(kōṭi)*, and 500 rupees on alcohol (for the men of the family and the musicians). Most villagers live on less than one thousand rupees a month.

15. For a Bengali version of this story, see Dimock 1963; for a Tamil version in dramatic form, see Bavanandam Pillai 1910.

16. Also see Hart's translation of this story (1979: 217–36).

17. In villages around Gingee, the Rati and Maṉmataṉ drama is staged during a temple festival that occurs during the Tamil month of Paṅkuṉi, March and April. The festival climaxes on the day of the full moon with the burning of Maṉmataṉ's straw effigy.

18. For another example of a marital dispute, see De Bruin's translation of the Tamil popular play *Karṇa's Death* (1998a). The central part of the play deals with the confrontation between Karṇa and his wife before he leaves for the battlefield, where he dies. De Bruin notes that, in the northern part of Tamilnadu, this play may be performed on the occasion of the *karumāti*, the ceremony that among non-Brahmin communities usually marks the end of the funeral obsequies on the sixteenth day after a person's death (xiii).

19. For another example of the juxtaposition of grief and comedy in a South Indian performance, see Stuart Blackburn's study of shadow puppeteers in the state of Kerala. Blackburn notes, "Nearly every major scene of mourning in the puppet play is similarly hedged with comedy, as an antidote, I think, to the intense sorrow that underlies the puppet play" (1996: 236).

20. To highlight their scene, singers sometimes perform in duo *(iraṭṭa kural)*, with one man personifying Maṉmataṉ and the other dressed up as Rati.

21. Ramanujan himself applied the old akam/puṟam (domestic/public) contrast to contemporary South Indian narrative genres (see his classification of Kannada folktales and myths, 1986). My research, however, does not support his

conclusion that, as "we move from akam to different grades of puṟam contexts, the language and technique of the telling become increasingly formal, varied, and complex" (45). As we have seen, the akam genre of Tamil dirges is just as fixed and formal as the puṟam genre of death songs.

22. Women are confined more closely to their homes than men are. In rural towns and villages, they have little social access to public spaces such as markets and restaurants for arranged social encounters and interactions.

23. This is not to say that feeling kuṟai is always automatic. Recall how the structure and dynamics of the crying clusters help a woman attain the emotional intensity necessary for expressing her crying song. Recall also that sharing grief validates a woman's suffering—a process that facilitates the general outpouring of comparisons.

CHAPTER FOUR

1. The stone is often a slab of granite etched with the figures of the king and his wife.

2. The middle stone is also sometimes referred to as "Kālī's temple" *(kālī kōyil)*, because the goddess Kālī is also said to reside at the entrance to the Tamil funeral ground.

3. Michael Moffatt notes that at the boundary of a village's burning ground in the Chengelput district "is a stone dedicated to Arichentiran, and here the Vettiyan [gravedigger] pauses and chants to the higher caste mourners." Moffatt's transcription of this "chant," however, appears to be incomplete, and his informants' assertion that the untouchable task here is one of "honoring the dead" does not conform to my findings (1979: 195). Josiane Racine's observation—that in villages near Pondicherry the king Ariccantiraṉ is requested to let the funeral procession proceed to the cremation ground—is more consistent with my research (1996: 203, 204). But she transcribes only a small section of this request (210).

4. South Arcot burying or cremation grounds are stark. Much as Anthony Good observes of those elsewhere in Tamilnadu, they "consist simply of untended plots of straggling thorn bushes and bare earth, with perhaps a few ashes or shards of pottery to indicate that a funeral has recently taken place. . . . The dead have no permanent monuments" (1991:132).

5. The refusal to link the end of physical being with physical decay is basic to many, if not all, mythological and philosophical traditions of classical and folk Hinduism.

6. Anthony Good also notes that villagers of the Tirunelveli district are not familiar with Sanskritic notions of death and rebirth, not even the theory that one's karma, the accumulated balance of one's past good and bad deeds, determines the nature of each rebirth. He writes, "Many villagers to whom I spoke seemed unaware even of its existence. Queries about what 'happens when someone dies' were greeted with amused incredulity. The question seemed never to have occurred to them, at least in such general terms." Good also notes that "local exegeses of funerals are fragmentary and inconclusive" (1991: 154).

7. Although the petition meets the other basic criterion of the classic anthropological definition of a myth—it is invoked or enacted over the course of a ritual, the funeral, and this is the *only* time it can be so used—I do not insist on this gloss of myth, for it has too many problems. To begin with, it is a Western category that predictably fails to convey the meanings that other peoples invest in their narratives or classes of narratives. In addition, the word *myth* is encoded with received methodologies and explanatory theories that, as I mention in a later note, impose serious limitations on our ability to understand the Tamil petition. Finally, "myth" has acquired so many notions of falsity and fiction that it is virtually synonymous with a lie. For a genealogy of the category "myth" from classical antiquity to modern scholarship, see Lincoln 1999.

8. This etymology is consistent with Tamil dictionaries, which gloss the prefix *vīra(m)* as "hero, heroic, courage or strength" and jāmpuhaṉ (or cāmpuhaṉ) as "the Pariah" or "the honorary appellation of a Pariah" and label it as a derivative of *cāmpu* or "drum" (a synonym for paṟai) (Fabricius 1972: 378, 893). A village headman once told me that in the old days the leader *(nāṭṭāṇmaikkāraṉ)* of Paṟaiyar communities was known as the jāmpuhaṉ. To him, *jāmpuhaṉ* was a title *(paṭṭam)*, "an old title that had been passed down for many generations." But none of my Dalit friends had ever heard of the world *jāmpuhaṉ* in connection with Paṟaiyan leadership. "In this world," one said, "no one is known as *jāmpuhaṉ*."

9. All four versions of the Vīrajāmpuhaṉ story that I recorded in 1990 and 1999 were irregularly performed at funerals in villages located within a radius of twenty kilometers from Gingee. The fullest versions were told by Vel and Ettyan, who respectively resided seven and twelve kilometers northwest of Gingee, a fact that suggests the story might be known in the nearby North Arcot district. We know that this used to be the case, for in Arthur F. Cox's *Manual of the North Arcot District in the Presidency of Madras* 1881–1895, H. A. Stuart reported a version very similar to the ones I recorded a century later in South Arcot (in Thurston 1987: 116).

Moreover, Michael Moffatt also collected a similar but shorter version from a high-caste man living in the Chengelput district (1979: 126–27). However, the story does not appear to circulate beyond North and South Arcot. I was not able to find it south of Gingee, and many of the classical village ethnographies of the southern districts of Tamilnadu—Madurai, Coimbatore, Kanya Kumari, and so on—do not allude to it. Robert Deliège's detailed study of the myths of origin of a Paṟaiyar community in rural Ramnad district makes no reference to it (1993). That the story is a local rather than a national expression is finally evidenced by the fact that none of the encyclopedias of Tamil Puranic or folk mythology gloss the name of its main hero, Vīrajāmpuhaṉ. However, one of the characters of the *Elder Brother's Story* collected in the Coimbatore district by Brenda Beck is called Cāmpukaṉ (1982, 1992). Like the hero of our petition, this Cāmpukaṉ is also a "servant," and "the [son of] the black Paṟaiyā woman" (1992: 421; also see 1982: 54–56). And according to David Shulman (personal communication), a character named Jāmpukaṉ similar to the one described in the ritual of the petition also turns up in classical Tamil in various places: for example, in Maṇimēkalai, one of the first two great Tamil epics (the other is Cilappatikāram) said to have been composed between the second century A.D. and the sixth or seventh century A.D.

10. The peacock is India's national bird. It is also associated with the South Indian god Murukaṉ, who is often shown seated on a peacock.

11. For a synoptic comparison of these four versions of the Vīrajāmpuhaṉ story, see appendix A. For Sivamani's version in Tamil, see appendix B.

12. The idea that Brahmā, the Hindu god of creation, causes the appearance of death is not unique to this Tamil myth. According to Greg Bailey, Brahmā is fundamentally associated with the advent of death (1983: 10). Also see no. 20 below.

13. In Tamilnadu the god Ganesh, the remover of obstacles and the embodiment of success in undertakings, is always invoked prior to a performance and ritual (Michael 1983).

14. My comparative approach makes no attempt to follow the structural analysis of myth pioneered by the French anthropologist Claude Lévi-Strauss. Lévi-Strauss's method rests on the basic premise that a myth consists of variants that, once broken, down and reorganized into bundles of binary relations, yield the myth's logical structure (1963). To him, this formal structure of oppositions is the fundamental significance of a myth. As he put it, "Myth is explained by nothing except myth" 215). Since myth is self-referential, Lévi-Strauss has no use for the storytellers' exegeses or cultural context. In fact, since myths are surface expressions of the unconscious, the French anthropologist does not even trust the narrators' commentaries.

What troubles me about the structural analysis of myth is precisely that it assumes to know better than the voices that expound myth. The method and not what the narrators may have to say, we are led to believe, yields the key existential contradictions that myth tries to solve. Yet there are grounds to suspect that Lévi-Strauss's formula might not be as reliable as it purports to be. First, his basic reliance on a totality of variants raises fundamental questions. How can we ever be sure that we have collected all versions of any myth? What kind of ontological reality should we attribute to whatever quantity we do happen to record? Since variants are recounted by different people in different circumstances, does their sum not exist only in the mind of the anthropologist? Second, the structural method is not easily replicable. I remember once attempting to analyze with a class of bright undergraduates four versions of a Tiwi origin myth according to Lévi-Strauss's instructions. We disagreed on how to cut and rearrange these four variants and compiled different lists of binary oppositions. Certainly we were amateurs, or *bricoleurs*, but our "variant" application of Lévi-Strauss's method suggests that identifying the key constituent units of myth and their relations is not a clear-cut matter of detached observation or statistics. If we are going to interpret—that is, read myth from subjective perspectives—we might as well start with the narrators' explanations, a procedure that has the advantage of telling us what they think about their own stories. This is what I have done, and I am convinced that without their exegeses I would never have grasped the basic issues of human identity, purpose, and self-awareness that lie at the heart of all their petitions.

15. The motif of rebirth out of total destruction appears in other Tamil cosmogony myths; see Shulman 1988.

16. The occurrence of the flood and other motifs and themes in the Vīrajāmpuhaṉ story (e.g., the origins of death, overpopulation, the hero's trickster-like behavior, and the connection between drumming and world regeneration) will surely elicit many parallels from folklorists and comparative mythologists, especially those who deal with the wider world of Indian traditions (cf. Shulman 1980: 55–89, 1988: 293–318; Doniger 1976: 243 ff.). It would be interesting to examine possible links between the "first man" Paṟaiyar drummer's regenerative associations and the tradition that associates the sound *(sabda)* of Siva's drum with cosmic restoration (Shulman 1988: 298). But in the present study, these questions would only tend to lead away from my real purpose, which is to explore the manifestation in performance and meaning of the story of Vīrajāmpuhaṉ for those petitioners whose life work it is to narrate it at the cremation and burial grounds.

17. Telling the truth seems to be a prerequisite for the position of publishing orders by drumbeat *(paṟaicāṟṟa)*. Vīrajāmpuhaṉ is first and foremost a messenger whose responsibility it is to make the correct announcement. This is all

the more critical because, as we will soon see, his medium presumes a dangerous theology of speech. Once drummed out, words create reality, and no one, not even God, can change it.

18. The same emotion, anger, is the cause of destruction and death in the pan-Hindu epic the Mahābhārata (Long 1977: 77; also see Bailey 1983: 11). In one of the many stories-myths recounted in this epic, the god Brahmā has created many beings, who have "multiplied so rapidly that no one has room to breathe" (Long 1977: 77). Not able to reduce the expansion of his creation, the god grows frustrated. His frustrations give way to anger, and from this anger springs a fire of cosmic dimensions. Much like the hero of the Tamil petition, Brahmā then plays down the true cause of his deadly fire. When the god Siva tries to pacify him, Brahma answers, "I am not angry, nor do I desire the death of all creatures. It is out of a desire to lighten the burden of the weight of the manifold creatures upon the Earth that I have brought about this destruction" (1977: 77).

19. In the version of this story recorded by H. A. Stuart in the late nineteenth century, the origin of untimely death is specifically attributed to the Paṟaiyar's need to make a living. In this version it is the god Siva who "ordered a Paraiyan to beat upon his drum, and cry 'Let the ripe decay.'" But the pay (some change, boiled rice, cloth, etc.) seemed to the Paṟaiyar "very little," so that "to increase the death-rate and consequently his perquisites, he cried, 'Let the ripe and the unripe decay.'" When later the god remonstrated with him, "the man pleaded poverty" (in Thurston 1987: 116–17). The same meanings resurface in a version narrated by a high-caste man to Michael Moffatt in the Chengelput district:

> The goddess Kali made the first differences. In those days, the Colony people were higher in caste. Therefore Kali gave them the right to announce, to beat the drums, and to honor the dead. The *uur* [village] people had to pay them a fee for this, so they had both honor and income in those days. One day, Kali asked a Colony person to beat the drums and to declare: "Let the unripe and let the ripe fall" [that is, let the young and the old die]. The Harijan added two or three more phrases: "Let the bud and let the flower fall" [that is, let the unborn and let small children die]. He did this in order to get even more income. Kali became angry with him and said: "Since you have changed my pronouncement, you are hereafter lower castes." Since then others have looked down on them as low, because they attempted to increase their income in this crude way." (1979: 126–27)

Elsewhere in India we find the same associations between death and profit making. Jonathan Parry, in particular, notes that, in Banaras, death is big business for the priests and other categories of specialists who perform funeral rituals for the thousands of people who wish to die in this North Indian city (1994). His chapters 3 and 4 focus on the manner in which funeral specialists are remunerated and on their fierce bargaining with mourners (1994: 75–150).

20. In his survey of the Vedic and post-Vedic literature pertaining to death, Bruce Long also finds that death is seen "as being both a necessity and a gift" (1977: 92). He writes, "All the myths are in agreement that[,] without the entry and continued operation of death in withdrawing from the temporal world those creatures whose terms of life have matured, and thereby providing living space for new beings, the universe soon would suffocate under the weight of its own superfluous progeny" (1977: 92).

21. The belief that human beings' volitions and deeds in the present life predetermine their nature, character, and social status in the next is one of the cornerstones of the Hindu worldview (see Long 1977: 81).

22. For another version of this part of the petition, see Racine 1996: 210.

23. Likewise, all four myths of the origin of the Paṟaiyars collected by Moffatt "describe a primordial fall, and all four attribute this fall to bad conduct on the part of the original Paraiyans" (1979: 127).

24. For another example of such identification between actor and character, see Zarrilli's study of Kathakali, the distinctive dance-drama of Kerala (2000: 40–64).

25. This notion of the firstborn hiding something resurfaces in one origin myth collected by Moffatt in the village of Endavur. In this story the eldest son is caught hiding a piece of cooked beef, and his younger brothers tell him, "Paraiyan, do not hide" (Moffatt 1979: 122).

26. In Tamil village culture, the cow is an auspicious and beneficent animal. Cows are not openly or willingly killed (also see Moffatt 1979: 114).

27. This would not be the first time that a South Indian performance did not engage a human audience. Stuart Blackburn shows that shadow puppeteers in the state of Kerala perform for themselves (1996). He adds that the lack of viewers stimulates puppeteers to perform their own unique version of the Tamil Rāmāyana story composed by the poet Kampaṉ. He writes, "Through a set of four conversations, which comprise the whole of performance, the puppeteers weaken the voice of the poet and speak in their own voice." Although not heard by an external audience, Blackburn argues that "these conversations create internal listeners inside the text and inside the drama-house" (1996: 224). It is possible that similar dynamics occur at the Tamil petition.

28. The washerman carries the ceremonial rice from the family home to the

grave. At the entrance to the cremation grounds, his only function is to give the rice to the village barber, who places it at the four corners of the middle stone.

CHAPTER FIVE

1. Bruce Tapper also notes that the "form of stylized wailing at funerals [in the state of Andhra Pradesh] . . . makes tangible the ideology that women are more emotional and less controlled than men" (1987: 146).

2. Sarah Lamb notes that older women residing in the village of Mangaldihi, in West Bengal, express similar views on the changing roles and attitudes of daughters-in-law. She writes, "Modern-day daughters-in-law, I was told, are better educated; they go out and get jobs, they are interested in make-up and movies, they desire their independence, and they are not willing to serve their husbands' parents as daughters-in-law once did" (2000: 92). Susan Seymour (1999) shows how innovations like schooling and delayed marriage are changing contemporary Indian women's attitudes toward family and gender roles. But Karin Kapadia (1995) argues that the changing context of marriage and dowry practices in rural southern India intensifies women's subordination and inequality.

3. Despite the state's efforts to ameliorate their condition, and despite the efforts of a new generation of political leaders who represent them, discrimination persists against untouchables. See Mendelsohn and Vicziany 1998; Lynch 2001.

4. The Anti-Brahmin Movement launched by Ramaswami Naicker was extremely influential in politicizing Tamil untouchables. For an exploration of the politics of identity change among Tamil untouchables, see Mosse 1999; Kapadia 1995: 175–78; Kannan and Gros 2002. Mosse concludes that, for all their acts of assertion, Tamil untouchables have failed to develop a unifying political identity. Kannan and Gros argue that Tamil Dalits have not yet developed a genuine literary production of their own.

5. Josiane and Jean-Luc Racine report hearing about similar feelings (1995).

6. Moffatt also notes that drumming is a task that the untouchables of Endavur village "take seriously." They feel compelled to honor the person who summons them 1979: 197.

APPENDIX A

1. Vaḷḷuvars are untouchable priests. They do not service caste Hindus.

GLOSSARY

ĀCĀRI: a member of the artisan caste (carpenter, ironsmith, etc.)
AKA VĀḺKAI: interior life, domestic or married life
AKAM: what is inner, interior; a house
AKKĀ: elder sister
AKKIṈI OR AGNI TĒVI: the five goddess
AḺU: weep, cry
AḺUTAL: weeping
AḺUVUHIRA PĀṬṬU: crying song, lament
AMMĀ: mother
AMMĀVAI TĒṬI: seeking mother
AMPAṬṬAR: barber(s)
AṄKALĀYPPU: the feeling of having less than others
AṆṆAṈ: elder brother
AṈPAḶIPPU: giving out of love
ANPU: love
APPĀ: father
ARICCANTIRAṈ: the king who never lied
ĀṞU: be appeased, comforted, cooled
ĀṞUTAL: comfort
ĀRVAM: pleasure, desire
AṬAKKAM: emotional control
ĀTĀVU. support, consolation
AṬI: beat, strike

ĀTI: beginning
ĀTI DRĀVIDA: native or South India
ATICAYAM: wonderful thing
ĀTICĒSHAṈ: primordial serpent that supports the weight of the earth
ATIHĀRAM: power
ĀTTIRAM: distress, anger
ĀVĒCAM: literally "without mask or disguise," a powerful emotional state
AYYŌ: expression of sorrow; alas.
BRAHMĀ: the god Brahma, creator of the Hindu world
CAHATĒVAṈ: the youngest of the five Pandavas brothers of the mahābhārata
CAHŌTARAR: brother-sister bond
CAMPANTAM: affinity, alliance, connection
CAMPANTI: one related by marriage, in-law
CĀMPU: drum, a synonym for paṟai
CĀMPUHAṈ: see vīrajāmpuhaṉ
CAÑCALAM: sorrow, trouble
CAṈṈAM: birth
CĀRĀYAM: arrack
CARITTIRAM: history, life of a person
CAṬṬI: pot drum
CĀVU: death
CĀVU MĒḶAM: death beat
CĒKKILĀR: twelfth-century Tamil poet, author of the ciṟuttoṇṭar story
CĒRI: untouchable settlement
CHETTIAR: member(s) of a landowning caste
CILAPPATIKĀRAM: a great Tamil epic
CIṞUTTOṆṬAR: the "little devotee" (of the god Siva); Ciṟuttoṇṭā: the oral form of the name
CONTAM: one's property
CŌṬI: fabricate a tale, circulate a false rumor
CUMAṄKALI: wife
DRAUPADĪ: goddess and heroine of the pan-Hindu classical epic the Mahābhārata
DUḤŚĀSANA: character in the Mahābhārata
EḺUTTU: letter
EṄAKKU: for me (dative case of the pronoun *i*)
ERICCAL: burning sensation in the stomach, heat of anger, envy, jealousy
IṈAM: present, gift

IRAṄKU: pity, commiserate
IRAṬṬA Kural: singing duo
IṬAI NILAI: middle position
JAJMĀNĪ: see mērai
JĀMPUHAṈ: see Cāmpuhaṉ
KĀCU: coin, cash
KAL: stone
KĀL: leg, foot, a quarter
KALAI: an art
KALAM: a dry or liquid measure
KĀLĪ OR KĀLĪAMMĀ: the goddess kalī
KĀLĪ KŌYIL: Kāli temple
KALIYĀṆA MĒLAM: marriage beat
KALIYĀṆAM: happiness, marriage
KAM: smith work
KAMMĀḶA: artisan(s) (smithworker[s])
KAMPAṈ: Tamil poet of the twelfth century
KAṆAVAṈ: husband
KAÑCI: rice gruel
KAṈI: ripe fruit (poetic)
KARṆA: god of love
KARTTAṈ: the creator
KARUMĀTI: the funeral ceremony that among most castes concludes mourning sixteen days after death
KATAI: story, narrative
KAṬAI NILAI: inferior position
KAṬAMAI: duty
KAṬAṈ: loan
KAṬANTA KĀLAM: the past
KATAVU: door, gate
KAṬṬAI: tree log
KAṬṬAḶAI: command, curse
KAṬṬI AḺUTAL: crying in a cluster of embracing women
KAṬṬU: bind, fasten
KAVAR: charm, seduce
KAVUṆṬAR: member(s) of the largest agricultural caste in the Gingee area
KĀY: unripe fruit
KŌLLAI: backyard, enclosed garden

KOṈAI: hunched back from kuṉi (stooping down, bending)
KŌPAM: anger
KOTI: bubble up (as in boiling), be angry
KŌṬI: new cloth (for ceremonial occasions)
KOTIPPU: boiling, raging
KŌYIL: temple, shrine
KŪCCAM: timidity, shyness
KULA: lineage, caste
KUMPAKŌṆAM: a Tamil town
KUṞAI: less, want, deficiency
KUṞAIPAṬA: to feel kuṟai, to feel depleted
KURAL: voice
KUṞAMPU PĀṬṬU: song of mischief
KUṬIPIḶḶAI: the children of a household; refers to service castes, such as the washerman and barber castes.
MAHĀBHĀRATA: a pan-Hindu epic
MAHIḺCCI: joy
MALAIYAṈŪR: a South Arcot town
MĀMĀ: mother's brother
MAṈACU: the heart
MAṈAM: the mind
MAṆIMĒKALAI: a great Tamil epic
MAṈMATAṈ: Rati's husband (the god of love)
MAṈUCAṈ: man
MARIYĀTAI: respect, reverence; also boundary, limit
MĀRKAḺI: the Tamil month of December-January
MĀYAVARAM: a tamil town
MĒḶAM: drum, a collection of musical instruments troupe of musicians, beat in music
MĒLMAI: superiority
MĒRAI: manner, way of doing, a quantity of grains given to service castes at harvest and ceremonial occasions
MOTCAM: release from the cycle of births and rebirths
MUṆṬAI: widow (also an abusive term)
MUṞAI: code of conduct
MURUKAṈ: a great Tamil god
MUTAL NILAI: first position
MUTALIYĀR: member(s) of a high-ranking land-owning caste

MUTALMEI: precedence
NAKALŌKAM: the underworld
NALLA KUṆAM: good nature
NALLATAṄKĀḶ KATAI: "good little sister" (heroine of a tragic folk story)
NĀṬṬĀṆMAIKKĀRAṈ: headman
NĀṬṬUPPUṞA PĀṬAL: folk song
OPPĀRI: comparison, lamentation
OPPUKKU: for conformity's sake
PĀKAM: a portion, share
PALAHAI: board, plank, a one-sided round drum played by Paṟaiyars
PAḺAM: ripe fruit, a very aged person
PAḶḶAR: member(s) of an untouchable caste (South of Tamil Nadu)
PAMPAI: drum
PAṄKIṬA TUKKATAI: to share grief
PAṄKUṈI: the Tamil month corresponding to March and April
PANTAL: ceremonial booth or shed made out of palm leaves
PAṞAI: information given by the beat of a drum
PAṞAIMĒḶAM: untouchable troupe of drummers who play at goddess festivals and funerals
PAṞAICĀṞṞA: to publish orders by beat of drums
PAṞAICĀṞṞAKKŪṬIYAVAR: the one who knows everything (vīrājampuhaṉ)
PAṞAIYĀ/PAṞAIYAṈ: an untouchable man
PAṞAIYAR: plural form of paṟaiyaṉ
PAṞATCHI: an untouchable woman
PĀRVATI: goddess, wife of the god Siva.
PĀṬAL: song, poem
PATIYAL: slave
PAṬṬAM: honorific title, distinction
PĀṬṬU: song
PĀṬUVAR: singer
PEṆ: girl
PERIYAMĒḶAM: "big drum," (same as tōṟikaṭṭai)
PERIYAVAR: a great man
PERUMAI: greatness, dignity, pride, vanity
PĒY: spirit of an untimely dead
PIÑCU: a new fruit from the blossom
POṄKAL: literally, "boiling,"; a festival usually held around the eleventh of January; Tamil new year

PORṞU: praise, applaud
PORUMAI: envy
POTU: public, common
PŪ: flower
PUHAḺ: praise, eulogy
PULAMPAL: lamentation
PŪMI TĒVI: earth goddess
PUNAI: fetters for cattle legs
PUṆṆIYAM: virtue
PUṞAM: outside, exterior, public
PUṞA VĀḺKAI: exterior life, public life
PŪRI: puffed unleavened bread
PURUṢĀRTHA: first man
PUTUMAI: newness, novelty
RĀMĀYAṆA: Hindu epic
RATI: wife of Maṉmataṉ (god of love)
ŚAKTI: goodness; goodness power
STŌTRA: praise
TAIRIYAM: courage, guts, nerves
TALAIVAR: headman
TĀḶAM: time, measure in music
TĀLI: marriage necklace
TĀḺMAI: inferiority
TAMPI: younger brother
TAṞ PERUMAI: self-pride
TAṞHAM: controversy
TARUMAM: charity
TAVACI: a type of tree
TĀY VĪṬU: mother's house
TEMPU: energy, boost
TERUKŪTTU: village theater
TĪṆṬĀ: untouchable
TĪṆṬĀ INAṄKAḶ: untouchable people
TIṆṬIVAṈAM: a South Arcot town
TĪṆṬṬAKĀTA: untouchable
TIṞA: open
TIṞAMAI: ability, talent
TIRUṬṬU: theft, fraud

TIRUVAṆṆĀMALAI: a temple town near gingee
TŌCAI: rice thin crepe
TOḺIL: work, action
TOḺIL KULA: caste work
TŌṞIKAṬṬAI: barrel-shaped wooden drum (also see periyamēḷam)
TUKKAM: sorrow, grief
TUṆAI: help, assistance, a companion
TUṆTU TUṆTĀ: piece by piece, little by little
TUṞAI: harbor, kingdom
TUYARAM: sorrow, grief
UḶḶAM: the inside, the heart
UṆARCCI: feeling, perception
UṆṬAI: a ball
ŪR: village (where caste Hindus reside)
UṞCĀHAM: enthusiasm
URIMAI: proprietary right, claim, peculiarity
URUMAI: poverty, destitution
UTAVI: help, assistance
UTIR: fall off, die
UṬUKKAI: hourglass drum
VACUTĒVAṈ: name of a sage
VAHAI: kind, sort, division, category
VAIRĀKKIYAM: absence of sexual passion or greed
VAḺI: way, road
VAḶḶUVAR: untouchable priest(s)
VAṆṆĀR: member(s) of the washerman caste
VARALĀṞU: source, origin, circumstances
VARI: line
VARICAI: order, regularity, turns by which ceremonial prestations are made
VARIMAI: right, relationship
VAṞUṆAM: poverty, emptiness
VAṬAI: steamed rice cake
VĀTAM: dispute
VĀYKKARICI: ceremonial rice fed to the dead at funerals
VEḶḶĀḺAR: member(s) of a landowning caste
VĒṄKAI: a type of tree
VEṞU: hate
VĒṬIKKAI: show, spectacle

VEṬṬIYAR: members of the lowest divisions of untouchable castes. at funerals, they drum, burn corpses, or dig graves

VIL PĀṬṬU: bow song

VIḺU: fall

VIṆṆAPPAM: humble address, petition

VĪṞAJĀMPUHAṈ: untouchable hero

VĪRAM: heroism, courage

VIṬU: let, permit

YAJAMĀNA: patron of rituals and festivals

YAMĀ: god of death

YŌṈI: form of life

REFERENCES

Abu-Lughod, Lila.

1986. *Veiled Sentiments: Honor and Poetry in a Bedouin Society.* Berkeley: University of California Press.

Appadurai, Arjun.

1990. "Topographies of the Self: Praise and Emotion in Hindu India." In *Language and the Politics of Emotion*, ed. Catherine A. Lutz and Lila Abu-Lughod, 92–112. New York: Cambridge University Press.

1991. Afterword to *Gender, Genre, and Power in South Asian Expressive Traditions*, ed. Arjun Appadurai, Frank J. Korom, and Margaret A. Mills, 467–76. Philadelphia: University of Pennsylvania Press.

Appadurai, Arjun, Frank J. Korom, and Margaret A. Mills.

1991. Introduction to *Gender, Genre, and Power in South Asian Expressive Traditions*, ed. Arjun Appadurai, Frank J. Korom, and Margaret A. Mills, 3–29. Philadelphia: University of Pennsylvania Press.

Bailey, Greg.

1983. *The Mythology of Brahma.* Delhi: Oxford University Press.

Bauman, Richard.

1986. *Story, Performance, and Event: Contextual Studies of Oral Narrative.* Cambridge: Cambridge University Press.

Bavanandam Pillai, Rao Sahib S.

1910. *Harischandra: The Martyr to Truth.* Madras: S. P. C. K. Press.

Beck, Brenda E. F.

1982. *The Three Twins: The Telling of a South Indian Folk Epic.* Bloomington: Indiana University Press.

1992. collector and trans. *Elder Brother's Story: An Oral Epic of Tamil.* Vols. 1 and 2. Madras: Institute of Asian Studies.

Ben-Amos, Dan.

1982. "Toward a Definition of Folklore in Context." In *Folklore in Context: Essays*, ed. Dan Ben-Amos, 2–19. New Delhi: South Asian Publishers.

Berreman, Gerald.

1971 "The Brahmanical View of Caste." *Contributions to Indian Sociology*, n.s. 5:16–23.

Blackburn, Stuart.

1986. "Performance Markers in an Indian Story-Type." In *Another Harmony: New Essays on the Folklore of India*, ed. Stuart H. Blackburn and A. K. Ramanujan, 167–94. Berkeley: University of California Press.

1988. *Singing of Birth and Death: Texts in Performance.* Philadelphia: University of Pennsylvania Press.

1996. *Inside the Drama-House: Rāma Stories and Shadow Puppets in South India.* Berkeley: University of California Press.

1998. "Looking across the Contextual Divide: Studying Performance in South India." Special Issue: *The Performing Arts of South India*, ed. Stuart Blackburn. *South Asia Research* 18 (1): 1–11.

2001. *Moral Fictions: Tamil Folktales in Oral Tradition.* No.278. Helsinki: FF Communications.

Blackburn, Stuart, and A. K. Ramanujan, eds.

1986. Introduction to *Another Harmony: New Essays on the Folklore of India*, 1–40. Berkeley: University of California Press.

Bloch, Maurice.

1982. "Death, Women, and Power." In *Death and the Regeneration of Life*, ed. Maurice Bloch and Jonathan Parry, 211–30. Cambridge: Cambridge University Press.

1988. "Death and the Concept of a Person." In *On the Meaning of Death: Essays on Mortuary Rituals and Eschatological Beliefs*, ed. S. Cederroth, C. Corlin, and J. Lindstrom, 11–30. Stockholm: Almqvist and Wiksell.

Bloch, Maurice, and Jonathan Parry,

1982. "Introduction: Death and the Regeneration of Life." In *Death and the*

Regeneration of Life, ed. Maurice Bloch and Jonathan Parry, 1–44. Cambridge: Cambridge University Press.

Bowker, John.

1991. *The Meanings of Death*. Cambridge: Cambridge University Press.

Briggs, Charles L.

1988. *Competence in Performance: The Creativity of Tradition in Mexicano Verbal Art*. Philadelphia: University of Pennsylvania Press.

Brubaker, Richard L.

1979. "Barbers, Washermen, and Other Priests: Servants of the South Indian Village and Its Goddess." *History of Religions* 19 (2): 128–52.

Bruner, Jerome.

1987. "Life as Narrative." *Social Research* 54 (1): 11–32.

1991. "The Narrative Construction of Reality." *Critical Inquiry* 18:1–21.

Butalia, Urvashi.

2000. *The Other Side of Silence: Voices from the Partition of India*. Durham: Duke University Press.

Caraveli, Anna.

1986. "The Bitter Wounding: The Lament as Social Protest in Rural Greece." In *Gender and Power in Rural Greece*, ed. Jill Dubisch, 169–94. Princeton: Princeton University Press.

Caraveli-Chaves, Anna.

1980. "Bridge between Worlds: The Greek Women's Lament as Communicative Event." *Journal of American Folklore* 93 (368): 129–57.

Cavarero, Adriana.

1997. *Relating Narratives: Storytelling and Selfhood*. New York: Routledge.

Clarke, Sathianathan.

1998. *Dalits and Christianity: Sulbaltern Religion and Liberation Theology in India*. Delhi: Oxford University Press.

Cutler, Norman.

1987. *Songs of Experience: The Poetics of Tamil Devotion*. Bloomington: Indiana University Press.

Danforth, Loring.

1982. *The Death Rituals of Rural Greece*. Princeton: Princeton University Press.

Daniel, E. Valentine.

1984. *Fluid Signs: Being a Person the Tamil Way*. Berkeley: University of California Press.

Das, Veena.

1986. "The Work of Mourning: Death in a Punjabi Family." In *The Cultural Transition: Human Experience and Social Transformation in the Third World and Japan*, ed. Merry I. White and Susan Pollak, 179–210. Boston: Routledge and Kegan Paul.

1990. "Our Work to Cry: Your Work to Listen." In *Communities, Riots, and Survivors in South Asia*, ed. Veena Das, 345–98. Delhi: Oxford University Press.

de Bruin, Hanne M.

1998a, trans. Karṇa's Death: *A Play by Pukaḻēntippulavar.* Pondicherry: Institut Francais.

1998b. "Studying Performance in South India: A Synthesis of Theories." Special Issue: *The Performing Arts of South India*, ed. Stuart Blackburn. *South Asia Research* 18 (1): 12–38.

Deliège, Robert.

1992. "Replication and Consensus: Untouchability, Caste, and Ideology in India." *Man*, n.s., 27 (1): 155–73.

1993. "The Myths of Origin of the Indian Untouchables." *Man*, n.s., 28 (3): 533–49.

1997. *The World of the "Untouchables": Paraiyars of Tamil Nadu.* Trans. David Phillips. Delhi: Oxford University Press.

Dimock, Edward C.

1963. *The Thief of Love: Bengali Tales from Court and Village.* Chicago: University of Chicago Press.

Doniger, Wendy O'Flaherty.

1976. *The Origins of Evil in Hindu Mythology.* Berkeley: University of California Press.

Dubuisson, Daniel.

1993. *Mythologies du XXe Siècle (Dumézil, Lévi-Strauss, Eliade).* Lille: Presses Universitaires de Lille.

Dumont, Louis.

1980. *Homo Hierarchicus: The Caste System and Its Implications.* 1966. Reprint, Chicago: University of Chicago Press.

Dundes, Alan.

1966. "Metafolklore and Oral Literary Criticism." *The Monist* 60:505–16.

Durkheim, Émile.

1965. *The Elementary Forms of the Religious Life*, trans. Joseph Ward Swain. 1915. Reprint, New York: Free Press.

Egnor, Margaret T.

1980. "On the Meaning of Sakti to Women in Tamilnadu." In *The Powers of Tamil Women*, ed. Susan S. Wadley, 1–34. Maxwell School of Citizenship and Public Affairs. Foreign and Comparative Studies, South Asian Series, No. 6. Syracuse, N.Y.: Syracuse University.

1986. "Internal Iconicity in Paṟaiyar 'Crying Songs.'" In *Another Harmony: New Essays on the Folklore of India*, ed. Stuart H. Blackburn and A. K. Ramanujan, 294–344. Berkeley: University of California Press.

Eliade, Mircea.

1977. "Mythologies of Death: An Introduction." In *Religious Encounters with Death: Insights from the History and Anthropology of Religions*, ed. Frank E. Reynolds and Earle H. Waugh, 13–23. University Park: Pennsylvania State University Press.

Emeneau, Murray B.

1971. *Toda Songs*. Oxford: Clarendon Press.

Fabricius, Johann Philip.

1972. *Tamil and English Dictionary*. 4th ed. 1897. Reprint, Tranquebar, India: Evangelical Lutheran Mission Publishing House.

Fernandez, James W.

1986. *Persuasions and Performances: The Play of Tropes in Culture*. Bloomington: Indiana University Press.

Flueckiger, Joyce Burkhalter.

1996. *Gender and Genre in the Folklore of Middle India*. Ithaca: Cornell University Press.

Freeman, James M.

1979. *Untouchable: An Indian Life History*. Stanford: Stanford University Press.

Fuller, Christopher J.

1992. *The Camphor Flame: Popular Hinduism and Society in India*. Princeton: Princeton University Press.

Geertz, Clifford.

1973. *The Interpretation of Cultures*. New York: Basic Books.

1986. "Making Experience, Authoring Selves." In *The Anthropology of Experience*, ed. Victor W. Turner and Edward M. Bruner, 373–80. Urbana: University of Illinois Press.

Good, Anthony.

1991. *The Female Bridegroom: A Comparative Study of Life-Crisis Rituals in South India and Sri Lanka.* Oxford: Clarendon Press.

Grima, Benedicte.

1991. "The Role of Suffering in Women's Performance of *Paxto.*" In *Gender, Genre, and Power in South Asian Expressive Traditions*, ed. Arjun Appadurai, Frank J. Korom, and Margaret A. Mills, 78–101. Philadelphia: University of Pennsylvania Press.

1992. *The Performance of Emotion among Paxtun Women.* Austin: University of Texas Press.

Handelman, Don.

1979. "Is Naven Ludic?" *Social Analysis* 1: 177–92.

Harlan, Lindsey, and Paul B. Courtright.

1995. *From the Margins of Hindu Marriage: Essays on Gender, Religion, and Culture.* New York: Oxford University Press.

Hart, George L.

1979. "The Little Devotee: Cēkkilār's Story of Ciṟunttoṇṭar." In *Sanskrit and Indian Studies: Essays in Honour of Daniel H. H. Ingalls*, ed. M. Nagatomi et al., 217–36. Boston: D. Reidel.

1995. "Archetypes in Classical Indian Literature and Beyond." In *Syllables of Sky: Studies in South Indian Civilization. In Honour of Velcheru Narayana Rao*, ed. David Shulman, 165–82. Delhi: Oxford University Press.

Hertz, Robert.

1960. "A Contribution to the Study of the Collective Representation of Death." In *Death and the Right Hand*, trans. Rodney Needham and Claudia Needham. London: Cohen and West.

Hiltebeitel, Alf.

1988. *The Cult of Draupadī.* Vol. 1: *Mythologies: From Gingee to Kurukśetra.* Chicago: University of Chicago Press.

Honko, Lauri.

1980. "The Lament: Problems of Genre, Structure, and Reproduction." In *Genre Structure, and Reproduction in Oral Literature*, ed. Lauri Honko and Vilmos Voigt, 21–40. Budapest: Akademiai Kiado.

Jakobson, Roman.

1971. "Shifters, Verbal Categories, and the Russian Verb." In *Roman Jakobson: Selected Writings*, 2: 130–47. 1957. Reprint, The Hague: Mouton.

Kakar, Sudhir.

1981. *The Inner World: A Psycho-Analytic Study of Childhood and Society in India.* Oxford: Oxford University Press.

Kannan, M., and Francois Gros.

2002. "Tamil Dalits in Search of a Literature." *South Asia Research* 22 (1): 21–66.

Kapadia, Karin.

1995. *Siva and Her Sisters: Gender, Caste, and Class in Rural South India.* Boulder: Oxford Westview Press.

Kapferer, Bruce.

1983. *A Celebration of Demons: Exorcism and the Aesthetics of Healing in Sri Lanka.* Bloomington: Indiana University Press.

1986. "Performance and the Structuring of Meaning and Experience." In *The Anthropology of Experience*, ed. Victor W. Turner and Edward M. Bruner, 188–207. Urbana: University of Illinois Press.

Khare, R. S.

1998. "The Body, Sensoria, and Self of the Powerless: Remembering/'Re-Membering' Indian Untouchable Women." In *Cultural Diversity and Social Discontent: Anthropological Studies on Contemporary India*, 148–261. Walnut Creek, Calif.: AltaMira Press.

Kumar, Nita, ed.

1994. *Women as Subjects: South Asian Histories.* Charlottesville: University Press of Virginia.

Lamb, Sarah.

2000. *White Saris and Sweet Mangoes: Aging, Gender and Body in North India.* Berkeley: University of California Press.

Langness, L. L., and Gelya Frank.

1981. *Lives: An Anthropological Approach to Biography.* Novato, Calif.: Chandler and Sharp.

Leavitt, John.

1997. "Poetics, Prophetics, Inspiration." In *Poetry and Prophecy: The Anthropology of Inspiration*, ed. John Leavitt, 1–60. Ann Arbor: University of Michigan Press.

Lévi-Strauss, Claude.

1963. *Structural Anthropology.* Trans. Claire Jacobson and Brooke Grundfest Schoepf. New York: Basic Books.

Lincoln, Bruce.

1999. *Theorizing Myth: Narrative, Ideology, and Scholarship.* Chicago: Chicago University Press.

Linde, Charlotte.

1993. *Life Stories: The Creation of Coherence.* Oxford: Oxford University Press.

Long, Bruce. J.

1977. "Death as a Necessity and a Gift in Hindu Mythology." In *Religious Encounters with Death: Insights from the History and Anthropology of Religions,* ed. Frank E. Reynolds and Earle H. Waugh, 72–95. University Park: Pennsylvania State University Press.

Lutz, Catherine A.

1988. *Unnatural Emotions: Everyday Sentiments on a Micronesian Atoll and Their Challenge to Western Theory.* Chicago: University of Chicago Press.

Lutz, Catherine A., and Lila Abu-Lughod, eds.

1990. *Language and the Politics of Emotion.* New York: Cambridge University Press.

Lynch, Owen M.

1990. "The Social Construction of Emotion in India." In *Divine Passions: The Social Construction of Emotion in India,* ed. Owen M. Lynch. Berkeley: University of California Press.

2001. "Untouchables in India's Civil/Uncivil Democracy: A Review Article." *Ethnos* 66 (2): 259–68.

Malamoud, Charles.

1982. "Les morts sans visage: Remarques sur l'idéologie funéraire dans le brâhmanisme." In *La mort, les morts dans les sociétes anciennes,* ed. Gherardo Gnoli and Jean-Pierre Vernant, 441–53. Cambridge: Cambridge University Press and Editions de la Maison des Sciences de l'Homme.

Malinowski, Bronislaw.

1984. "The Role of Myth in Life." In *Sacred Narrative: Readings in the Theory of Myth,* ed. Alan Dundes, 193–206. 1926. Reprint, Berkeley: University of California Press.

Mattingly, Cheryl.

1998. *Healing Dramas and Clinical Plots: The Narrative Structure of Experience.* Cambridge: Cambridge University Press.

Mattingly, Cheryl, and Linda C. Garro, eds.
2000. *Narrative and the Cultural Construction of Illness and Healing.* Berkeley: University of California Press.

McGilvray, Dennis B.
1983. "Paraiyar Drummers of Sri Lanka: Consensus and Constraint in an Untouchable Caste." *American Ethnologist* 10 (1): 97–115.

Mencher, Joan.
1974. "The Caste System Upside Down, or the Not-So-Mysterious East." *Current Anthropology* 15:469–93.

Mendelsohn, Oliver, and Marika Vicziany.
1998. *The Untouchables: Subordination, Poverty, and the State in Modern India.* Cambridge. Cambridge University Press.

Metcalf, Peter, and Richard Huntington.
1991. *Celebrations of Death: The Anthropology of Mortuary Ritual.* 2nd ed. Cambridge: Cambridge University Press.

Meyer, Rachel S.
2000. "Fluid Subjectivities: Intertextuality and Women's Narrative Performance in North India." *Journal of American Folklore* 13 (448): 144–63.

Michael, S. M.
1983. "The Origin of the Ganapati Cult." *Asian Folklore Studies* 42:91–116.

Moffatt, Michael.
1979. *An Untouchable Community in South India: Structure and Consensus.* Princeton: Princeton University Press.

Moreno, Manuel.
1981. An Untouchable Funeral in a Village of South India. *Chicago Anthropology Exchange* 14 (1–2): 152–63.

Mosse, David.
1999. "Responding to Subordination: The Politics of Identity Change among South Indian Untouchable Castes." In *Identity and Affect: Experiences of Identity in a Globalising World,* ed. John R. Campbell and Alan Rew, 64–104. London: Pluto Press.

Nabokov, Isabelle.
2000. *Religion against the Self: An Ethnography of Tamil Rituals.* New York: Oxford University Press.

Narayan, Kirin.
1986. "Birds on a Branch: Girlfriends and Wedding Songs in Kangra." *Ethos* 14:47–75.

1995. "The Practice of Oral Literary Criticism: Women's Songs in Kangra, India." *Journal of American Folklore* 108:243–64.

1997. *Mondays on the Dark Night of the Moon: Himalayan Foothill Folktales.* New York: Oxford University Press.

Nenola-Kallio, Aili.

1980. "Two Genres for Expressing Sorrow: Laments and Lyrical Songs in Ingria." In *Genre, Structure, and Reproduction in Oral Literature*, ed. Lauri Honko and Vilmos Voigt, 41–54. Budapest: Akademiai Kiado.

Nishimura, Yuko.

1998. *Gender, Kinship, and Property Rights: Nagarattar Womanhood in South India.* Delhi: Oxford University Press.

Nuckolls, Charles W.

1993. *Siblings in South Asia: Brothers and Sisters in Cultural Context.* New York: Guilford.

Panourgia, Neni.

1995. *Fragments of Death: Fables of Identity: An Athenian Anthropography.* Madison: University of Wisconsin Press.

Parry, Jonathan P.

1994. *Death in Banaras.* Cambridge: Cambridge University Press.

Personal Narratives Group.

1989. *Interpreting Women's Lives: Feminist Theory and Personal Narratives.* Bloomington: Indiana University Press.

Peterson, Indira Viswanathan.

1988. "The Tie That Binds: Brothers and Sisters in North and South India." *South Asian Social Scientist* 4 (1): 25–52.

Racine, Josiane.

1996. "Chanter la mort en pays Tamoul: L'Héritage reçu et le stigmate refusé. *Puruṣārtha* 18: *Traditions orales dans le monde Indien*, ed. Catherine Champion, 199–218.

Racine, Josiane, and Jean-Luc Racine, with (Viramma).

1995. *Une vie Paria: Le rire des asservis.* Paris: Plon and Editions UNESCO.

Raheja, Gloria Goodwin, and Ann Grodzins Gold.

1994. *Listen to the Herons' Words: Reimagining Gender and Kinship in North India.* Berkeley: University of California Press.

Ram, Kalpana.

1991. *Mukkuvar Women: Gender, Hegemony, and Capitalist Transformation in a South Indian Fishing Community.* North Sydney: Allen and Unwin.

Ramanujan, A. K.

1967. *The Interior Landscape: Love Poems from a Classical Tamil Anthology.* Bloomington: Indiana University Press.

1986. "Two Realms of Kannada Folklore." In *Another Harmony: New Essays on the Folklore of India*, ed. Stuart H. Blackburn and A. K. Ramanujan, 41–75. Berkeley: University of California Press.

1991. "Toward a Counter-System: Women's Tales." In *Gender, Genre, and Power in South Asian Expressive Traditions*, ed. Arjun Appadurai, Frank J. Korom, and Margaret A. Mills, 33–55. Philadelphia: University of Pennsylvania Press.

Ramaswamy, Sumathi.

1998. *Passions of the Tongue: Language Devotion in Tamil India, 1891–1970.* New Delhi: Munshiram Manoharlal.

Ramaswamy, Vijaya.

1994. "Women and the 'Domestic' in the Tamil Folk Songs." *Man in India* 74 (1): 21–38.

Randeria, Shalini.

1999. "Mourning, Mortuary Exchange, and Memorialization: The Creation of Local Communities among Dalits in Gujarat." In *Ways of Dying: Death and Its Meanings in South Asia*, ed. Elizabeth Schömbucher and Claus Peter Zoller, 88–111. New Delhi: Manohar.

Rosaldo, Renato.

1976. "The Story of Tukbaw: 'They Listen as He Orates.'" In *The Biographical Process: Studies in the History of Psychology of Religion*, ed. Frank E. Reynolds and D. Capps, 121–51. The Hague: Mouton.

1984. "Grief and a Headhunter's Rage: On the Cultural Force of Emotions." In *Text, Play, and Story: The Construction and Reconstruction of Self and Society*, ed. Stuart Plattner and Edward Bruner, 178–95. Washington, D.C.: American Ethnological Society.

Rosenwald, George C., and Richard L. Ochberg, eds.

1992. *Storied Lives: The Cultural Politics of Self-Understanding.* New Haven: Yale University Press.

Scheper-Hughes, Nancy.

1992. *Death without Weeping: The Violence of Everyday Life in Brazil.* Berkeley: University of California Press.

Schömbucher, Elisabeth, and Claus Peter Zoller.

1999. *Ways of Dying: Death and Its Meanings in South Asia.* New Delhi: Manohar.

Scott, James C.

1985. *Weapons of the Weak: Everyday Forms of Peasant Resistance.* New Haven: Yale University Press.

Seremetakis, Nadia.

1991. *The Last Word: Women, Death, and Divination in Inner Mani.* Chicago: University of Chicago Press.

Seymour, Susan C.

1999. *Women, Family, and Child Care in India: A World in Transition.* Cambridge: Cambridge University Press.

Shulman, David.

1980. *Tamil Temple Myths: Sacrifice and Divine Marriage in the South Indian Saiva Tradition.* Princeton: Princeton University Press.

1988. "The Tamil Flood Myths and the Cankam Legend." In *The Flood Myth,* ed. Alan Dundes, 293–318. Berkeley: University of California Press.

1993. *The Hungry God: Hindu Tales of Filicide and Devotion.* Chicago: University of Chicago Press.

1995. "First Man, Forest Mother: Telugu Humanism in the Age of Krsnadevarāya." In *Syllables of Sky: Studies in South Indian Civilization: In Honour of Velcheru Narayana Rao,* ed. David Shulman, 133–64. Delhi: Oxford University Press.

Strenski, Ivan.

1987. *Four Theories of Myth in Twentieth-Century History: Cassirer, Eliade, Lévi-Strauss, and Malisnowski.* Houndmills, U.K.: Macmillan Press.

Tapper, Bruce Elliot.

1987. *Rivalry and Tribute: Society and Ritual in a Telugu Village in South India.* Delhi: Hindustan Publishing Corporation.

Thurston, Edgar.

1987. *Castes and Tribes of Southern India.* Vol. 6. 1909. Reprint, New Delhi: Asian Educational Services.

Tiwary, K. M.

1978. "Tuneful Weeping: A Mode of Communication." *Frontiers* 3 (3): 24–27.

Trawick, Margaret.

1988a. "Spirits and Voices in Tamil Songs." *American Ethnologist* 15:193–215.

1988b. "Ambiguity in the Oral Exegesis of a Sacred Text: Tirukkōvaiyār (or, the Guru in the Garden, Being an Account of a Tamil Informant's Responses to Homesteading in Central New York State)." *Cultural Anthropology* 3 (3): 316–51.

1990. *Notes on Love in a Tamil Family.* Berkeley: University of California Press.

1991. Wandering Lost: A Landless Laborer's Sense of Place and Self." In *Gender, Genre, and Power in South Asian Expressive Traditions*, ed. Arjun Appadurai, Frank J. Korom, and Margaret A. Mills, 224–66. Philadelphia: University of Pennsylvania Press.

1996. "The Story of the Jackal Hunter Girl." In *Culture/Contexture: Explorations in Anthropology and Literary Studies*, ed. Valentine Daniel and Jeffrey M. Peck, 58–83. Berkeley: University of California Press.

1997. "Time and the Mother: Conversations with a Possessing Spirit." In *Poetry and Prophecy: The Anthropology of Inspiration*, ed. John Leavitt, 61–76. Ann Arbor: University of Michigan Press.

Turner, Victor W., and Edward M. Bruner, eds.

1986. *The Anthropology of Experience.* Urbana: University of Illinois Press.

Vallikkannan, K.

1990. "Songs of Mourning." In *Encyclopedia of Tamil Literature*, ed. G. John Samuel, 1: 456. Madras: Institute of Asian Studies.

Venugopal, Saraswathi.

1982. *Folk Songs: Social Status Comparison.* Madurai, India: Madurai Kamaraj University.

1985. "Persuasion as a Sign in Tamil Folklore." *Journal of the Institute of Asian Studies* 3 (1): 133–40.

Willis, Paul.

1977. *Learning to Labor: How Working Class Kids Get Working Class Jobs.* New York: Columbia University Press.

Zarrilli, Phillip B.

2000. *Kathakali Dance-Drama: Where Gods and Demons Come to Play.* New York: Routledge.

Zvelebil, Kamil V.

1995. *Lexicon of Tamil Literature.* Leiden: E. J. Brill.

INDEX

Compositor: Integrated Composition Systems
Text: 10/15 Janson
Display: Janson